William George Hamley

Captain Clutterbuck's Champagne

A West Indian reminiscence, originally published in Blackwood's magazine

William George Hamley

Captain Clutterbuck's Champagne
A West Indian reminiscence, originally published in Blackwood's magazine

ISBN/EAN: 9783337057763

Printed in Europe, USA, Canada, Australia, Japan

Cover: Foto ©ninafisch / pixelio.de

More available books at **www.hansebooks.com**

CAPTAIN CLUTTERBUCK'S

CHAMPAGNE

A

WEST INDIAN REMINISCENCE

ORIGINALLY PUBLISHED IN BLACKWOOD'S MAGAZINE

WILLIAM BLACKWOOD AND SONS
EDINBURGH AND LONDON
MDCCCLXII

CAPTAIN CLUTTERBUCK'S CHAMPAGNE.

CHAPTER I.

THERE is, or was some quarter of a century ago, in the Port Royal Mountains of Jamaica, a military station called Stony Hill, about 1300 feet above the sea. It had been established at this altitude in the hope of procuring increased comfort and health for the troops. It was certainly cooler than the plain, and therefore answered its intent in respect of climate; but experience had shown that it was far from being beyond the range of that scourge, the yellow fever. However, it was quite in the country, though within a moderate drive of the city of Kingston, and thus it afforded an agreeable change to one who had been quartered on a lower level.

We glance back over the quarter century of which mention has been made above, and introduce the reader to a room in the officers' quarters. 'Twas a lodging that had held many inmates, and seen incidents well worthy, perhaps, of remembrance—all absorbed into the same voracious past whence we are humbly endeavouring to rescue this our tale. With submission to the 'Spectator's' captious Dervise, we venture to affirm that, spite of its frequent changes of inhabitants, this chamber was not a caravanserai, and that, if he had been silly enough to spread his carpet there unbidden, he would have had his holy head punched, and suffered summary ejectment at the hands of Lieutenant Arthur Brune, who considered himself for the time being its rightful and sole possessor. Judged of from the fireside of a snug English drawing-room or study, 'twould seem a bleak and desolate apartment; but it must be borne in mind that, in tropical regions, coolness is comfort, and that for this reason rooms are kept as bare of furniture and hangings as convenience will allow. It contained a small oak table furnished by his Majesty, and two strong and cruel-seated elm chairs from the same gracious source. This was all the regulated furniture; but the barrack-master had, at his own proper risk, lent a soldier's iron bedstead, mattress, and pillow, which, being covered with a chintz envelope, answered passing well for a sofa. There was a portable arm-chair—private property; and a deal slab to hold glasses, bottles, and goblets, fixed against the wall, whose fixing, being a breach of regulation, would, on surrendering the chamber, be paid for at the rate of twopence per nail, and a trifle for lime-whiting to the Royal landlord, who, towards his military tenantry, was an austere man, and kept a lot of factors, called his Barrack Department, to squeeze them of their miserable substance: at least this is the subaltern's version of the matter. The table stood between the sofa and the arm-chair, each of which held an occupant looking particularly *ennuyé*, and puffing a cigar. On the board was some porter-cup, an agreeable and bilious mixture, well known in the island as a promoter of good-fellowship and yellow fever. The foaming beverage was contained in a *jorum* or huge glass, from which the parties drank at their convenience, preserving each his own side of the rim. For one or two this answers very well, but when a dozen or eighteen come to pull in turn all at the same jorum, it requires some familiarity with the method before the last drinkers become reconciled to the marks of thirsty lips, and plunge boldly into the surge from which not the minutest arc of the crystal circle is free, refreshing their souls at the expense of their fastidiousness. One of our seedy subjects was Arthur Brune, aforesaid; the other was a chance guest of his—allow us to introduce him.

Old Tom Gervaise was fat, indolent, and slovenly. His countenance was handsome, and his complexion had probably been good before grog blossoms established a right of commonage on his person, and exercised their prerogative without order or reserve. The head was nearly bald on the top, but its contour was so good and its proportions so massive, that the loss of hair was hardly a disadvantage. At heart he was a voluptuary, but as he had not a grain of energy or patience, he appeared simply as a dirty, surly, lazy old sloven. Incapable of amusing himself, he spent such hours as were unavoidably solitary in lolling on a sofa, dozing gently, or improving the minutes between his slumbers by the study of illustrated fictions, of which he possessed a small but objectionable assortment. Solitude, though, he invariably eschewed when company could be obtained without trouble or exertion; and he drank, gamed, or sported, not so much from love of these things, as because they were means of procuring society. Long compliance with dissipated companions had, however, without decided excess, shaken his constitution and made a wreck of him. A small quantity of liquor affected his head, and he had not the self-command to refrain from mixing several kinds together, but recklessly swallowed one sort after another as they were presented. To the *agrémens* of companionship he contributed nothing except the opportunity of cracking a chance joke on his peculiarities. Too indolent even to talk, his custom was to loll in an arm-chair, smoking, and to speak in monosyllables or very curt sentences, more remarkable for force than for suavity. If his cigar happened to be in his mouth, he would not always take the trouble to remove it to make a remark, but would push or pat, sometimes not gently, any one who rallied or contradicted him, with a thick stick, which his uncertain gait obliged him to carry, and which was a well-known and celebrated staff. Whenever any sort of entertainment was going on, Tom was sure to be present. What made his presence acceptable it is difficult to explain, if it were not that the fellows liked to laugh at him, and hear him growl. Certain it is that he was always more than tolerated, and allowed to say and do with impunity things for which another man would have been called to severe account, but for which he seemed to possess a general prescription. One reason of this may be that he had not always been the sort of old sinner that he now was; and possibly habit, without an effort of his own, kept him within bounds, and caused him in some sort to discriminate character, and to adapt the intensity of his style to the person he addressed. Indeed, there was a tradition that Tom had once been the most fastidious dandy in his regiment. He seldom or never himself alluded to a period when he was not an eagle's talon in the waist. Yet it could not have been so very long ago, for, though called old Tom, and though lazy and helpless enough for an octogenarian, he had not passed middle age. Even now, those who had known him in his exquisite days took a pride in the remembrance; and, upon occasions when they desired the regiment to look its best, as at a public dinner or a governor's *levée*, would invade Tom's quarters, heedless of the inhospitable growls and curses of the proprietor, and wash him by force, and dress him decently by contributions from their own wardrobes. A very fine old fellow Tom looked, too, at such times! His head bore the stamp of a lawgiver or a historian, and a most audacious forgery it was. Nature got thimblerigged, and found the skull under which she thought she had placed a double portion of brain, lamentably empty. Poor old Tom! It is hard to read over what truth has compelled to be written concerning him, and still harder to explain why any kindly feeling should exist towards him: yet the foregoing paragraphs were penned with regret. He was an example, and unfortunately not a rare one, of the destructive effects of a warm climate upon a person of undisciplined mind and indolent disposition.

An injustice has, however, been done to Tom in representing him as in all things listless and inert. Stuck on the box of any vehicle drawn by horses, with the whip and ribbons in his hands, he would show you that he knew something of putting a team along: four-in-hand was the only style which he thought worthy of his science, but he was content, *faute de mieux*, to run a tandem; and it was on that equipage that he commonly effected locomotion, in a most disgraceful old frock-coat, and a broad-brimmed white beaver with an aperture cut on either side below the crown for ventilation, and a series of greasy circles rising from the rim upwards, and telling of many seasons, as the age of a palm-tree is known to the naturalist by its rings. From this elevation Tom smacked his whip at all passengers, where he dared making its lash excite the skin a little, which, in that drowsy country, where very light clothing is worn, was no doubt an agreeable stimulus. In return he would get a mango, orange, or possibly a brickbat, at his head. Sometimes a thin-skinned ensign was known to hoard up his wrath, and at a future meeting express with black ingratitude his dissatisfaction at Tom's passing notice; whereupon the latter would remind him that the touch did not hurt, and explain how pungent his scientific arm could have made it, had it so pleased him; which explanation would cause the ensign to marvel greatly what the real tickler must be like if the one he received was considered painless.

Tom's regiment lay at Up Park Camp, about a mile from Kingston; but their mess having been very quiet for some days past, he had driven over to Stony Hill, in the hope that his presence would induce the officers stationed up there to put on a little extra steam in his honour; in which hope he had not been disappointed. His cart was quartered on some one who happened to possess the luxury of a gig-house, his leader on another, his shaft-horse on a third, and the honour of entertaining his highly respectable self he had conferred on Arthur Brune, in whose sitting-room he took a shakedown if he chanced to go to bed. They had had a great jollification the night before, for these country folks did not dislike an excuse for a chance merry-making.

It would be unfair towards Arthur Brune to judge him by his present appearance. He does not often look thus. It is wrong, the writer knows, to introduce him in this exceptional condition; but there are duties towards the narrative as well as to its characters, and the history will have it so. Deal mildly with him, however, reader!—that is, if you be masculine (many soft eyes, we flatter ourself, will read Arthur Brune's story, whose owners require no caution in respect of charity); say, if you like, how grieved you are to see a fine handsome young man with that debauched look. Pity his pale gills, his weak-looking eyes, his jaded expression; but no lofty denunciations, remember—no thanking God on him! You have perhaps in your virtuous mind already piled up a goodly battery of stones. Pause a moment before you discharge one. If you were a fine, generous, warm-hearted fellow at three-and-twenty (which of course you were), and never in your life picked yourself up of a morning in a somewhat similar condition, shy away! But if Memory, spite of the ingenious manner in which you have barricaded your bosom against her, and puttied up the minutest chinks, doth ever percolate the fence, and lure you back, and rock you pleasantly in days and nights when you were as other men are, then, we charge you, forbear! We know exactly how things are with you now; are we not human? have we not sipped, and suffered, and profited? If you are an exemplary member of society, so are we. If your spouse is a paragon, and can attribute to you no earthly failing, present or past, ours is as unexceptionable in her own attributes, and more blind to our demerits than we deserve. Are your little people "sweet innocent cherubs?" we call ours " dear angelic lambs;" that is the only difference. Are you orthodox? so are we. Is your name respected throughout the district? we hope ours is so too. Do men cut short their jokes, and take the twinkle out of their eyes, when you come within hearing? 'Tis exactly the same with us. It is possible that in the article of charities, moral associations, and philanthropic endeavours, you and we are much on a par. We will measure phylacteries with you, or enter into judgment concerning neck-ties. In short, it is plain that both of us are correctness itself. This is in 1861, you know; but it was not always '61. We used to write the figures 35-6-7-8-9, &c. How if our biographies during these years could be revealed! What should we feel when the many checkered and the occasional dark pages should come under review! Shall we quote? No, not unless you force us: all the sweet souls read Maga,* therefore we forbear; but—be charitable to Arthur Brune.

There was, as will speedily appear, a reason why Arthur for a time consented to dissipation. On his breast lay a heavy disappointment, which he sought to stifle, but could not. And he called in idle company, and walked in their ways, to lure him from himself, and support him in a trial which his resolution —though he was a youth of strong mind—hardly enabled him to endure. The young man had suffered

* It was in Maga that this story first appeared.

cruelly in his affections, and was, moreover, perplexed to determine how his duty required him to act. Hitherto he had followed the dictates of his pride; but reflection, which he could not wholly shut out, persuaded him more and more to a bolder course. The conflict was so grievous, that he could not bear to think of his trouble.

Well, the immediate cause of Brune's condition was, as has been said, a great symposium which had taken place last night in honour of old Tom's visit. It had ended in a squabble, as was too often the case; and, but that some one present had sense and influence enough to compose the matter before it had reached the seventh cause, there would have been a duel. The cool morning air, which probably contributed much to the rational termination of the dispute, also disposed the party to dispense with going to bed. It is a question whether the freshness inhaled without doors an hour before sunrise be not a stronger restorative than a feverish slumber. Brune and Tom appeared to think that it is, and so took coffee and a *chasse* at daybreak, strolled about the stables and negro-paths for half an hour, proclaimed themselves "all right," and, in the strength of their morning ramble, made a tolerable essay at breakfast. As the sun mounted, however, and the air began to boil, and the shadows shrank up to almost nothing, and the sea-breeze, which chose to be a sluggard that morning, was anxiously waited for, the gentlemen found that last night's account was not yet settled. They relapsed into a rakish discreditable condition, fit only to loll about, half alive, and sip porter-cup, that they might not utterly waste the morning; for improvement of the fleeting hour was insisted on by Tom Gervaise, who remembered that with each sun came its appointed duty of getting tipsy before bed-time. Happier than Titus, Tom never, to our knowledge, suffered remorse for having lost a day!

"Hollo you, sir!" shouted Tom to a negro who passed the window; "come here and fetch me Massa Brune's cigar; my light's out."

"Yes, massa."

It did not astonish the negro, as it probably does the reader, that he was called into the room to perform a service which, by simply rising up, or even stretching across the table, Tom might have executed for himself. The sable minister received, as his guerdon, first a rap on the shins from Tom's stick, which made him hop with his leg in his hand and cry "Hie!" and, secondly, a Cuban cigar, shot by Brune with the accuracy of a Tell, so as to graze his scalp and bury itself in the woolly covering, which made him turn on the whites of his eyes and grin delightedly as he did obeisance with his naked foot, and pocketed the prize, and went his way.

"'Pon my soul!" said Tom, between the inspirations from his newly lighted weed, "this climate is the devil. See how weak and helpless it makes us. How I have borne it so many years is a marvel. If I had not attentively supported the system during my residence, I must have turned up my toes long ago. And yet you get neither credit nor thanks for this at home. By Jove! nothing they can give is a sufficient reward for passing a large slice of one's life in such a furnace: a peerage wouldn't be too much!"

"If they ever should give you one, Tom," answered Brune, "it's to be hoped that you'll 'purge and live cleanly as a nobleman ought.'"

"That's a bit of chaff you picked out of Hannah More or 'Tristram Shandy.' I know I saw it in print somewhere when I used to read books. Can't read in this climate," said Tom, as if the latitude alone stood between him and scholarship.

"You'll have the papers to read soon. You know the packet from England was signaled this morning," replied Brune.

"Was she?" grunted Tom. "I think little about packets now. I hardly feel that I've any connection with England, except to look out for the St Leger and Derby."

"Wonder whether Clutterbuck has got poor old Swillhard's company without purchase," mused Arthur. "Abominable shame! he's been refused two death vacancies, though he never left the headquarters since they came out here. In each case a youngster at the depôt was allowed to purchase by their bringing in some old sinner from the half-pay to sell."

"Well, you'll soon be out of suspense," said Tom; "here comes the postman. We shall have the letters in ten minutes. I bet five dollars they've disappointed Clutterbuck again."

"Then they deserve the pains of Tartarus," said Brune. "You talk of a peerage, Tom: all they are likely to give one here is a grave. One's legitimate promotion is jobbed and bartered away. Heigho! I can stand disappointment pretty well, but patience has limits."

"There's one of your disappointments that I fancy you may get rid of and turn on your opponents whenever you like," said Tom.

"What the devil do you mean, Tom?" asked Brune, sharply.

"Mean!" answered Tom, "nothing but what every fellow with half an eye sees and knows as well as I do. You may cut out that Melhado whenever you like—even now his wedding-day is fixed; ay, and by Jove! I'd do it too. I'd do it for the fun of cheating that creole savage, let alone the splendid little filly."

The young man blushed scarlet as Tom began to speak, and then turned pale; his colour came and went rapidly. "Gervaise, I can't stand this," said he, hurriedly.

"Nobody wants you to stand this or anything else. 'Tisn't my affair." And Tom leisurely replaced his cigar, and began coaxing back the fire, which had nearly expired during his exhortation. "Devil take the girl," he recommenced, puffing only interjectionally, now that he saw a cheerful glow under his nose; "let Melhado have her if he likes. I wouldn't, though—feed me on slops if I would. I'd carry her off in spite of all. Hollo! here's the letter-bag."

Brune was pacing the little room with a flushed face and a rapt gaze. He seemed quite unconscious of the mail's arrival until Gervaise, having turned over the packet, shouted, "Look here, I say; here are a dozen letters for you. Only two for me, and they'll keep till I've seen how the betting is, and to whom they've given the step." So saying, Tom pocketed an epistle from his sister, and another from his tailor.

Brune opened one letter after another, skimmed over their contents, and glanced at the signatures. He came at last to one without postmark, and evidently despatched from some station in the island, and this he read with interest. Tom turned over the newspapers, throwing each down after a short examination. "I've found three gazettes," said he, "but not a word of our regiment. Just look; here's an interesting gazette for a whole week: '*Erratum in the Gazette. of the* 20*th instant.—The Christian names of Ensign Bogg of the* 55*th are Salusbury, de Vere, Gubby, Plantagenet, and not Salusbury, de Vere, Grubby, Plantagenet, as previously stated.*' Ensign Bogg, indeed! Still nothing of Clutterbuck. They can't have filled the vacancy; they must be keeping it open for some rascally job."

"Make yourself easy," replied Brune; "Clutterbuck has it all right. 'Tis a letter from him I have here."

"Ugh!" grunted Tom; "there was no pet who wanted it, I suppose, or he'd have got it."

Brune read through the epistle, and afterwards read it aloud to Tom. It ran as follows:—

"My dear Brune,—I've got it at last—
'Candidior postquam tondenti barba cadebat,
Respexit tamen et longo post tempore venit'—
and there's time enough before the letters go to Stony Hill to write a line and tell you so.

"I can't in conscience use the seal any more, and

so send it to you as the best fellow I know, hoping that you, too, will soon have reason to discontinue its use.

"I thought I was too old now to value rank or anything of that sort; but I'm ashamed to say I'm as pleased to feel myself a captain, and to be addressed as such (they've all been to congratulate me), as if I was two-and-twenty.

"Good-bye, old fellow, and believe me ever yours,
"S. T. CLUTTERBUCK."

There followed a postscript, which Brune with hesitation read. It was this:—

"*P.S.*—I shall probably give champagne on the —th; so keep yourself disengaged. Won't we have fun! I must ask old Arabin and Melhado, as they've been very civil; but you won't mind that; our mess-room is large, and you needn't be near them."

The seal enclosed and alluded to in the letter was well known pretty nearly throughout the island. 'Twas engraved as follows:—

"PSALM LXXV.
Verse 6th." *

A witty conceit went at that time a long—a very long way in Jamaica. The seal was not of Clutter-

---

* Verse 7 in the Prayer-Book version.

buck's invention; neither did he know the gifted originator, whose name and local habitation had become an antiquarian question by reason of the changes of quarters. Perhaps he was in England, over a seacoal fire, relating stories about Jamaica—perhaps he lay under the sod of the Antilles. Messes contended for him as of their numbers; cynics said he never belonged to any mess, but was an accomplished civilian—a devilish deal sharper fellow than messtables often produced; while profound thinkers maintained that such a witticism was beyond an individual, and was probably the joint work of confederate Millers. Clutterbuck got the gem from some one who parted with it for the same reason that induced Clutterbuck to transfer it now to Brune,—it was no longer applicable to his condition.

"Umph! So you've got the ring," said Tom, who had a good deal of passive jealousy in his composition.

"I've got it," said Arthur, "and I shan't be sorry to part with it for a good reason."

"Rather a stale joke," Tom said; "but never mind the ring. I was thinking Clutterbuck's night will just suit for the enterprise of which we were speaking. You see, old Arabin and Melhado are to be there. They'll sit all night—that's your chance."

"Tom, you old sinner," Brune replied, "I believe

the Evil One is tempting me out of your mouth at this moment. Say the truth—have you let him your old temple?"

"He hasn't half good enough taste to come my way. He likes serpents—hate snakes—always make my blood run cold," said Tom, shuddering, and taking a pull at the jorum.

"I'm afraid," said Brune, "he has a turn at all sorts."

"Well," replied Tom, "I don't pretend to be better than my neighbours; perhaps the old enemy takes a night's lodging with me now and them."

"Lodging!" echoed Arthur; "he's got a confounded long lease, if not the fee-simple."

"So much for that," Tom answered; "but it's nothing to do with what we have been speaking of. Be it devil or angel that prompts, I'd have her off on Clutterbuck's night. Look here! we'll see them well primed and fast at hazard: you shall go up and pilot the prize to the mountain's foot, where I will be waiting with the cart; and if I don't take you to any church in the island, and see you spliced before pursuit has begun, my name isn't Gervaise."

Tom had struck the chord which had of late been vibrating so painfully, and whose thrill now amounted to agony. His voice was like the hair that breaks the camel's back. Brune's mind had been oscillating so miserably between the promptings of two different spirits, and was so desperate with their importunities, that even the suggestion of Gervaise served to fix his determination. Nothing tries a vigorous mind like uncertainty; but once decision takes the place of doubt, though it point to trying or desperate measures, there is a relief in collecting the energies for action which is akin to pleasure. Before that morning passed, Brune had formed a resolution out of which springs this tale of *Captain Clutterbuck's Champagne.*

CHAPTER II.

On the afternoon of the day which we began in the last chapter, Brune left old Gervaise snoring on the sofa after second breakfast (*Anglicè*, lunch), and mounted on a rough, fast-trotting pony, was clearing the paths which lead from Stony Hill to another branch of the Port Royal Mountains. He travelled with the unconscious speed of excitement. All flushed, he pressed the pony's reeking sides, devouring the way, yet heedless of his passage; spurring faster yet, and faster, while inwardly he revolved some all-absorbing thought. Brune's route descended first from Stony Hill to the plain, across which he rode with his face towards the principal mountain-chain. That road is not one for a traveller to pass unnoticed. Varied and ever varying rise the broken heights clad to the summits with herb or forest, the tops fading, from distance, into the softest purple. A thousand prongs and ridges push out and court the sunbeam, hugging between them shadowy channels and dimples where the dazzled eye may rest. Even faces of perpendicular rock are covered by verdure and blossom, for the daring creepers weave themselves across. Only where a slight landslip has recently happened, or where the zigzag path has been newly made, is the bare soil exposed. All earth is gay, all heaven is serene, and the transparent vapours that float between earth and heaven catch every colour from the burning rays, and bathe the landscape in a fairy flood. Glorious hills: witnesses of everlasting summer! He who has seen them will retain for ever, but he cannot communicate, the impression. It is not awe of the grandeur, but admiration of the beauty, which possesses him. Overwhelming power in the Creator, conscious insignificance in the beholder, are not the first ideas which the scene excites. Neither are strong and sublime emotions aroused. The soul is content to live and look. For Nature has put on glorious apparel, her face is lovely as a rainbow, and her breath like the happy sigh of a mother over her first-born.

The hill rose abruptly from the plain. After being scorched by the sun, and consumed by his own impatience and speed, Arthur suddenly entered a pass between two beetling rocks, and felt a new rush of life from the delicious shade and already fresher air. The road turned to the left, and led with a gentle rise along the mountain's base. Trees, shrubs, and creepers now abounded on both sides; sometimes the way was overshadowed with foliage, sometimes only the centre of the arch above was open, and the eye, upturned, saw the clear blue sky like a strip of ribbon, solving the question asked so long ago—

"Quibus in terris
Tres pateat cœli spatium non amplius ulnas?"

Along the path grow mango, and orange, and star-apple trees, whose fruit is free to the parched passenger. In the bush are forest trunks, among which stand tamarinds, palms, silk-cotton, and bread-fruit. The mountain is broken into endless projections and recesses, along the contour of which winds the ever-changing road, showing through occasional openings to seaward the richly burdened plains of Liguanea, studded with villas (called *pens*), estates, and buildings, and churches: some of the highest parts of Kingston sparkle in the distance, and beyond them is a narrow belt of sea touching the horizon.

The air, the grass, and the foliage, resound with shriek and hum. Everywhere is animation, more apparent, if not more abundant, than in severer climes, and every sense is appealed to by the infinite forms of life. Myriads of insects, humming-birds scarce bigger than insects, parrots and parroquets, are above and around him. Beneath his feet are the chameleon turnings of the lizard, and the silent creep of the black snake. The great convolvulus, and a profusion of gay flowers, garland his path. The rich full tints of the trees indicate not autumn, foreshadow no decay: biting winter comes not hither. If, as a celebrated living author * has said, *that only is real joy which is likely to endure*, then is the pleasure of beholding these woods a truth, for to-morrow will not rob them of their charms.

Suddenly the road turns; our traveller faces about, and recrosses at a higher elevation the same spurs whose feet he has just threaded in the opposite direction. Soon again the zigzag way is reversed. Another and another tropic, the lines becoming shorter in proportion to the heights. The hill-side is now less uniformly clad: he is in the region of coffee. Estates divide this altitude with the forest, their buildings and barbecues at last standing out sharply from the blending colours. The flat land beneath begins to look like a map; the sugar-buildings are mushrooms, the villas are specks, and the whole fair city of Kingston glitters in the sun, with its flashing harbour, the long line of sand, called the Palisades, terminated by the little town of Port Royal, and then a burning sheet of sea. All round the windings of the hills, houses and cottages send back the sunbeams—*sent back*, for on a sudden the erewhile laughing scene is

* Sir E. L. B. Lytton.

eclipsed by vapour. A few yards in front of Brune, so it seems, rises from the valley a lurid cloud; the lightnings flash; the rocks reverberate the thunder; yet all is clear immediately around the traveller, who expects, but does not feel, the sudden storm. His observation of it is for a time impeded by reason of an inequality in the road, and when he recovers the prospect it has begun to change. The cloudy veil becomes less dull and regular; the outline of the higher mountains is once more seen, and underneath them, as by magic, springs a gorgeous arch, its bases hidden in the valleys. For, evermore, in climes like this, amid the fitful moods of nature, which threaten wreck and woe, is seen this lovely presence, toiling man's charter, assuring him that, while the earth remaineth, seed-time and harvest shall not cease. Anon the vision disperses, the fleecy wreaths depart hither and thither, and the hills, glittering with dewdrops from the recent shower, show their varied faces once more.

Brune heeded not these scenes; he rode as though for life; he noticed none who passed, though every passenger turned to stare after him, negroes ejaculating the everlasting "hi," and white men marvelling at the young man's rapt countenance and hot haste. Few of those who saw him would have desired to contend with him, for the rider is young and active, and there is *purpose* written on his features. The pony, too, is hard and sinewy, and fears not his work. Yet, swelter as they may, thou and we, oh reader, know how to outstrip them. Swifter than light divine Imagination glances. Let them toil, and sweat, and palpitate; we leave them far behind, and lo! we have forestalled that panting spirit, and are already in the house to which he is yet toiling!

A bower in the mountains of Jamaica, erected by the hand of Taste, is indeed a pleasurable spot. Such was the house of old Arabin. He did not build it, neither was it in his nature to create such a paradise; but he had just discernment enough, when it was offered for sale, after the death of him who conceived and formed it, to pay down at once the heavy price, and so to strangle competition. A small piece of table-land had been chosen as the site. 'Twas overlooked on three sides by hills more or less distant, which, opening wide toward the south, repeated from a higher level the view of Kingston and Port Royal with which Brune was so often playing bo-peep as he traversed the steeps below. This way, of course, looked all the principal rooms.

The plateau was bounded by a fringe of foliage composed of the tops of mango and other tall trees, which, rooted on a lower level, towered just high enough to be seen without obstructing the view.

The part of its area nearest the house was laid out in ornamental forms, and covered, except the walks, with Bahama grass, whose deep green was grateful to the eye. On it grew a few lofty trees, the principal of which were a tamarind and almond, whose branches, interlacing at a great height, overspread the sward, giving momentary passage as they waved about to piercing sunbeams, round which the gentle shadows sported incessantly. A fountain bubbled between the trees, and as its light silver was scattered this way and that by the breeze, the transient rays, dissolving through its mist, figured the ground like the field of a kaleidoscope. The lower trunks, being well pruned, allowed to be seen beyond the greensward a garden bright with tropical blossoms. All hues shone upon the beds, and above them waved the oleander, frangipane, and a profusion of shrubs.

There was an advantage in the dark-green foreground, for it allowed the windows of the principal room to be open during the heat of the day, and thus to admit the air, which, charged with the scent of orange and jessamine, rioted through the apartment, disturbing every article that was not well weighted down, causing the music on the piano to crackle, table-cloths to be violently agitated, pictures to rattle against the walls, and blowing about the light-brown tresses of Violet Arabin as if they had been Zephyrus his private property. If not an owner, he was at least a welcome guest, and had every reason to be flattered by his reception; for Violet had waylaid the wind, placing herself right in its path, and enjoying its caress as it breathed on her fair face and neck. She lay half reclined on a couch; her air was languid, and her manner subdued. It had been much subdued of late, though her health could scarcely be thought to have suffered; for, spite of many months' residence in the tropics, the bloom which she brought out from England had not disappeared, though its brightness was dimmed. Her eye, too, had lost its quick and laughing glance, and beamed pensively from below the long downcast lash. Climate was made answerable for the change; and yet, among those fresh mountains, a healthy girl, you would have thought, might long have preserved her European bloom. But no subterfuge ought to have been resorted to, or to have been necessary in the matter, and *we* see no reason for reserve, and mean not to maintain any. Be it confessed then, that Violet, young and fair and fascinating as she was, had felt already the power of grief.

> "A foe to rest
> Had stained the current of her sinless years,
> And turned her pure heart's purest blood to tears."

And yet she was betrothed; another fortnight, please

Heaven, would see her a bride! And all Jamaica would flock to congratulate and admire her, and to offer in a new form the incense which had greeted her presence since the day she landed. Poor girl! there is something cross in this.

"My child," said Mrs Arabin—we beg pardon for not having introduced the old lady—" my child, you never touch the instrument now—that is not wise. Husbands should not be allowed to complain that their wives have abandoned their accomplishments with their maiden names."

Violet, being deep in thought, was some time before she apprehended her mother's observation. "I don't mean to give it up, mother," she said at length; "I shall play and sing more than ever I did, after—after——"

"After you are married, my love. I am delighted to hear you say so. Mr Melhado is particularly fond of music, and I think understands it. He would be sadly disappointed if he found you after marriage indifferent to a gift in which you excel."

Her daughter sighed "O yes!" and fixed her eyes again on the floor.

"There are those songs of Bishop's, you know, 'The Soldier Tired,' and 'Bid me discourse,' and so on; you were never weary of singing them, while now we never hear a note."

"But you know, mother, the same things cannot please for ever. I had for that music a passing fancy, whose very excess has now changed it to indifference."

"Nay, Violet, it was not only here that they were your favourites. Long before your return home you sang them constantly; and on the voyage out you entertained the company on board with them every day—at least you said so, and Captain Gibbs said Mr Brune used to sing with you."

The fair girl moved impatiently, and almost rose from her seat; but she instantly resumed it, sighing again. Her eyes became suffused with tears.

"My sweet child," resumed the old lady, "you grieve me more than I can tell by this sadness. You surely do not allow yourself, now, ever to think of this Mr Brune, after the many admonitions I have given you on the subject. And you about to be married, too! Quite dreadful! It was very well some time ago to have a handsome gentlemanly young man pay you attentions, as he of course was very ready to do, you being Mr Arabin's daughter, and, though I say it, a girl that nobody could help admiring. But then you know it is different now: you have made your choice, and must forget all fancies. This one, in particular, I wonder at your retaining, after the shocking accounts which your father heard of the young man's behaviour."

"Mother, mother," said Violet, "this is too much. Whatever my father has heard to his discredit, is a falsehood—nothing less—the utterance of some base malignant spirit! I have obeyed my parents in all things with regard to him: I meet him as a stranger, and I try to banish him even from my thoughts; but hear him slandered I will not!"

Violet had risen as she spoke. Her eye was uplifted now, and there was no lack of colour in her cheek. Mrs Arabin was startled at her unusual vehemence.

"Why, Violet, my dear, how can you?" said the old lady, rising also, and putting her arms round her daughter. "Why, what can it signify about this young officer? Perhaps it may be as you say. I daresay he is innocent."

"He is, he is," sobbed Violet, on her mother's breast; whereupon Mrs Arabin sobbed too, and, taking the infection profusely, she wept and mingled her tears with those of her daughter.

Mrs Arabin was the first to recover. She dried her child's eyes and her own, and then, gently kissing Violet, replaced her on her seat.

"What a foolish thing it is," she said, "and all about nonsense, too—the merest nonsense; because, you know, your papa's position being what it is—a member of Council, and one of the most influential men in the island—the idea of a young lieutenant having any serious thought of you is perfectly absurd —ha, ha!" And with her lips contradicting her red eyes, she laughed mockingly, inviting Violet's responsive laugh, which did not come.

"Yes, mother; but let us talk of some other matter."

"Well, that is sensibly spoken—so we will. Let us be cheerful, as I'm sure we ought when we think of the beautiful, the magnificent wedding you will have—your elegant dresses, and the bishop to marry you, and the bridesmaids, and the carriages, and the favours. O my!" And the weight of the splendid anticipations so oppressed Mrs Arabin, that she was obliged to set down her load and rest for a moment before she could proceed.

"Then there will be the announcement in all the papers : 'Daughter of the Honourable Christopher Arabin, of Crystal Mount and Dirty Gully Plantations, Member of His Majesty's Council, Colonel of the Kingston Horse Guards (bright scarlet), Receiver of Rum Customs, Clerk of the Market, Head Scavenger,' and I don't know what besides. What a sensation it will create in London when it appears in the 'Times' and 'Morning Post!'"

Violet *did* smile now. "Why, mother, you don't suppose that any people in London, except acquaintances of our own, would trouble themselves about our affairs?"

"Of course, my love, it will be the talk of the country. How young and simple you are! Don't we see the precision, the absolute toadyism, with which they record the union of the most noble duke or marquess of so and so with the lady this or that, the fair and accomplished daughter of the earl of something, and all the particulars of the two families, and the list of their seats and possessions? And isn't your papa here quite in the same position as a duke is in at home—a legislator, a great landowner, and a holder of most important offices under the Crown? *Of course* your marriage will be the topic of the day. I shouldn't wonder if it made the people forget all about Mr O'Connell, and created a little popularity for the poor King."

Again Violet attempted to correct her mother's creole hallucinations, but in vain. Mrs Arabin wound up a prolonged recital of the grandeur of their house by remarking, "Thus you see, love, how important it is for people of note to consider well even their private and domestic acts. Mr Melhado is a member of Assembly, and, your papa thinks, a talented and rising young man. His speech on the John Crow* bill was a masterpiece. Many people think him quite the equal of Sir Robert Peel. Then his large fortune and his capacity for business point him out as one of our future wealthiest proprietors. All these advantages bespeak your marriage with him a most proper and prudent connection, as well as, I hope, a source of lasting happiness to you both; while, had you allowed your head to be turned by any silly fancy—a preference for some obscure person like this Mr Brune, for instance—the great inequality of the match, as well as——"

"Stop, mother, I implore you, stop," faltered Violet, the fountain of whose tears having been so recently opened, could not bear tampering with. "Assist and strengthen your poor girl; do not trifle with— with——" And again the poor maiden's passionate sobs were vented more vehemently than before on the matron's shoulder, who, after a more temperate indulgence in the same refreshing luxury, seemed at length to be awakened by a sudden idea.

"My darling girl, my sweet child, is it possible— no, no, Violet, tell me—you cannot—you, Mr Arabin's daughter, you cannot have given your heart to this

---

* A loathsome vulture (*vultur aura*), which, being very useful in the removal of carrion and garbage, is protected by an act of the Legislature.

young man—O dear, O dear—your father—speak, Violet, speak, my sweetest."

But Violet spake not. A long-pent torrent was rushing like an avalanche from her heart; she gasped and sobbed, and clung to her mother's neck, and buried her face upon her mother's bosom, as if her eyes might never again face the daylight. Her mother returned the embrace half unconsciously. She was agitated by opposing emotions, any one of which might have sufficed to distract her, but which, by conflicting in her breast, and neutralising each other, produced a stupified equilibrium. The possible defeat of the projected grand alliance—Mr Arabin's disappointed wrath, which *might* make the house very unpleasant—the effect of a *contre-temps* on a society whose highest stratum she considered no small object of ambition, and whose pointed finger seemed to her a terrible weapon—rushed simultaneously on her perceptions, and created this awful calm. But fortunately no meaner feeling searched to the depth of her nature, where, underlying ignorance and vanity and conjugal timidity, was a true and valiant affection for her child, which presently asserted a pre-eminence, and made her speak as unlike herself as noble instinct is unlike selfish folly.

There was an interval during which the light rushed strongly upon Mrs Arabin's mind. That mind, as the sagacious reader is already aware, was not of the most perspicacious order, and it required direct prompting and powerful motive to inspire it with either clearness or vigour. She had now chanced to receive a right impression, and maternal instinct did the rest. Her former quiet adoption of the views of others, more especially those of her husband, as regarded Violet's feelings, seemed now quite marvellous to herself. How readily had she overlooked every sign of her poor girl's struggle with herself, or explained in some simple way what she could not help observing! And Violet's sufferings—what must they have been while maiden feeling kept her silent, and her heart was bursting for lack of confidence and counsel! From regarding herself, in the first place, as strangely blind and negligent, the mother, as she more and more clearly realised her child's misery, began to accuse herself of culpable indifference to her duties, and finally she voted herself the most unnatural monster alive. Rushing now, with the facility of a weak disposition, into a different extreme, she was visited with a series of most heroic conceptions, the risk of which she was quite ready to encounter on Violet's behalf, but they were unhappily not of a practicable description. Soon, however, came more rational resolves, if no very clear solution of the difficulty; and Mrs Arabin saw that there was one anodyne which she might at once afford, in assuring poor Violet of her sympathy. This, of course, was effected with a further grand accompaniment of tears and embraces, of which we pretend not to convey an adequate impression: we merely allude to their occurrence, lest fair critics, observing the omission, should pronounce this true history a bungling fiction; and with this observation we proceed to give the heads of what passed.

"My girl! my darling! trust to your own mother. She will make you happy, not break your heart. Violet, I would never willingly have given you a moment's pain; all that has been done seemed for your advantage and future happiness. I have erred. I see it all; but it is not too late. Cheer up. I will myself see Mr Brune."

"Mother! mother!" again sobbed Violet, in deprecation — " mother, I never said, never thought of that. I can bear the sacrifice which my parents require of me; my prayer, in return, is only that my feelings may be respected."

"How, Violet? I do not understand you. You do not wish to marry this young man?"

"I do not wish to wed another—that—that is my misery."

"But Mr Brune—is he an object of indifference to you?"

Silence again; and her rosy neck answered for Violet, though her cheeks were hid.

"I must go on now, child, and learn the whole of your case. I take for granted that my sweet daughter, in giving her heart, believed fully that another had been given in return."

And Violet murmured "Yes."

"Has he told you so?"

"No."

"And yet you believe it!"

"Mother, there is an eloquence more convincing than words."

"But men have been known ere now to feign a passion; and recollect, my darling, that this one, though he may be fully sensible of your beauty, and the advantage of our connection, lies under grave imputations, and we are warranted in at least testing his sincerity."

"I have observed him through the trying ordeal of a sea voyage. I have seen him risk his life to save the life of another. When others were launching boats and seeking appliances, he, without hesitation, dashed overboard after his drowning comrade, while all was dismay and stupefaction. If you had watched him, mother, gloriously struggling with the waves and supporting the lifeless body, while tardy prudence pulled dryshod to their aid—had you seen his drenched form hoisted on to the deck, the chest scarcely heaving, the countenance deathlike—had you seen the languid eyes turned still upon him whom he had rescued, and making the inquiry which the tongue could not, whether he still breathed,—you would have known as I do, that he is neither base nor selfish."

"Heaven send it prove so, my child, for I see that your happiness is wrapped up in him. But now to think how our arrangements may be altered—postponed we will say at first. Dear me, what a vexation!" And the perplexities of Mrs Arabin began at length to look formidable again. "Your father will be frantic—what a house we shall have! And the odious ill-natured remarks—that Mrs Simons, how delighted the wretch will be! Your trousseau, to be sure, will not be entirely thrown away; but the cake now—I do believe there has never been such a cake as this will be! All yesterday and half the day before did Zenobia and I spend in mixing it. I would not trust even her on such an occasion; the least indiscretion, you know, might have impaired its excellence, and they have all such whims and fancies, even white ladies. There is Mrs Turner, now, never adds the almonds till it is three parts kneaded, and Mrs James lets it rise twelve hours. But I know my mother's recipe, which I have always followed, drives them all mad with envy. To be sure, such a cake! It is the best I ever compounded, and I have made enough to know something about them. Mrs Turner indeed! Well, but after all, the cake is not the first consideration." (Mrs Arabin's mind, very much frightened, had been trying to steal away from its difficulty, but was obliged to turn back and face the matter in hand.) "How shall we move your father's determination? How shall we, or how can he now recede from engagements so clear and determinate?" And as Mrs Arabin pondered on her difficulties, they expanded like thunder-clouds, and threatened to overwhelm her. "Oh!" she groaned—"oh, that I were a man! Oh, that I had some one to advise and help us!"

And in truth the situation did call for energy and decision and prompt action. Some subtle association of ideas suggested to the bewildered woman a quarter where these qualities were to be found.

"Violet," she continued, "I have undertaken your cause, and will omit nothing to secure your peace of mind. I will myself see this Mr Brune, and if I find his demeanour answerable to your hopes, he shall have an opportunity of clearing his character and of avowing the sentiments——"

"Nay, mother, mother; you would not, could not," said Violet, clutching her mother's dress as if to prevent an immediate execution of the appalling project.

"My dear," said Mrs Arabin, with some spirit, "this is not an occasion for refinement. Some assistance I must have, and if the thoughts which you have revealed to me do not deceive yourself, there can be no impropriety in my permitting an interview. Of course I shall use discretion in bringing it about. I shall—I shall—send—yes—no—that won't do—I will contrive to—'um, that's not it—I have it—I'll——"

"Missy," screamed a coloured servant, running in with small regard for ceremony, "Massa Brune come again. My king! me see him go to the stable-yard wid his horse. I glad, for true!"

The raw magician who has faltered his first doubting spell, and cowers before the spirit he has raised, can scarce be more astonished than was poor Mrs Arabin at this announcement. So scared was she that she thought the negro sported with her trouble, which he did not even know.

"How dare you, Leander," she said, trembling with emotion—"how dare you practise your jokes upon me, sir? Your master shall know your behaviour when he returns, and shall teach you better manners."

"Hei, missy, me no joke. Massa Brune really

come. Me see him 'pan de brown pony. My, dat horse sweat! moast wash away."

"Do you mean seriously to tell me that Mr Brune is here?"

"Av coorse, missy, me say so. He here—here he come, faba* king."

And as he spoke did Arthur Brune approach, his noble form and air justifying the negro's comparison.

His appearance had created some excitement in the establishment. A round yellow laughing face, surmounted by a kerchief and flanked by two enormous ear-drops, was thrust across the doorway behind him. The owner of it was pretty Miss Rosabella, *femme de chambre*, who, exhibiting a brilliant set of teeth, said gleefully, "De lubly buckra!"† and withdrew. At the same moment was seen at one of the front windows the apparition of Nick Chitty, *soi-disant* butler, who, with a half-cleaned soup-ladle in one hand, and a piece of chamois skin in the other, presented his black visage, with a horrid scowl on it. He, having inspected the new-comer, muttered "Chaw! what bring you dis side?‡ Who de debil want you?" Then he shuffled away again, polishing severely.

---

* *Favour king*—i.e., like a king. The word *favour*, in the acceptation of the Jamaica negro, means to *resemble*—e.g., he favours you, means, he is *like* you.

† White person.   ‡ Here.

Leander, the negro who had announced Brune, cast at Violet a look which he intended to be congratulatory before he withdrew.

Arthur's reception was of course, spite of his self-possession, sufficiently embarrassing to all. Violet could not effect a retreat so rapidly but that he detected the traces of her recent emotion, and shaped his plan according to the hopeful symptom. He was to be subjected to what Mrs Arabin, poor woman, intended for a very searching examination. Of course the "honour of his visit" was the first thing to be accounted for; and, on this invitation, Brune went straight and manfully to his object.

"He was there," so he said, "to supply an omission, which, had it concerned himself alone, he would never have sought to repair. But it had occurred to him strongly that the happiness of another might possibly be affected by his course; and this view of his duty had but now presented itself. Pride and anger, and they only, had deterred him, some months ago, from declaring his passion for Miss Arabin, and asking her hand. Events had happened since that period such as to make a declaration *now* appear not only useless, but impertinent. Nevertheless he viewed his duty, as he had said, in a new light, and he had taken a sudden resolution. He had come thither to make known his affection for Miss Arabin, and to say that it would be showing him the highest favour to allow him to plead his cause to herself. He had his reasons for preferring to say so to Mrs Arabin rather than to her husband."

Mrs Arabin, grand inquisitor, was completely confounded by this candour. The confession which her ingenuity was to have wormed out of the unsuspecting youth was voluntarily poured into her ear. Her attempted air of dignity, and her murmurs of "most extraordinary"—"astonished"—"quite unprepared," were pitiably done; and it did not aid her perplexity to find herself immediately subjected in her turn to the question—

"Madam," said Brune, "I believe that you love your daughter as she ought to be loved, and that you would purchase her happiness at the expense of your own? You have heard my declaration. Let me implore you to act upon it like a loving parent. If, as a mother, you dare not tell me that my suit is as hopeless and out of place as it must appear to the world, aid, I conjure you, in arresting the threatened course of events."

Perceiving that she was not quite mistress of the situation as she had intended to be, Mrs Arabin now made a dignified effort to recover the command.

"I am at a loss to comprehend, sir," she said, "by

what right you presume thus to dictate to me in matters concerning my domestic affairs."

"I claim no right whatever, madam," replied Arthur; "I have not even an excuse to offer for my conduct. I thought it just possible that my behaviour might explain and justify itself. Since it has not done so, I have only to render my intrusion as short as possible, and to assure you that you need not apprehend a repetition of it."

Saying which he rose, and, bowing low, turned to withdraw. Instantly her difficulties overshadowed the matron once more. The aid which fortune had sent in the very moment of need she had contrived to alienate. The dignity disappeared, and the perplexed mother sobbed out—

"And are you really going to desert us? Oh, the fickleness, the hollowness of men!"

"Pardon me," said Brune, with becoming gravity, "you remarked on my presumption."

"How can you sport thus with a mother's feelings?" said Mrs Arabin. "You know not half my embarrassment, or you would not—could not. Oh, if those who envy my position could but feel these anxieties, they would know the insufficiency of rank to confer happiness! What is all that I possess, if I have not an adviser in my distress? Ah, me! I wish I was dead!"

"Mrs Arabin," answered the young man, taking her hand, "you shall command my best advice and assistance. I ask in return but two concessions. Give me your confidence; and suffer me to have a short interview with Miss Arabin."

From what has been seen of Mrs Arabin's diplomacy, the reader will already have divined that she was not long in making a clean breast; and that Mr Arthur Brune found the existing state of things in the Arabin family not very unlike what his imagination had painted it. Shortly after the old lady's confession, she was to be seen in her accustomed seat facing the front window, while Violet Arabin and Arthur Brune stood by the cool fountain, under the shade of the dark tamarind. Motionless were both, and their attitudes seemed sad; but Violet's face wore the startled expression of returning joy, and Brune's eye, while gazing on it, seemed to retain by an effort its grave and monitory aspect. Already had the young soldier learned the value of time, and to repress emotion when action or decision was required of him. We might divine their thoughts—we might reveal their language—we might regale our reader with a love scene in which good sense, strong affection, and difficult circumstances, render both the actors incapable of insipidity. We might retail argument and remonstrance, and depict the strength both of principle and passion. But we prefer to consider knowledge of this kind sacred, and forbear to make any revelation, withdrawing with delicacy to the other side of the house, and amusing ourself with what there passes up to the time when Mrs Arabin again joins the pair, and, shortly after, Brune bids both ladies a short adieu.

CHAPTER III.

BEHIND the house the ground soon began to fall. There a winding road led through a shrubbery to the stables and offices, and finally to the negro houses—these buildings being kept out of sight by the bushes and the brow of the hill. Loitering along this road was the pleasing form of Miss Rosabella, who, sometimes picking a flower or a leaf, sometimes gazing abstractedly at the prospect, while she wrought her mouth into a foam by fretting her teeth with chewstick,* and sometimes kicking the small stones with her pretty foot,† gave evidence that she was not bound upon a mission requiring despatch. Looking leisurely up from a lizard which she had three or four times turned over on its back with her shoe, and which seemed to join in the sport as blithely as the dragon on a guinea, she smote her upraised foot smartly on the ground, and uttered the

* A fibrous creeper. A piece of it is generally seen in the hand of an unemployed negro, who rubs his teeth with it at intervals.
† The dreadful negro hoof disappears when the race is mixed.

monosyllable "Chaw!" Miss Rosabella was displeased—most unreasonably so, one might suppose; for that which met her view was the form of Mr Nicholas Chitty, the butler, attired as we saw him a short time since at the drawing-room window—that is to say, in a shirt and trousers not over clean. It might be that these accidental meetings with Mr Chitty were too frequent, or that his manner, which was somewhat cynical and caustic, was not appreciated by her, or, haply, because he was declined into the vale of years, that Miss Rosabella was wroth at the sight of him. She, however, smothered her irritation, and received with maidenly propriety the address of this important personage.

"Hah, my 'pring-flower!" said Mr C., looking sweetly—that is, trying to subdue a settled sneer, which reminded one of the untameable hyæna—"you is de pusson I always like to meet when I 'troll out for a airing, 'pon my life you is. Leetle chilly dis afternoon, don't you tink so, Miss Rosy?"

The sun, which had been vertical an hour or two before, was at that moment darting his beams into Mr Chitty's grizzled wool and over his respectable person, so as to make the observation unintelligible to a European.

"It is not too cold," replied Rosabella; "you always so delicate, Meesta Chitty."

"Of course," said Mr Chitty, "me has got finer feeling dan dose common negro people. Dat is de reason why I admires you so all time, Miss Rosy, becausin you is so genteel; and you is werry 'andsome too—make me can't help in lub wid you."

"Meesta Chitty, don't bodder me; you is always talkin' dis same nonsense," replied the fair one.

Nick looked up after the manner of Mr Romeo Montague, as if seeking among the spheres for some object to attest his truth; but he apparently found none worthy of that distinction. Had he enjoyed a histrionic education, he would unquestionably have sworn by his gracious self, whom he thought aptly formed to be the god of any "nyoung woman's" idolatry. Language thus failing him, he advanced with a hideous grin and offered to take Rosy's hand.

"Hei, Meesta Chitty, what is you doing, sar?" said she, in a smothered exclamation. "You no 'fraid somebody see we? Meesta Brune's horse come dis way direckly, and a pretty sight for the groom you would make!"

Satisfied, since the objection proceeded from prudential and not from personal considerations, Mr Chitty waived the proposed attention and withdrew a pace, promising himself usurious compensation. He gracefully turned the conversation to general topics. "Dis Massa Brune, now, Miss Rosy, what make him bring him ugly face dis side again? After we no see him so long, I hoped him gone to de debil, and not come no more."

"La, Meesta Chitty! who you call ugly? My king! de hansummest nyoung sojer buckra in de harmy—he, he, *ugly!!* chaw! Come? Why, of course, him is come for coort Miss Wily; what else?"

"Tought she going to marry Massa Melhado, eh? How dis, eh? Someting not quite right here. Wonder if Massa understand what going on!" marvelled Nick.

"Of course he understand," rejoined Rosy, sharply. "Any pusson who was to speak to de Massa about it, I wouldn't look at him if there didn't anoder man alive."

"Chaw! who goin' to 'peak to him? what me care about deir lub-making?" said Nick, intimidated by the lady's threat.

Both Nick and Rosy had evidently interpreted Brune's visit in some degree correctly, and had ranged themselves on different sides according to their instincts—the girl the abettor of true love, the cynic the marplot of the piece. When he so readily consented to refrain from communication on the subject with "Massa," he had had time to reflect that old Christy would show little gratitude for any revelation, while there was another quarter from whence it would be well paid for. Thus deference to his ladye-love sorted well with self-interest.

"So long as my 'pring-flower look pleasant 'pon me, why is me to tell massa?" said Nick, ogling frightfully. "Now look here, my lub; supposing you is to be in de Mango Walk dis evening; it just possible dat me might come dat side too; and if we should happen to meet, you know, lubly Rosy, why den — hei! who dis?" At this unlucky moment another person came upon the scene. It was Leander, who had announced Brune to the ladies—a smart, intelligent, young mulatto, who, having been in England, was a cut above the ordinary coloured class, however profaning the name of him whom

> "Love who sent forgot to save
> The young, the beautiful, the brave,
> The only hope of Sestos' daughter."

The balked Chitty grinned sardonically at the newcomer, with a wrath which was more than doubled when his quick eye detected a glance of intelligence and deprecation passing from Rosabella to Leander.

"What de dooce you want here, sar?" yelled Nick. "Is dis for you* English manners, when a lady an' a

---

* In the Jamaica dialect, the possessive pronoun is generally formed by placing the word *for* before the personal; thus, for you face, means *your face;* for him name, *his name;* house da for me, *the house is mine.*

gentleman is discoorsing, to push for you dam black face atween dem, eh?"

"Don't vex," replied Leander, smiling; "I really tink, Mr Chitty, that I have a right to go down to the stable to order up Mr Brune's horse widout your leave."

"Den pass on, sar," said Nick, highly incensed. "I is 'peaking important business, and don't want to be boddered wid negro boys."

"Hah, hah, hah!" tittered Leander, "I must laugh. It is better than a fun to hear you talk about negro boys. Why, you is as black as de debil yourself, and a near relation too, I should tink, Old Nick."

"If you says dat," observed Mr Chitty, urbanely, "you is a cussed liard."

Hard words do not necessarily lead to hard knocks among negroes, but they often produce a railing match of the most energetic description. Such a passage of tongues appeared now to impend between these sable champions. The issue no man might foretell, for in prowess and accomplishments they appeared equally matched. Mr Chitty's tongue was an embossed club or two-handed sword with which he rained a shower of stunning vituperation fitted to prostrate an unwary antagonist in the first encounter; while he of Abydos, less affecting the crushing ruin of the mace or battle-axe, preserved his temper and his wit, dexterously parried or evaded the pelting opprobrium of the foe, and, watching his opportunity, longed a pointed sarcasm through the joints of the armour, Mr Chitty's moral hide being plated like a rhinoceros. Both stood prepared and eager for the fray, while the fair Rosabella, sole arbitress of the lists, should rain influence and judge the prize. Fate decreed, however, that the interesting duel should not take place, for as the combatants addressed themselves to the assault, Arthur Brune, whose mood it did not suit to wait for his horse, appeared in the road on his way to the stables, his brow still bearing traces of anxiety, but cleared of that engrossing cloud beneath which we saw him ride up the mountain.

"Hah, Leander," said Arthur, "why, you look as you used to do on board ship when it began to blow: and pretty Miss Rosy, also, you don't look sea-sick now at any rate, though I have seen you miserable enough. My old sweet-tempered friend, Menelaus too, I declare! How d'ye do, old boy? you seem to have imported a fresh cargo of gall and verjuice, and look as if it would burst you. Long time isn't it since you saw me or my money, so I shall just give you a dollar apiece." The gratuity, received with the usual scrape of the foot, relaxed immediately Leander's countenance, and even mitigated the severity of Mr Chitty's. Rosy expressed her delight at seeing

"Meesta Brune" again, and told him personally that she thought him handsomer than ever, for reserve is not a characteristic of the coloured maiden. Brune, having but few thoughts to waste on the group, hurried on to the stable. As soon as he was beyond hearing,—

"Hei!" said Mr Chitty, "him begin 'bout dat dam Mennylaiss again, time he forget him shildish foolery. Wha de debil him mean wid him *Mennylaiss, Mennylaiss?* 'Pose dem all begin again now to call me *Mennylaiss.* It not a gentleman's name."

"It de name they give the dogs and pigs in England," said Leander; "b'lieve it 'riginally belonged to a hangman." Now, *hangman* is the very lowest term of negro reproach.

This worthy was indebted to Brune for the nickname of Menelaus, which had almost superseded his acknowledged appellation. It was suggested by a misfortune which befell him, similar to that which the angry gods inflicted upon the son of Atreus, though its effects were not so direful. His third or fourth helpmate—the writer is uncertain which—was a free coloured girl of considerable personal attractions, who, in her early and undiscriminating youth, had suffered herself to be proclaimed the mistress of his affections and establishment. Their union was not felicitous. After a very short time the lady's ideas became sufficiently matured to enable her to reject the evil and to choose the good; the practical result being her sudden abandonment of Mr Chitty, and elopement to the north side of the island with a bandsman of one of the regiments.

Now the weakness of the soubriquet "Menelaus," and the thoughtless haste with which Brune had applied it, are apparent at this stage of the narrative, for the affair did not so much as contribute a bloody nose to the encouragement of the Epos; and, as an impassioned foreign poetess once remarked, "The blind old man of Scio might have chawed upon it from July to eternity without creating a dollar's worth of hexameters from the transaction."

However, though no hero, Nick discovered the route and followed the fugitive; and endeavoured by promises, blandishments, apologies, and protestations, to induce her to return, but without effect. He had likewise addressed himself to the destroyer of his peace, but that Lothario heaped insult upon wrong, and withered his victim with a refined and lofty disdain. "Him cuss me, and tell me to go to ———, sar," said Menelaus, when relating the adventure to Brune. Nick obeyed this mandate, not according to its letter, which would have killed, but in its spirit, and took himself off.

The misfortune, however, did not trouble him long.

In a very few weeks another lady belonging to the estate had succeeded the faithless free-woman; but neither did this alliance establish Mr Chitty's happiness on a solid foundation. Incompatibility of temper, that frequent queller of domestic joys, caused their connection to terminate by mutual consent, after, alas! a brief duration. They separated: he, however, who would test the veracity of this account by a reference to the Lords' Journals would probably lose his labour. No legislator, nor judge, nor gentleman of the long robe assisted in dissolving the knot; but the solution was effected in a simple and unostentatious manner. Mrs C., on departing one morning for the cane-field, remarked, "I not coming again." To which Menelaus replied, "I rejice to hear it;" and thus he was once more master of the affections which he had now so freely bestowed on Miss Rosabella.

But we have lost sight of our lover.

A man who has traversed a road under the pressure of a burden so heavy that it allowed him not to note an object or incident of the way; and who, after depositing his load, returns rejoicing and refreshed, his senses all awake, and his mind yearning for pleasant impressions, might be taken as a type of Arthur Brune's varying dispositions in his rides to and from Crystal Mount. As he went, every thought turned inwards, and he recked not if it were Paradise or Tophet through which he journeyed. Returning freed in spirit and confirmed in resolution, his mind seemed eager to repay herself for the severe strain that had been put on her; and, instead of revolving definite or practical ideas, sailed buoyantly into the realms of fancy, abiding nowhere, but floating through a succession of delightful images. In this reactionary state the liberated imagination hovered about its newly-secured treasure, as yet too elated and astonished to grasp and feed upon it. Violet's image filled his soul, but was so far from occupying his intellect that it seemed to set free his powers, and bid them luxuriate where they would; there was a great, calm, inseparable joy in the heart, so let the fancy range. It is the *doubting* lover who knits his brow and grinds his mind against his fears! And Arthur thought of lofty deeds and godlike men of old, and then, remarking and dwelling upon each feature of the landscape, he called up as the day declined forms that had walked those hills and vales, and lived, and sinned, and suffered there—the gentle Arowauks and the cruel and haughty Spaniards. Surely if blood can cry to heaven, there is even now ascending from every corner of this island a memorial of the desolation wrought by their conquerors upon the inoffensive red men. Not a rock nor a glen which now reflects or absorbs the moonbeams but has its deep romance, its terrible tragedy. Earth, if it be true that thy legendary spots which have witnessed sublime powers and sufferings and affections of the flesh, can for ages attract the disembodied spirits, then must the surface of Jamaica be as that hill where the young man's eyes were opened at the prayer of the man of God. It must be thick with airy forms seldom unveiled to mortal ken. And forasmuch as these wretched ghosts had neither bard nor sculptor to record their wrongs, and that not one of their race was left alive to transmit the fell tradition, how great must be their indignation, how intense their desire to commune with mankind; how in their restless and invisible swarms they must feel as do the souls of those who were slain for the testimony, and with what impatience must they cry "how long!"

Then Arthur thought how all this infatuated guilt belonged to the fellow-countrymen and immediate successors of the mighty discoverers of those western realms; how but a brief time before the advent of destruction that day might have been pronounced glorious for the islands which saw approach them the grandest adventurers of the eastern world. And then came the reflection how this land had been hallowed to history by the presence of one of nature's greatest, who, within the narrow circle of her shore, had walked and burned and groaned; how, underneath the same sky, and in view of these unchanging hills, the strong body had been weakened by disease, and the mighty spirit had poured forth its plaint! These are the words:—

"It is visible that all methods are adopted to cut the thread that is breaking; for I am in my old age oppressed with insupportable pains of the gout, and am now languishing and expiring with that and other infirmities among savages, where I have neither medicines nor provisions for the body, priest nor sacrament for the soul. My men in a state of revolt; my brother, my son, and those that are faithful, sick, starving, and dying; the Indians have abandoned us, and the Governor of St Domingo hath sent rather to see if I am dead than to succour us, or carry me alive from hence."

Thus from Jamaica in 1504 wrote CHRISTOPHER COLUMBUS to the King of Spain.

The legends of the Antilles, too traditionary for the historian, what might they not become in the hand of the poet or the fiction wizard? Shadowy facts, here and there displaying their outlines sufficiently to guide the mind from point to point, admit of being informed with a connecting spirit, and of being made life-like by the master's hand. But no master has been there. The jolly mariner painting youthful recollections in broad farce, or the puling philanthropist seeking to verify the dream which he dreamed in England, and blind to all facts but those which suit his purpose—these have written of the West Indies, but without the power which seizes on men's hearts, and turns them whither it will.

To Arthur's delighted mind as he rode through the warm night, how interesting seemed the tales of Indian eld—how fit to charm and soften! And with the spell of moonlight on those scenes, as fireflies sparkled through the forest, and the rocks and hills showed like embattled fortresses, meet holds for giants, and the bamboos waved gloomily as over hallowed spots, the time was fit for inspiration.

Before leaving England he was well read in Jamaica scenery, having studied it in the graphic pages of Tom Cringle; and never did he verify with greater pleasure than now the descriptions of that delightful author.

In this mood he alighted once more at Stony Hill. The sounds of revelry were heard from the mess-room, where Arthur would have been hailed as the one person wanting to complete the enjoyment of the evening. But gay company waited for him in vain. Hugging in his heart the new-found happiness, he stole with it to his chamber, and barred his door lest any chance wassailer should profane his blissful solitude. His frame was soon refreshed, and his limbs stretched on his couch. Waking or sleeping, he was in a dream; and it was not until the peeping of the day-beam through the jalousies, and the blowing of the shell upon the hills, that he resolutely dismissed his visions, and prepared like a man of this world for the difficult adventure that lay before him.

CHAPTER IV.

ABOUT a twelvemonth before the period at which our story commences, two young subalterns had been suddenly ordered from their depot at Cork to join headquarters in Jamaica. Some irregularities had been reported to be going on, such as were but too frequently practised in garrison towns — gambling, flirting, drinking, and fighting; and the Horse Guards avoided the trouble of investigation by ordering the officers whose names were prominent in the scandal at once on foreign service. Accordingly, Lieutenants Edward Knox and Arthur Brune, instead of waiting for the transport which was to take out the next draught, proceeded to Gravesend, and embarked on board the freight-ship Sophia Brown, in which passages had been provided for them by the Admiralty. The ship was a fine West Indiaman, and her state-rooms were filled with passengers. There were two or three creole* professional men with their wives

* This epithet is often misapprehended in England, and supposed to mean *coloured* or *crossed with the negro blood.* Its proper

and some children, a barrack-master and his helpmate, a luxurious old planter or two, and others, of whom it is necessary to mention only Miss Violet Arabin, who, having completed her education near London, was returning to her parents and home, watched over by the master of the ship and Mrs Wingrove, a doctor's wife and fellow-passenger, and attended by Leander and Rosabella, who had been sent home expressly that Christy Arabin's daughter might sail in befitting state. Mrs Arabin had suggested a large retinue as indispensable, but her husband reasonably objected to the expense of the double voyages ; wherefore the matron contented herself with exhorting the soi-disant *Captain* Gibbs before he left the island with Leander and Rosy, to make known to all the company on the return voyage how that, partly from accident and partly from the unostentatious temper of herself and her mother, Miss Arabin crossed the Atlantic in a style very much beneath what her condition warranted. Thus were Violet and Arthur placed in that propinquity and communication which were unavoidable in ships of the Sophia Brown's class. They who now scud across the ocean in La Plata and the Magdalena, knocking off their 240 knots a-day, and sitting down hundreds together in the huge

meaning is *born in the West Indies.* Thus there are white creoles, black creoles, and brown creoles, creole horses and creole beef.

saloons, must not marvel that we have described the old freight-ships as bringing their passengers into close relationship. The voyage to Jamaica used to occupy from six weeks to three months: the party was comparatively small, and the arrangements did not admit of isolation. Among young people the constant intercourse was almost certain to become intimacy, and thus it was that our two lovers began the acquaintance which appears to have conducted them to perplexity and sorrow. Handsome, energetic, clear-headed, and good-humoured, Arthur almost immediately became the leading man of the little community. In fair weather he kept them alive and merry, on rough days he cheered and ministered. Before they reached Madeira they encountered a serious gale. The ship's bulwarks were partly carried away; the caboose or deck-kitchen was washed overboard: the master and his mates were absorbed with the care of the ship; all hands, even to the steward and cabin-boys, were required to assist in the navigation; and the helpless passengers would have fared ten times more miserably than they did had it not been for the resources of Arthur Brune. At the commencement of the storm he made all snug within the cuddy, set the passengers to some amusement, and, making frequent excursions to the poop, brought in as comfortable reports as his conscience would permit. As the danger

E

increased, and nearly all the company betook themselves to their cabins, he it was who took possession of the steward's locker, prepared over a lamp refreshment for the ladies, and brought them periodical reports of the state of things, making his announcement always close to the door of Miss Arabin's cabin, and demanding from Miss Rosabella, after every bulletin, a particular account of her young lady's condition. Knox, willing and active, made a capital second, but would have been of little use without the direction of his comrade. When the danger became undeniable, when the ship strained and pitched, and there was scarce twilight at noonday, and the winds and the sea contended in the loudness of their roarings, and the hatches were down, and voluminous seas rushed over her prow and half filled the saloon and cabins, within which latter arose shrieks and prayers and moanings, Mr Brune, who still kept his legs, stationed himself almost constantly at Violet's door, advising, explaining, exhorting, and nourishing —in short, making love by every method proper for such an occasion. It is not certain that, when the tempest had so far abated as to restore confidence and serenity, Miss Arabin's feelings were wholly pleasing. The storm left some tinge of regret, and the remembrance of it had more of joy than terror for many a year after. At length the gale gently subsided. The male passengers one by one appeared in the wet cuddy, and, gathering their feet on to the benches, assisted at a luxurious repast which was presided over by Lieutenant Brune, and consisted of raw ham, wet biscuits, pickles, raisins, and cheese. These viands, washed down by libations of brandy-and-water (thank God, the fore-hold was all tight), were found to be of an excellence quite beyond belief; and when the poor drenched skipper and his mate for the first time put their heads between decks and indulged in a few delicacies, the meeting grew undeniably jovial. In the next stage of improvement, Violet, leaning on Brune's arm, surveyed from the dry poop the traces of elemental strife. Tattered sails, crippled spars, broken ropes, and bestrewed decks, attested the violence of the commotion. They had tried the pumps and found the old craft as tight as a bottle. Seamen therefore alow and aloft were busy splicing, knotting, fishing, reeving, and otherwise occupied in processes which it is not lawful for a landsman to utter. The carpenter was patching up as best he could, and had got a rough rail across the great breach in the gunwale. Well that he did so, for as she still gave occasionally vicious kicks and rolls, the barrack-master, who had suddenly become very active in a flowered dressing-gown and slippers, was tilted clean across the main hatchway, and only brought up by the aforesaid make-shift. Poor man! had it happened a quarter of an hour sooner 'twould have been his last caper. The consciousness of this made him, when he recovered his legs, assume a look of horror. But the whole incident was ludicrous, and, as he was no great favourite in the ship, it gave rise to a general though quickly suppressed titter, the first burst of merriment heard since the gale began. And now the scene changed as in a theatre. Rosy tints succeeded frowning clouds, azure waves replaced the tumbling vitreous billows, light and warmth revived the soul, and a gentle air, wafting her like a fairy craft towards Madeira, effaced for a while the memory of the thundering blast. A day or two to refit and transact a little business at Funchal gave opportunity for excursions on shore, bright Madeira seeming a paradise after those inclement days. Mr Brune, in pleasure as in danger, was generally at Miss Arabin's side, and, with a difference, continued his attentions. And there were summer and witching prospects, and newness everywhere, and strange delight, and re-awakened senses, and young love and transient happiness. Leander and Rosabella burst into ecstasies at the sight of some sugar-cane exposed for sale at a stall. With sparkling eyes they purchased the congenial plant, and *nyaming* greedily its fibre, were entranced with the luscious joy. The short sojourn flew away on silken wings. And now once more on board! but not to boiling surge or bursting sky. There are both wind and sea in plenty, but they are working the right way; all are by this time accustomed to her motion; and though she bounds and frisks, every gambol sends her nearer to her goal. With fixed sails and unswerving helm she rolls lazily down before the trade-winds. It is the very reign of indolence, and those nervous mariners who lately sprang to brave the unchained winds and the raging deep, growled and languished, and made bitter jests about the deck, finding no work worthy of their mettle. Furs and wrappings cast aside, the passengers eschew the hot berths, and, under sleepy awnings, yawn or laugh or love away the hours. To-day but repeats yesterday, the same and still the same. A nautilus, a dolphin, come now and then to cheer them, and a little element of terror appears in the shadow of a dusky shark who occasionally looms astern, and intimates that he has his eye on them. Appalling monster!

"What the deuce shall we do, Brune?" says Knox. "I am dying of ennui."

But Brune, who lay at Violet's feet, found agreeable occupation in abundance, and marvelled how a rational being could think the minutes heavy.

"Ennui!" replied Arthur, "how odd! why, there are hundreds of things you can do. You can—you can—why, hang it, you *must* know fifty things. Go and read Shakespeare. You've read till you're tired? Well, challenge old Wingrove to backgammon,—twenty hits this morning? Then sing psalms. Don't think that'll suit you, though. I have it. Ask Jack Fidd to show you how to catch a dolphin: there are lots about the bows. Mind you hold fast if you get on the bowsprit."

And, having rid himself of the intruder, Arthur basked once more in Violet's sight, and dreamed away the day.

There was a sudden alarm.

"Halloa, there. Back the sails!—let go life-buoy!—man overboard!—lower away a boat. Move and be —— to you!" shouted the master.

But Jack's machinery had contracted the thinnest possible coating of rust from inaction. Three weeks ago he started on the instant to grapple with twenty whirlwinds. His sinews and senses were braced beyond surprise or hesitation. Now even *he* felt the power of idleness and security. Soon, though, he shook off his slight lethargy, and addressed himself gallantly to his duty. But, alas! it is by seconds that the Fates in such cases decide the lives or deaths of men, and Edward Knox had sunk to everlasting night had his rescue depended upon the crew alone. No sooner had the first alarm started every one from doze or dalliance or reverie than a small knot rushed to the stern, whence could be descried, not yet twenty yards off, among the waves, the unhappy cause of the commotion awkwardly striking out — the features repeatedly immersed, but, when seen, stamped with a terror and anguish that must haunt every beholder to his dying day.

"Good God!" exclaimed Violet Arabin, "I see the unfortunate man drowning;" and she clung to the ship's side fainting, until roused by a splash in the sea beneath where she stood. Arthur Brune, for whom she looked in her fright, was not to be seen on the deck, and a strong swimmer was striking out in the direction of the drowning man.

"It is Mr Brune—save him, save him!" she shrieked; and rushed frantically, she thought not whither, in quest of aid. On the quarterdeck she found the master stimulating all hands to the necessary exertion. The way was already partly off the ship, and a boat's crew were collected and ready to launch.

"Quick, for the love of Heaven," gasped Violet; "Mr Brune has jumped overboard after the first man!"

"Mr Brune!" passed from mouth to mouth, and seemed to inspire every one with redoubled ardour.

"Now then, smartly, lads!" grunted an old mate

who was directing the boat's crew. "We'll save that young chip if men can do it. He's been and jumped arter t'other. Blow my old heart, I know'd he was the right sort!"

Owing to the altered position of the ship, her late path was now visible from the waist where Violet stood straining her eyes towards the spot where she supposed the struggling men to be. Every glass on board was levelled in the same direction.

"I see them!"—"I see one of them—Brune, I think, but where's the other?"—"Oh! yes, there they both are."—"No, by Jove!—Yes!"—were the eager exclamations uttered by the gazers.

"Now, Miss Arabin," said the master, "I think this focus will suit you. Rest the glass on the gunwale, and you'll see what they're doing."

But Violet's eyes were dim, and her heart was throbbing, and her hand quivered. She could see nothing.

Many minutes had elapsed since the accident. They seemed hours.

"Well, then, I still see one head, for certain," said the skipper, "and, it may be, two. The boat is nearing them gallantly. Pull away, my hearties. Now I've lost them again. There, that must be one of their heads. Gone again. Pull boat, pull like grim death! She's close now to where they were. The mate sees something. Strange, now, I've lost them. Boat's head coming round again,—men looking about. God help 'em, they can't have sunk."

"Oh, no, no!" gasped Violet. "They have not—cannot. You—you will see them."

"By Jove, you are right, ma'am," replied the skipper after looking again. "They are hauling something on board sure enough. But, as I live, it's a dead body."

And he closed up the joints of the glass with a sharp ring, indicative of his honest regret.

"Don't agitate yourself, my dear young lady; the boat will be back in a few minutes, and we shall see; but 'tis prudent to prepare for the worst."

The fainting form of Miss Arabin was borne to her cabin by the honest master and Mrs Wingrove, the former observing, "Ah! you haven't seen so many of the miseries of the sea as an old tar like me, and a mishap troubles your nerves. Lie down a little, and you'll soon come round. Accidents will happen. I pity that gallant lad, though!"

"Boat ahoy! What have you got?" roared the first mate.

"Got 'em both."

"Alive or dead?"

"Mr Brune is breathing. All over with t'other."

Dead to all other sounds, Violet's ear was alive to

this colloquy. She was once more on her trembling feet, and managed to totter on to the quarterdeck. The exhausted figure of Arthur Brune was being *whipped* on board. Already there lay on the planks Knox's inanimate body. The medical passenger was directing the steward to prepare the necessary appliances.

"Come away, my love," said Mrs Wingrove, "do come in. Such a scene will quite unnerve you." But Violet watched the doctor's face, and asked with her looks if she might hope. Attracted by Mrs Wingrove's repeated solicitations to Violet, the doctor at last answered the appeal of the latter, and said,

"Not a bit alarmed about Brune; alive, and strong constitution. Less sure about the other. Go in with Mrs Wingrove, that's a good girl."

That evening all on board breathed freely once more when it was announced that, thanks to the doctor's skill and care, both young men were doing well. The shadow of death passed away from the ship, but at the same time the shadow of the dread shark became visible to those on the poop, and reminded them of the twofold danger that had been escaped.

"What!" said the old mate, who had steered the boat, and who was now standing behind the wheel, about to heave the log—" what, old lawyer,* are you there ? Why, if I was you, blow me if I wouldn't disrate all my pilot-fish and give 'em four dozen apiece into the bargain! A set of lubbers! What was they about? and what was *you* about, old un, eh? Was you in your parlour down there keeping the watch below, spinning of a yarn with a friend; or was you taking of a constitootional cruise; or having of a few words with your missus; or writing up your log; or minding the fractious baby cutting of his nine row of teeth; or what *was* you a-doing of? My eye, old cock, if you ain't lost the daintiest morsels, and missed the chance of scrunching up the finest young feller as ever walked a deck! Ah, you may lick your old chops long enough now; you gets no sich opportunity again, you bloodthirsty varmint! D-a-m-n y-o-u-r e-y-e-s!"

After these observations, the last of them in linked sweetness long drawn out, Mr Taut turned his quid squirted an amber mouthful at the attorney of the deep, and betook himself to the log-line.

Soon, hearts beat calmly again: the old monotony returned, and the ship bowled along without further particular incident; the passengers steeped

* Jack calls a shark a *sea-lawyer*, possibly because he has such a quantity of *jaw*. Other explanations have been suggested, but they have a somewhat illiberal tinge.

in idleness, and two of them up to the necks in love.

What a break-up does a landing make after a long voyage! People, who for months have lived like one family, find suddenly their relationship terminate, and quietly separate, some for ever, others to lapse into new associations and altered habits. Our party dispersed, some to their fields, others to their merchandise, and some to the duties of their professions. Brune landed with a halo round his head: his general merits and his particular exploit being sounded before him as with a trumpet. It was the very reputation to make him at once popular in the service; and, among civilians, always here disposed to hospitality, a full recognition awaited him.

The arrival of a daughter—and *such* a daughter—caused, of course, the doors of old Christy's house to open wide, and brought out in strong light the magnificent condescension of his wife. Friends and neighbours likewise gave entertainments in honour of the sweet arrival, and at all of these was to be seen Mr A. Brune, looking very handsome in a red skeleton jacket, and not far from Miss Arabin's side. His pony spent as much time in Christy's stable as in his own stall at Stony Hill. He was most intimate with the negroes, and had his fun with them all. And so matters continued till, on a sudden, his reception at Crystal Mount appeared to become less and less cordial, and a Mr Melhado, a wealthy merchant, who dealt in everything from a skewer or a yard of tape or a coffin, to a carriage, set of emeralds, or a three-masted ship, became a constant visitor at the house. This gentleman's appearance there was, it would seem, the result of a secret negotiation between Christy and Melhado's mother, an ambitious old lady, who had held out large inducements to bring about a connection. And, indeed, as far as means and position went, the match seemed quite reasonable and suitable. The objections to it were that Mr Melhado, though not an ill-looking nor a stupid youth, was of a vulgar type, in no way harmonising with Miss Arabin's; and that Miss Arabin had already, as the reader has seen, given her affections in another direction. For some time the two young men met occasionally, without, of course, fraternising very kindly. Melhado's visits became frequent; Brune's, who was nettled at the apparent caprice with which he was treated by the old couple, and by the sudden reserve of the young lady, became more and more rare. At last came the announcement of an engagement between Violet and Melhado, whereupon Brune was seen at the house no more, until the day of which we are now writing. Rumours reached Brune to the effect that he had forfeited Arabin's good opinion in consequence of some irregular conduct imputed to him; and, to do the old man justice, he really had heard and believed things to Brune's discredit before he listened to old Mrs Melhado's overtures. Christy took some pains to satisfy himself, and did feel satisfied on the subject, but he gave Brune no opportunity of rebutting the charge. Indeed, he was not sorry to have a good excuse for terminating the acquaintance; thinking, as worldly old parents always have thought, always do think, and always will think (vide Library of Love *passim*), that his daughter felt but a transient fancy which would soon yield to absence and the attentions of another. Like most fathers who keep ledgers, he had an instinctive idea that young soldiers stood to him in the same relation as rats do to a cornmerchant. This had its influence in deciding his behaviour, though he couldn't help liking Arthur personally any more than his neighbours.

Now then, we think, the thread of our narrative may be resumed.

CHAPTER V.

WHILE Crystal Mount was witnessing the scenes which we recorded before our late digression, its lord was employing himself in various ways on a lower level. He had been at Spanish Town attending to his legislative duties as a councillor of the island, and was now on his way back to Kingston, where he proposed to transact a little further business before he should return home to dinner. Nowadays there is a railway along the thirteen miles that intervene between Kingston and Spanish Town, and senators, like their neighbours of all colours, are ingloriously rattled to and fro in the trains. Of old it was far otherwise: then all men had to whip along the highway, and the style in which they travelled this much-frequented road was a criterion of the travellers' wealth or acumen, and of their horses' value. To give an idea of a gentleman's importance, negroes would desire you to remark the "'tyle" in which "him trabel de 'Panish Town road." If his knowingness were to be illustrated, you were informed that he was always fifteen minutes less than his neighbours between Government House and Kingston ; while of a horse it was high praise to say, " Him will take you to 'Panish Town widin de hour, sar." Such a road as it was too ! They were eternally patching and mending it, and incredible sums were reported to be spent on its repairs ; yet, except the first mile out of Spanish Town, it was always in a scandalous condition. One-half its breadth was villanously paved—perhaps it might be more correct to say *unpaved*, since the large stones were always knocking about it in independent profusion. The other half was by courtesy said to be macadamised : in wet weather it was a mire, and in dry a sample of the great Sahara. Somehow or other, however, all the world managed to get along it, though perhaps with a little trial of the temper. Our friend Tom Gervaise, for instance, when threading his devious way between the frequent blocks, or when up to the axles in sand, would afford beautiful examples of patience. In a playful mood he would wish that his hand were on the lever of a vice within whose jaws might be the head of the contractor : or if the case were too serious for fanciful language, he would discharge great point-blank oaths, the wind of which might knock a man down, and whose blow must have been annihilation. Along this road, then, was Christy

Arabin being bogged and jolted. He was beautifully turned out, and had the journey lightened by well-conditioned horses and a comfortable carriage, in which he was shaken about very harmlessly. He was clad wholly in white, the jean jacket on his back not exactly becoming his figure, which was short and portly. He wore no neckcloth, and his shirt-collar, which was doubled down, had lost all its starch from dampness of some kind. On his head was a Panama hat, with a low crown and broad brim turned up at the sides, tied with a narrow black ribbon. His face was round and reddish, and would have been better without the keen twinkle which appeared every now and then in his eyes. Like his aspect, all his qualities were marred by some defect. He was good-natured, but uncertain, and suddenly, though not often, irascible; liberal in the main, but occasionally too shrewd; reasonable and moderate in his opinions, but arbitrary and unjust in some of his dealings. These contradictions did not prevent his being a popular and respected character, for he had graduated very notably in colonial virtues and accomplishments—that is to say, he liked, and was not over-choice of, society; enjoyed good eating and drinking; troubled no man with moral remarks; dealt neither more nor less scrupulously than his neighbours; and was ready to submit any difference of opinion to the arbitrament of the pistol, as he had already done more than once in his lifetime. He carried usually a cigar in his mouth, which caused a waggish and profane legal functionary to compare him to Israel in the wilderness, seeing that he had always a cloud before him by day and a fire by night. By the time we get up with him he is near Kingston, and has nearly recovered his equanimity, which has been somewhat shaken by the bishop vigorously opposing him in council. The prelate often had occasion so to do, but Christy was accustomed to blow off his wrath on the spot by retorting upon his right reverend opponent, if not good arguments, very strong and often unseemly language. To-day he had been tongue-tied, and therefore carried his pent-up indignation several miles before he could smoke it off. His forbearance arose from no newborn sense of propriety, but from an interested motive. The bishop had promised to marry his daughter to Melhado, and it was of importance not to quarrel with him till the ceremony should be over. Not that Christy cared for this distinction on his own account: if he had laboured for such vanities, he never would have earned the wealth which now enabled him to obtain them. But the expected honour was highly agreeable to Mrs Arabin. And thus again it becomes necessary to explain why Christy, who seldom troubled himself to gratify his wife, was now so anxious to secure compliance with her ambitious fancy. Christy, whose mind was not speculative, knew nothing about his motives, and nobody about him read his heart distinctly. Ourself alone, who possess the key to his conduct, can reveal this important *why;* and here is the interpretation. Deep down in the old gentleman's mind—so deep, indeed, that it had never taken the distinct form of thought—lay an unpleasant conviction that he was not acting truly by his daughter, and that all the specious arguments with which he quieted his conscience and deceived other people were fallacious. He had a great dread lest the mother's heart should put sight into her eyes, and make her perceive the iniquity that was designed ; for, armed with such knowledge as she would then possess, even her voice would be powerful against his schemes : nay, to say truth, he felt uneasy concerning his conjugal supremacy when he should stand at such a disadvantage. But she had readily deceived herself; and all that her husband had to do, therefore, was to feed her vanity, and keep her mind fixed upon the bishop's promise to officiate, and all the pomp which was to accompany the marriage.

As he entered the city he was quite serene again, and to the coachman's inquiry whither he should drive, he answered quite graciously, "to Mrs Melhado's." Accordingly the carriage stopped in one of the upper streets before a large house which stood back behind some dusty shrubs and flowers, and whose whole front was covered with jalousie work, the frames painted white and the blades light green. Christy was received in a large drawing-room, richly furnished after the fashion of the country, by a tall, spare, aquiline-headed old lady, who could at first be but dimly distinguished, so great was the contrast between the dazzling glare without and the subdued light within. Whoever desires a graphic description of the effects of this contrast should refer to 'Tom Cringle's Log,' and study his first meeting with his cousin Mary, by which it will appear that the strongest ties may be broken, and things made manifest which should for ever be concealed, through this sudden transition. Mr Arabin, who was pretty well experienced in the vicissitudes of a Jamaica life, was not disconcerted by the change, but he returned the lady's cordial grasp, and, seating himself at her invitation, began to mop his countenance with high-bred ease, while they recited the usual prefaces to a morning conversation. After these, Mrs Melhado took occasion to remark, "Mr Arabin, sir, you would like a drink after your drive." And before Christy had time to express his entire concurrence with this opinion, she had sounded a hand-bell, and desired that a liquor-case might be brought in, with the proper accompaniments of glasses, goglets, and ice.

"You see I don't ask *what* you'll take," said she, unlocking the casket, "knowing your appreciation of poor Melhado's brandy. Poor dear man! there's a good drop of it left yet."

"Quite right, ma'am," Christy answered: "none of your compounded drinks for me. Good brandy, properly diluted and cooled, is the finest morning-draught in the world. Yours is the best I ever tasted. I'm glad to find it holds out so well."

"Oh, and it's likely to last," said the lady; "for, except my little drop every day—I don't care who knows it, and it's a pity other ladies are not equally candid—it's only our discriminating visitors, and friends like yourself, that ever get any. Manuel still likes sangree and malt liquors best: he will come to brandy-and-water by-and-by. You and I and another person must see that he doesn't get too fond of it."

The late Mr Melhado had imported the brandy for his own use. There was an internecine strife between them, and the brandy, much exhausted, was the survivor. A hereditary feud was therefore much to be deprecated.

Christy replied, that if Manuel should evince any taste for strong waters—which, fortunately, he had not yet done—they must use every means to check him.

"It's very little *we* shall be able to do with him," replied the old lady : "if his wife can't keep his head straight, nobody else can ; but of course she will."

Christy, with great uneasiness, thought of his daughter's hapless lot, if once her charms and gentle influences should cease to sway her husband. He answered—

"As long as legitimate feminine control can move him, he is quite safe ; but once beyond its reach, I should expect him to take his own course unrestrained." The old man shuddered as he said this, but Mrs Melhado retorted sharply—

"Why should he ever be beyond its reach?"

"Well, we'll hope not, ma'am—we'll hope not. He has good sense, no doubt, and good feeling; and, indeed, I don't see why they should not be very happy. He has a little bluntness of manner and an arbitrary style of expression, but these are very readily changed when affection rules."

"Oh, the way they speak don't signify a rush," said the lady. "Melhado swore dreadful."

Christy, who was aware that, whatever was Mr Melhado's command of language, he did not command in his own house, was able to join these remarks in a syllogistic form, and to deduce from them the truth which they contained—viz., that a loud voice and domineering manner are not necessarily evidence of domestic ascendancy. But Mr Melhado's subjugation was quite an exceptional case, and by no means argued the certainty of his son's humiliation. For many years he waged with superhuman gallantry an unequal war, up to the time when, beaten and despairing, he surrendered at discretion, and turned for comfort to the brandy. There sat his conqueror, still able to subdue the spirit of any man —ay, or the spirits of any dozen men. What a capital fellow he had been, and what a life she led him! He was worth a score of her. And a shade of regret came over Christy's mind when he thought of the fiery trial which had tried his old chum, and how much pleasanter affairs would have been now had the contest ended the other way. Well-a-day!—

"Victrix causa deis placuit, sed victa Catoni."

"Well now, Mr Arabin," said the old lady, as she observed the pensive mood into which Christy had fallen, "I wonder what's come to you to make you so thoughtful! I suppose it's that abominable tobacco that you can't dispense with. Well, you know, I don't allow it in *this* house—never *did*, and never *will;* but I'll tell you what I'll do now, as we ought to be on the most friendly terms; I'll go and sit in the verandah with you while you have a cigar; will that do?"

Christy protested that he had smoked that morning quite enough to satisfy him, and that the little absence of mind of which he had been guilty was attributable to his long drive in the sun. When she hinted at his beloved weed, the old fellow's system yearned for its accustomed anodyne; but a craven feeling overcame his desire. He wanted to lead the conversation into another direction, and with that aim he summoned his flagging spirits, and began to talk with animation of passing events. This humour Mrs Melhado was quite ready to join with, and they soon wandered far among gossip and scandal. The lady was wont to describe herself as "none of your mealy-mouthed pretenders," and to boast that she said what she thought, and was none the worse for it. Howbeit, she was not agreeable when in a sprightly mood; and old Christy, though his worst enemy could not accuse him of squeamishness, said he never could endure her in her frolicsome moments: it seemed so unnatural, he said, that it set his teeth on edge and made his flesh creep. We fancy this sensation was the only approach to bashfulness which the old gentleman had experienced for many a day. He felt now that the conversation must be changed at all hazards, and so he charged abruptly into the business which had occasioned his visit.

"To be sure, ma'am, you'll be astonished at something I heard in Spanish Town. Dan Bumper, who is in London, wrote to Archy Calipash by the mail which arrived this morning, that Mr Venables is much better, and actually coming out to reside, and manage his property himself, with a view to clearing it of its mortgages, which possibly he may be able to do."

" You heard that, did you?" remarked Mrs Melhado, shortly.

" Yes, ma'am," answered Christy, "and from authority that seems good."

" And you think that if he does come he may clear the Cinnamon of its encumbrances by his management?" asked the old lady again.

" Well, the thing is possible," said Christy; " it's a fine estate, and the man's not a fool."

"And there goes, you would say, Manuel's chance of passing from attorney to proprietor of this splendid estate?"

" His chance will certainly not be improved by this arrangement."

" And what do you think my son would be about in case it took place? will he do nothing to hold his ground and keep his prospects open?"

" No doubt," replied Christy, "Manuel will exert himself, like a clever young man as he is; but when the proprietor shall be on the spot 'twill be hard to keep him in the dark as to the capabilities of his estate, and the case would require much caution and experience."

"Right!" said Mrs Melhado, with a grim smile. "'Tis a delicate matter, and Manuel is somewhat young to handle it. But what say you if an older head were to look to it? How, if it had been already looked into by a person considerably Manuel's senior?"

"Mrs Melhado, your look and manner reassure me, ma'am," said Christy; "you already know of this matter, and can inform me concerning it."

"Yes," said Mrs Melhado, "make yourself easy; I heard of it some time ago."

"And you do not believe he is coming?"

"Certainly not."

"Your authority may be mis——"

"His physician!"

"Ma'am!"

"His physician!" repeated the lady, looking hard at Christy, and clenching her lips.

"Mrs Melhado, you'll pardon me for doubting one moment your watchfulness and ability," said Christy, much impressed. "I thought the information I got was reliable, and you'll do me the justice to admit that 'twasn't of a nature to be indifferent to."

"Certainly not," replied the old lady, dryly; "it might, if true, have disconcerted some notable arrangements. But you may make yourself easy, as I said before. Mr Venables's visit is not a bit more probable than many former ones which he projected; and he'll neither come hither nor move anywhere else. His days are numbered. The mortgage is quite safe, and will be foreclosed—not paid off; so that's all right. Now, have you heard anything more?"

"No, ma'am—no, no, nothing more. By Jove, ma'am, you've a head of your own! No—nothing more."

"Then I have something to communicate," said Mrs Melhado. "Manuel has just got a similar mortgage on the Nutmeg, and as there's very little chance of *its* proprietor coming this way, I think that may end as prosperously as the other is like to do."

"As I live, ma'am," burst out Christy, "you beat the cleverest of us. You are—by Jove, you ought to be a legislator! You'd manage the House of Assembly and the government too—hang me, if you wouldn't! Well done, ma'am—well done; I see there's little danger of your—of *our* interests suffering while you are awake. Your very good health, ma'am!"

Had the late Mr Melhado survived to a patriarchal age, it is certain that he would not have transacted business as keenly as his disconsolate relict. Christy began to think that the gods might possibly have known better than Cato. His soul had not only been relieved of an anxious doubt, but it had received an unexpected cause for rejoicing. His morality, as has been before hinted, was not of a delicate order, and both he and Mrs Melhado thought it perfectly fair to practise a little upon an absent proprietor, and relieve him of a possession for whose management he showed an ineptitude.

The lady did not deign to notice her visitor's compliments, but proceeded to remark upon the business in hand.

"Thus, you see, my son has the attorneyship, with the possible succession to the Cinnamon and Nutmeg in Surrey, two of the finest estates in the island, and of Beggar's Bush in Trelawny; while he already owns the Diamond Vale in Middlesex, and Pernambuco in Cornwall."

"A pretty little roll," said Christy, grinning, "worth, I should think, not less than——"

"Don't let us get to figures," replied Mrs M. "It's a pretty property just now, there's no denying it; but they've a capricious way in England of dealing with colonial produce, and therefore I don't put my trust altogether in land. But then, in any case, we've the store, and see what a business we are doing, and what mercantile openings these attorneyships afford. I don't suppose there's a firm in the island turning half so much capital as Melhado, Huggins, and Bamboo."

" I'm sure there's not, ma'am," said Christy, whom this conversation had filled with delight and awe—delight that Melhado's possessions and prospects so completely justified the approaching connection, and awe at the superior powers of the strong-minded woman. They had pretty well cleared off their business topics, and Mrs Melhado gave evidence of a disposition to relapse into that sportive vein which affected Christy so unpleasantly; it was therefore a relief to him when the young man, whose future had been the subject of their conversation, returned home and joined their company.

Mr Manuel Melhado deserves a short description, as he believes himself destined to the distinguished honour of wedding Violet Arabin. He was slight and well formed, and of the average height. His complexion was olive, and his hair jet black, curled, and profusely oiled. His features were good, especially the eyes; and, except that the forehead was somewhat low, the profile might have been pronounced handsome. But the full face was not so good: the expression was mean, and there was a repulsive breadth across the jaw. As yet there was little beard or whisker, and the smooth open neck suited his countenance well. So common fame seemed justified in calling him a very handsome young man. Though that is a climate where loose light clothing is an especial luxury, this youth was habited in a cloth coat and waistcoat, made to fit his figure accurately, and drill trousers tightly strapped under Wellington boots. His collar was turned down, and he wore below it a scarf fastened with two pins, a major and a minor, connected by a gold chain, and the former headed with a brilliant stone. Round his neck was a double watch-guard as thick as a jack-chain, and his waistcoat buttons, of yellow metal, were linked together very sumptuously. Small spurs projected from his heels, and he bore a riding-whip in one hand, while the other held his black beaver hat— a most unpleasant substitute, one would think, for the cool shady Panama. Mr Melhado, however, was a man of fashion, and did not choose to follow any rules of dress, but rather claimed the right to dictate those rules. Among the brown ladies he was the observed of all observers; and indeed we ought not to confine his celebrity to that class, for there were many white ladies who pronounced him charming, and showed every disposition to cultivate his good opinion. By Kingston youth his precedence was acknowledged; yet this was, in his estimation, but a light thing, for his ambition led him to be on easy terms with the young military officers, whom he was never tired of entertaining, and for whose countenance and familiarity he was willing to undergo a great deal. They ate his dinners, rode his horses, and tolerated his society, but he was not a favourite with any among them. He had neither a good disposition nor very good sense to guide him, and his attempts at fashionable ease were disagreeable, if not offensive. We have seen how Tom Gervaise felt towards him; and Tom, except in matters of adornment and purification, commonly held the opinion of the majority.

The youth set down his hat, and sauntered across the room to grasp the hand of old Christy, who, greatly comforted by the intelligence just received, gave him a cordial squeeze, and inspected him from head to foot with an approving smile.

"Well, ma'am," said he, addressing the old lady, "if this is the penalty one has to pay for youth and fashion, I hardly regret that my day is past: we had our fancies, no doubt, like every other rising generation, but to suffocate ourselves wasn't one of them."

Mrs Melhado had too good sense not to see the impropriety of dressing thus in such a climate; but she liked to see her son look to advantage; therefore she said, apologetically, "Oh, Manuel has been making some visits, and been at the barracks with some of his military friends. It wouldn't do, you know, to appear careless or slovenly among *them*."

"By Jove," said Christy, "they are the most sensible fellows going! You never see them in anything but a white jacket when off duty, while our young city bucks think they must dress as men do in England. But never mind, Manuel, dress as you like—that's your affair, you know, now, and it will be a thing for you and your wife to settle between you a month hence, eh? Are you coming up to Crystal Mount with me? because if you will, I shall be ready in half an hour, and will drive you to the foot of the mountain, where we shall find horses."

Melhado accepted with much readiness, and went to make a change in his toilet, while Christy proceeded into the city to order some cigars, and transact other pressing business. Didn't he stick a havannah in his mouth and pull out his tinder-box before he was at the bottom of Mrs Melhado's door-steps!

The lover, of course, did not wish to omit any elegancies of costume when dining at Crystal Mount: he therefore summoned a yellow female with a lean wrinkled neck and skin, but nevertheless wearing her hair dressed, and an enormous pair of ear-drops, and bade her get a portmanteau packed for him. This personage was his mother's factotum, lady's-maid, housekeeper, confectioner, laundry-woman, and general superintendent. The duties of a house are very differently divided in that country from the method we are accustomed to at home; and these brown domestics, when they reach a certain age, attain a neatness and an aptitude for household duties which is rarely found in the other sex. The use Mr Melhado made of his own male attendant was this: when the portmanteau was packed, he made him strap it, and then ordered him to take it on his head and trudge off with it to Crystal Mount.

On the journey up the gentlemen held little conversation worth repeating. In fact, Christy, who wanted to ponder on the pleasant intelligence received from Mrs Melhado, pressed a cigar upon his companion, and stopped his own mouth with another. He saw that Melhado, if he played his cards well, might become — never mind by what means — the wealthiest proprietor in the island. He felt, too, how these improved prospects would feed the vanity of his helpmate, and increase her satisfaction with the match; and with this reflection the little bit of remorse which played about outside his heart seeking an entrance, was kicked sturdily from the door, and peremptorily forbidden the premises.

Violet met her father with a smile, and the old man, intent on her grand prospects, and imagining himself the most devoted of parents, kissed her affectionately. Melhado, too, had a gracious welcome. As the character of the evening there depended very much upon the host's humour, this promised to be a cheery one. Christy was in spirits, and talked and joked. Melhado, after his manner, was assiduously attentive to both ladies. So they dined very pleasantly. The conversation, when the servants had disappeared, turned upon some superstitious excitement which was agitating the negroes, and leading them to hold frequent and large nocturnal meetings. The overseers and book-keepers on the estates thought that these assemblies might lead to mischief, and had represented their misgivings to Mr Arabin as proprietor of Crystal Mount, and to Mr Melhado as representing the owner of the Cinnamon estate, a little farther down the hill. *Obi* is the name of the religion, incantation, or devil-worship, whichever it may be, that prevails among the negroes. Obeah men, their high-priests or professors, are always native Africans, so are the women who practise its crafts. Hence there is no doubt that the whole of its mysteries are of African origin. When their orgies are more than usually solemn, it is to be dreaded that they mask some insurrectionary move, and the whites are uneasy while they continue.

It is never wise to speak on this subject before black servants, as nearly all of them are in thraldom to the superstition, and they may be chiefs and ringleaders; for there is a peculiar mystery most carefully maintained concerning the rites, professors, and votaries of Obi, and the whites have never been able to sift it, though now and then they get a little insight into its abominations.

Melhado said that he would send up to the Cinnamon to-morrow a brace of Spanish dogs, to be let loose on occasion of the next Obeah gathering. At this plan old Christy shook his head. He had no dislike of the proposal, but he doubted its prudence, and thought that while there was such a disposition to pet the negroes, it would read badly in the newspapers, and be turned to account by the party to which he stood opposed. Violet, from motives of humanity, combated the design, for some of these dogs are exceeding fierce, and they might not have simply dispersed the crowds, but perhaps maimed or killed some. Melhado laughed at these feminine objections, and thought it became him as a man of determination to persist in his plan; but when Violet reiterated her horror at the idea, he made a show of gracefully yielding to her wishes, while he winked at old Christy in token that he would adhere to his first intention nevertheless. The conversation was then led to a visit which the family was to make a day or two later to Spanish Town, partly to visit friends, and partly to arrange preliminaries of the marriage; for these matters are conducted in the island somewhat differently from the English customs; for instance, the governor is the person to grant the licence, not the bishop. To make the excursion pleasanter, it was agreed that the party should go to Spanish Town by water as far as Port Henderson, Melhado undertaking the arrangements for the short voyage. And thus the evening wore away. There was no music. Violet could with difficulty maintain her self-possession after the events of the day; and she excused herself from singing, and retired immediately after tea.

Poor girl! it had been a cruel evening for her. Not till she retired at night had she an opportunity of collecting her thoughts, and balancing the reliefs and anxieties of which this day had been the parent. But reason would not, could not, now measure the gain and loss; for, welling up through the tangled doubts and cares, came one fresh and thrilling consciousness, beside which no meaner idea might gain attention. Arthur loved her; and who should set a price upon Arthur's love! Not that Violet had been ignorant or doubtful of his affection; but now it was hers, not by implication or inference—told with his own lips, yea, poured from his heart of heart. And the murmurs still lingered in her ear, and evermore came again the blessed words, like the echoes of a spirit's song, holding her mind entranced, and charming away farther and still farther all other sound. The cares were there—she knew it: outside the magic circle, fierce and eager, there they waited, sure to have their hour; but that hour could not be now. And so it was that Violet, happy suddenly, but happy without stint, cast trouble afar; and, even with the consciousness that Melhado, to whom she stood in such unmeet relation, lay under the same roof, felt only the new-born joy. We have stolen in through the warm spangled tropic night to catch but one glimpse of this trance ere it is gone. Soon—perhaps to-morrow—cross chance may resume its sway, for we know the difficulties that impend. Let us linger, then, but a moment with bliss and Violet, and then, leaving with a sigh the fair and happy girl, let us hasten to another part of the house, and a far less pleasing scene.

Mr Arabin, before seeking his bed-chamber, usually retired to his dressing-room to meditate and grow cool, in addition to which processes he smoked a cigar and sipped a pleasant mixture of gin and cocoa-nut milk. If his mind chanced to be discomposed, this treatment soothed it; if it were pleased or jocund, the treatment enhanced his satisfaction. To-night he blew a mighty cloud, indicative of the calm joy which possessed him as he thought how his schemes drew towards their consummation, and how they looked brighter as their day approached. In the lightest of wrappers, stretched at length near the open casement, his mind looked forth into the fancied future, which, like the starry night, seemed only the more soft and lovely for its dimness. Wealth and consideration, power even, for him and his, promised to abound while his energies should last; and when, tired and satiated, the old man should court repose, there would be the luxurious retirement, the life in others, and the honoured age. And this prospect of good was of his own creating. Let your weak or lazy noodles excuse their unreadiness and incapacity by prating of a patience in well-doing, and a humble trust for the event. Men of energy and sense carved out their own fortune, ha! ha! And Christy waxed presumptuous, and blew out long arrogant placid wreaths, and said in his heart, Tush! And while yet the vision tarried, came a low nervous knock at his door, and the dreamer said, "Who the devil are you? what do you want? come in and be d—— to you."

The handle turned gently, and with hesitating gait Mrs Arabin entered the apartment.

"Hollo, Susan! why — what — who could have thought of it being you? Nothing the matter, eh?" said Christy, much disturbed by the apparition.

"Nothing the matter, Mr Arabin—nothing," faltered the lady; "only I thought I should like—that is, if you are at leisure—I thought I might——"

Mr A.—"Ah, well, Susan, perhaps 'tis just as well you came in. Take a seat, my dear. I've something pleasant to tell you."

Mrs A.—"Indeed, Mr Arabin, I'm glad to hear that—very glad; but I hope it isn't that you've been setting down the poor bishop again. You do give such keen and sarcastic replies that his feelings mightn't bear it, and then——"

Mr A. (conscious of much greatness of mind).—"Never fear, Susan; all is right there. To be sure, I let him go on to-day till I thought I should have burst. I knew exactly, too, where to hit him, but I held in. No, it's all right in that quarter. What I wanted to tell you is nothing concerning the council; it's about Manuel. What do you think, now? he's got a mortgage on the Nutmeg. 'Twill surely be his own as well as the Cinnamon. What d'ye think of that?"

Mrs A.—"Indeed, Mr Arabin, 'twill be a grand thing, no doubt. But I was thinking——"

Mr A.—"Well, what were you thinking, my dear, eh?"

Mrs A.—"I was thinking, you know, whether, with all this prospect of wealth and grandeur, we can feel confident that our poor girl will be—quite—quite happy, you know!" (Mr Arabin wouldn't allow his own heart to hint at such an idea as this on any consideration, and now here was his silly wife blurting it forth as if it were the most ordinary remark. Flesh and blood couldn't bear it.)

Mr A.—"Happy, ma'am? Why, what the de——, what nonsense has got into your head! Of course they'll be happy. The bishop's to say the blessing, remember, and think of the noise the marriage will make. Happy—I believe you!"

Mrs A.—"Ah, the bishop and the fine doings are all very pleasant; but if she—if our Violet—should —should ever regret—ever find that her lot is not so enviable as it has been pictured, we should never— never——"

Mr A.—"Bless my soul, ma'am, what is all this humbug? You can't be well. Some silly fancies have got hold of you: go to bed, now, and get some rest. Your nervousness will be gone by the morning."

Mrs A. (a little more firmly).—"'Tisn't any fancy, Mr Arabin. I want to speak seriously to you before it is too late. Think of how Violet has been brought up, and how gentle she is. I cannot feel satisfied of this young man's principles and disposition."

Mr A.—"You can't, ma'am, eh! Upon my word!"

Mrs A.—"No, I *can't*, Mr Arabin. Violet is your

daughter, as well as mine, and we ought—you *know* we ought——"

Mr A.—"To behave like two confounded fools, eh, and make ourselves the laughing-stock of the island? After securing the best match that has been heard of since Miss Molasses married the governor's second son, to lose all by our own timidity and folly!"

Mrs A.—"You don't understand me, Mr Arabin. I wish to talk over these matters with you. If everything is right, we shall do no harm by discussion; and if anything requires our attention, now is the time."

Mr A. (who thinks that, after all, this may proceed from some mere whim or misconception).—"Go on, ma'am; let's hear."

Mrs A.—"First, then, I doubt whether our dear Violet's heart assents to this marriage at all."

Mr A.—"Pooh! since when have you doubted?"

Mrs A.—"Since very recently."

Mr A.—"What's next?"

Mrs A.—"Coupled with my former suspicion, I think it very questionable whether Manuel *can* make her happy—whether his nature is at all suited to hers."

Mr A.—"Anything else?"

Mrs A.—"There seems so much to object to, once

one begins to think. His mother now—I never could bear her."

Mr A.—"By Jove, ma'am, she's a clever woman—a right clever woman. I only wish that some others I know were like her—that is, that they were half as wise."

Mrs A.—"Well, I'm not questioning her abilities, Mr Arabin; but don't you think now that, all these things considered, the marriage might be at least postponed for a little?"

Mr A.—"Postponed, ma'am! Fire and fury! what's this you say? Postponed! why, you rave. Some of the Obeah people have bewitched you. I must send for Granny Nip to disenchant you."

Mrs A.—"A mother doesn't need witchcraft to make her anxious for the welfare of her child."

Mr A. (mocking).—"Anxious for the welfare of her child! Why, you're a sillier fool than I thought you were, and that's saying a great deal."

Mrs A.—"Oh dear, Mr Arabin! how can you——?"

Mr A.—"Let's have no more of this nonsense. Go to bed, and never speak to me on the subject again, unless you've something pleasanter to say."

Mrs A.—"Mr Arabin!"

Mr A.—"You idiotic fool, will you go to bed?"

Mrs A.—"You will be sorry——"

Mr A.—"The devil take you, will you go, eh? I

can stand baiting or begging or arguing as well as my neighbours, but when a cursed fool begins twaddling, I own I can't control myself. That's right, be off before I say something to be sorry for."

The last words were uttered as he let Mrs Arabin through the door, and closed it behind her. Mrs Arabin, as she passed to her own apartment, presented a figure unlike her former self at any epoch. Her step was firm, her hands were clenched, her head was thrown back, with the nostrils wide open, the eyes glittering, and the lips compressed, while at intervals it moved suddenly to and from the right shoulder. The mother's and woman's blood was up.

CHAPTER VI.

The officers' quarters in Up Park Camp are in two wings, each wing consisting of two pavilions or ranges, with a mess-room dividing them.

A young officer walked out of his bedroom into the verandah of the eastern pavilion about eight o'clock in the morning after Brune's visit to Crystal Mount. He was slight and well grown, with handsome features; but his eyes were sunken, his complexion was sallow, and his forehead showed lines which his years did not warrant. He paced with a varying step the portion of the gallery in front of his apartments, occasionally making a sudden stop, and peering through the jalousies with corrugated brow, as if in anxious observation. Suddenly he called, "Sampson!" whereupon a little bandy-legged negro, with a squeaking voice, came waddling out of the room next to that from whence the officer had issued.

"Breakfast immediately!" said the latter, sharply.

"Massa, de milk no come," piped Sampson; "dat Miss Asher gal reelly too bad!"

"Milk not come!" repeated the master; "then why the devil isn't it come, eh? I've no doubt 'tis some negligence of your own. Bring it immediately, or I'll——"

Sampson fled from the menacing hand and angry countenance as a Philistine would have shunned his unshorn namesake.

"Sampson," called the young man, mildly, "let me have breakfast as soon as the milk comes. I'm not angry; I daresay the goats are wild this morning. Tut!" he went on as soon as Sampson had disappeared, "what on earth makes me so irritable with this wretched devil, and with everybody!"

"Ah, Lorton, my boy, how's yourself? Monstrous hot, eh? I've just ridden down from Crystal Mount, and I took you in my way; for hang me if I could go on to Kingston now, or eat any breakfast if I got there!"

The above was the salutation of our young friend Melhado, who had passed the retreating Sampson on the stair, and come hastily on to the verandah. He was excessively hot and moist, but looked very well.

"Good morning, Melhado!" replied Lorton, with rather more reserve of manner than the other. "You must be in league with Miss Asher and the goats.

But for them I should have breakfasted, whereas they have managed the meal so as to be just in time for you."

"Devilish lucky that! Then I'll be ready in a jiffy, if you'll just let me wash my hands. I'm too hot to get into the bath, or I should enjoy a plunge. Suppose you've been in already?"

"I have," Lorton said, "and I think I must have remained in too long, for I have a little shivering and headache."

"Breakfast's the thing for that, my buck," said the free-and-easy visitor as he retired into Lorton's bedroom to perform the desired ablution: "you get up the grub, and I'll be with you sharp."

That chapter of the natural history of young Englishmen which treats of their habits in the mother country is so thoroughly understood, that it would be an impertinence in us to detail the food consumed at a home breakfast; but the modifications produced by migration to Jamaica may be a subject of interest to the curious reader.

First, then, Sampson brought in a dish of flying-fish lately caught—a real treat, we assure you; then came ortolans or butter-birds, a dainty procurable only at certain seasons. Roasted plantains, and yampees browned and buttered, served as accompaniments to the hot dishes; while avocado (vulgarly, *alligator*) pears might either be eaten with the cold ham, or, discussed alone, might cool delightfully the palate. Fruit or vegetable, which shall we call them? Flavoured with lime-juice and sugar, they claim the former name ; but at breakfast pepper and salt must be the dressing, and vegetable the denomination. Delicious they are ; and so dearly do we hold the memory of them, that if it were possible in this frigid land to place before us one of them fresh from the tree, we feel that neither our dignity as the writer of this interesting narrative, nor a restriction as to green esculents which has come upon us with advancing years, could for an instant restrain our eager assault. Sanitary considerations scattered to the winds, and this our grey goose quill trampled under foot, we would renew our accustomed delight, scrupulously bisecting the treasure, then extracting its hard heart, seasoning with salt and pepper the hemispherical cavities where lay that stony inmate, and then scooping out and enjoying the grateful pulp as it should melt like cream on the palate, till the well-scraped rind alone should remain in memory of the too-quickly-fleeted delight. *Subalterns' butter!* yes, that was the familiar name we gave them in days when fresh butter was a thing unknown in Jamaica, and when that which was by courtesy called salt butter should have been spurned with opprobrium as rancid oil! Bread, plain and toasted, was on the table to fill crevices, and wild fragrant honey and guava jelly to eat therewith. On the farther end, to be brought into action at the end of the meal, were bottles of claret and brandy, with dishes of mangoes and oranges, and a huge pink shaddock, whose rind had been cut by the ingenious Sampson into arabesque forms; coffee is generally taken immediately on rising, therefore tea alone may be looked for at breakfast.

"'Tis plain you have had no ride this morning, Lorton," said Melhado, attacking his second pigeon; "never saw a pecker so lamentably down: four lumps, please: never do out here not to eat, you know: sure to end in toes upwards, march in Saul, and that kind of thing."

Lorton shuddered. "I'm certainly off my feed," he said; "must keep quiet, and avoid the sun for a day or two. You appear as brisk and hearty as a bridegroom ought to be. Is it true that the happy day is fixed?"

"No doubt of it, my boy. I shall be turned off in less than a fortnight. Rather pleasant, isn't it, to find all right, after the fears and anxieties of courtship? Yes, by Jove, all settled. Before long I hope to see you congratulate Mrs Melhado. She doesn't know how much we owe to you for our happiness, but I'll take care she shall."

"*Owes me!*" repeated Lorton, with an inquiring stare.

"Certainly; but for the timely information you furnished concerning that fellow Brune, I daresay I might have had some trouble and delay, though I should probably have won her at last," answered Melhado, modestly.

Lorton coloured. "You will be good enough to remember," he said, "that I simply showed you passages from my cousin's letters, which were not very clear as regarded Brune, and that I in nowise vouched for the truth of what was reported."

"Oh, of course not," replied Melhado, with a wink which made the young officer's colour rise still higher. "I'm not the man to compromise a friend."

"Ah!" uttered Lorton, with disgust.

"Devilish fortunate that we managed as we did, and got him to haul quietly off. I thought at one time I should have been obliged to warn him off the premises, but you see he had the sense to go, like a wellbred dog!" This was said with a swagger.

"You seem to have received an erroneous impression concerning Brune's disposition," said Lorton. "I have no doubt he will be anxious to correct it, if it reaches his ears."

"Why, how! what the devil!" asked Melhado, looking up astonished, with an ortolan poised on his fork, for which his jaws had already opened when Lorton's remark arrested the intended bite, and caused the fountains of expectation to regurgitate coldly on his system. . . . "Deuce take it! I thought you hated the fellow as much as I do!"

"I thought you hinted at having scared Mr Brune. There are few men that could do that; and if he should hear that you suppose yourself to be one of them, I *think* he would bring that question to a speedy issue, that's all."

Melhado looked very pale; it is doubtful whether he could have swallowed the ortolan if he had tried. "You don't mean," said he, "that you intend to repeat what I have said in all the unsuspecting confidence of friendship?"

"I mean nothing of the sort, certainly," Lorton answered, with a sneer. "You surprised me by the tone in which you spoke of your rival's secession from the field. Now finish your breakfast; there are some hot ortolans."

"Well, I'll be hanged," said Melhado, his colour creeping back, "I didn't certainly expect a word on Brune's side from *you*. If there was a fellow I could have counted on to cross him through thick and thin, you were the man."

"Brune is a man that I cannot like; so far you are right. It has happened that, in the pursuance of what I considered a just and friendly line of conduct to you, I have been obliged to thwart his plans. Possibly," added the young man, with some emotion —" possibly personal dislike may have prompted me more than I was aware of. If so, I shall extremely regret it. But do not fancy that I am his unscrupulous enemy. God help me! why do I allow revengeful feelings to sway me at all?"

Mr Melhado was not given to moral speculation, neither did he associate much with persons that were so addicted. He stared for a moment at Lorton, but finding that occupation unprofitable, and being quite unequal to a reply, he ate the ortolan, to which act he was by this time perfectly competent. Then, seeing his companion still silent and pensive, he began to feel an awe that it was necessary to dispel. Accordingly, after adroitly brushing out the hiatus by choking himself with his tea, and spluttering and swearing himself up to a proper equanimity, he said, carelessly—

"Never told you, now, what brought me here this morning. Fellows begin talking of all sorts of nonsense, and forget business. Mustn't do that. Now I say, Lorton, will you, like a good fellow, let one of your Africans go up to the Cinnamon and take charge of a pair of dogs that I am sending to Jenkins the book-keeper? I promised Mr Arabin to send them there for a little while, to let loose in case of the Obeah nocturnal meetings not being discontinued. The creole negroes are so confoundedly afraid of dogs that I should expect them to let these go if they should be at all unruly, notwithstanding their muzzles."

"You shall have an African certainly," said Lorton; "but your fellow must show him the way up. Do you mean that these are bloodhounds?"

"Yes, and beauties too—the scent of an eagle, and savage as the devil. You never saw such darling dogs. Old Orritt, one of my skippers, brought 'em from Cuba. They really are treasures. Cursed if I don't believe they would eat a nigger up in royal style like lions. Oh, they're regular pets! Precious few people, you may depend, that I would part with 'em for; but Arabin, of course, is privileged, and we've got a careful book-keeper, who knows when it's necessary to let 'em loose."

"You'll be killing some of the people with these ferocious brutes," Lorton said; "surely some other means can be found of keeping the Obeah people quiet, if they make themselves troublesome?"

"Troublesome! hang 'em, they're the pests of the country; and, between ourselves, 'twouldn't be a bad thing if the dogs did make free with a little of their carrion. But never fear. Whatever I may wish, I shan't do anything to compromise myself or anybody else. Jenkins the book-keeper is as safe as a parson. I'll just take a claret cup, and then be off to Kingston, where I'll look up Master Domingo, who always loiters, and send him on here with the dogs: you can then hand them to a steady African to lead, and Domingo will show the way." Then tossing off his draught, which made his skin look as if he had just stepped out of a shower-bath, he treated Lorton's hand to a warm clammy shake, and relieved him of his presence.

The negro of whom Melhado was in quest was not unjustly accused of a disposition to loiter. He had been sent forward at once, while his master halted in camp, to ask for the dogs, and bring them back thither immediately, Melhado's house being only about a mile or a mile and a half from the military post. But Domingo construed the word *immediately* according to a glossary of his own, and found it to be accurately rendered by a periphrasis to the following effect—" After having transacted all your own business, attended to all your own pleasure, and lounged and gossiped and loitered till you are tired, and the service required of you becomes quite a relief." He had a dozen friends to visit on all imaginable errands. He sold a paroquet, brought down from the mountains in some mysterious manner; for he had no cage, and had been required to use his hands in his master's service. He made inquiries concerning the health of a young woman, whose mother he comforted, on taking his leave, by remarking, "Him will die; I sure of it!" He looked in at the court-house, and heard various offenders sentenced by the magistrates; then he indulged in a bottle of spruce beer, and stole off the stall a cigar, which he lighted on turning the next corner, begging a "fire-tick" for that purpose from a most unamiable old lady of some ninety or a hundred years, whom he addressed as "Granny." Furnished with this mark of caste, he got up a swagger, cocked his hat, and assumed the air of a man of fashion. That the reader may conceive how admirably he looked the character, we mention that his hat was of the coarsest straw, guiltless of a crown, girt with only half a rim, and not clean; his shirt was striped with pink, gorgeously wrought on the bosom, and in holes all over; his trousers, likewise considerably disintegrated, were of Osnaburg. This—if we take no account of dirt—completed his costume, with which he himself appeared to be well pleased. He stopped at last by a small newly-painted house with a cool green verandah, and having first settled his hat into its original unpretending fashion, and then put out the cigar, and stuck the unconsumed portion behind his ear as a clerk sticks his pen, he walked into the yard and bowed politely to a domestic who was rubbing a bridle-bit in a mild manner, which did not seem inimical to the rust, and said courteously, "Marnin', sar; how you do?" Whereupon the gentleman who mildly rubbed the bit executed an elaborate courtesy, containing some passages of inexpressible sweetness and dignity, and replied, "Quite well, sar; tank you, sar."

Domingo then remarked, "It not so hot dis marnin', sar;" and the other gentleman replied, "Me doan't feel de cold, sar; me is berry robuss. I 'fraid you is not well, sar; you look leetle pale."

"I is not sick, sar, but I is delicate; dat make me look fair. You is robuss for true, sar; your cheeks like rose-bud," responded Domingo.

The complexions of the interlocutors both resembled a pair of boots that had been worn for a day, dirt included.

"Is Massa Grant at home, sar?" at length inquired Domingo.

"Him is in de tuddy, sar, making sarmint: you wish to see him?"

"If you will hab de goodness to say I call on him, sar, I shall be obleege," Domingo said.

"Perhapsin, sar, you will take a seat upon de cask while I axes," said this courteous negro; and then, depositing with great gentleness the bit on the ground, he retired very leisurely towards the house, but had no sooner reached the back verandah than he turned again to request the visitor not to sit too heavy on the cask, as "de top loose, and window-glass inside."

After a second expedition, he conducted Domingo into the presence of a rather young gentleman in clerical costume, except his coat, which had been replaced by a white jacket. The clergyman sat at a writing-table, with a manuscript before him. He had a bright eye and a benevolent countenance, with an expression of complacency rather than of power. The Rev. Mr Grant belonged to the Church of England. He firmly believed that he was a man calculated to do an immense amount of good to both negroes and planters; nay, that he had already effected great improvement. The influence of dissenters, which was at the time paramount in the island, he had determined to supersede. Confidence and hard work will go a long way towards the achievement of most designs; and, so far as these sufficed, Mr Grant accomplished the object of his mission. He looked up with a pleasant patronising smile as Domingo entered.

"Well, Brutus—no, Domingo—yes, to be sure, Domingo—well, Domingo, how d'ye? Calisto is quite well, I hope?"

"Him is too well, sar," said Domingo, trying to

spin his hat upon his hand, but unable to maintain rotation on account of the heavy rim being on one side only.

"Too well! ha, ha! curious expression that," said Mr Grant, rubbing his hands—"not a common complaint. You mean, in excellent health, eh?"

"I mean, sar, dat him is too well: no chance for him fall sick and die."

"Oh, shocking! shocking!" said the clergyman; "you are joking, surely. Married men mustn't talk that way. You're a Christian now, you know, and must love everybody, your wife especially."

"Massa," said Domingo, grasping the hat tightly, and looking up with an air of determination, "ever since you make me marry him, me hab no peace wid him. Him temper dreadful, him canduck vile; him is altogether wortless."

"Oh, my good man, this will never do, you know! There will be little misunderstandings, perhaps, between man and wife, in spite of all that can be done; but I'm sure Calisto does not deserve the character you give her. She will make you a good wife, depend on it. You must have patience, you know."

"So me hab, massa. Me mash him head tree or four time, but he no better. I come now to beg you, sar, to unmarry we, and take him back, becausin me can't tand him no longer."

"Hah! there, you see! you've been fighting. That's not the way, you know. You must learn to bear with one another. I daresay Calisto would say the blame was not all on her side."

"Him wicious as de debil, sar; you must take him back."

"Impossible," said Mr Grant, smiling. "You know, I thoroughly explained to you that the contract was for life. You took her for better or worse."

"Yes, sar—yes, Massa Grant, I quite 'greeable for dat, sar; but dis one all wuss and no better."

"Not at all—not at all," said the clergyman; "you are impatient, and both your tempers want controlling. You are far too apt—so we are all—to complain of your little troubles; but you take no account of the blessings you possess."

"Blessin', massa! what blessin' we got, poor negers, eh?"

"Why, you ought to be ashamed to ask the question, Domingo. What blessings! have you not an Established Church and faithful ministers? Don't you live under liberal laws and institutions?"

During this last remark Domingo inclined his head to one side as a parrot does when listening. He did not appear convinced—indeed, he did not clearly comprehend the meaning—but he replied—

"Iss, massa."

"Very well, then," said Mr Grant, "reflect on these things, and let the thought make you patient and forbearing. Bring Calisto down next Sunday, and let me speak to you both. There's a tenpence to buy something to carry home with you. Now, good morning, and no more fighting."

Domingo drew his bare foot along the floor in acknowledgment of the sixpence,* and still stood awkwardly, as if further disposed to show cause why his nuptial contract was not binding; but the minister's head was bent down, and his pen was running over the paper, so that the baffled husband, after balancing himself from leg to leg, and making a last effort to spin the eccentric hat, had nothing for it but to ejaculate "Cha!" and make a lingering retreat. As he came out he saw his friend still polishing the bit, at which occupation he probably continued till nightfall, when he sought the repose earned by such a hard day's work. Having exchanged parting compliments with this conscientious domestic, Domingo emerged from Mr Grant's premises, and encountered a negro funeral on its way to the burial-ground. Such a procession could, we believe, be seen nowhere but in the streets of Kingston. The body, which was that of some grown person, was rapidly borne or rather swung along by eight or ten people of both sexes,

* *Tenpence* currency equal *sixpence* English.

scrambling on either side of it without the slightest order or decency, and followed by a mixed crowd, attired in rags of all colours, and covered with dirt. Some were shouting, some quarrelling, some eating mangoes. Whether a hope arose in Domingo's mind that he might some day be carried to his long home with similar marks of respect and sorrow cannot be determined; but his interest was sufficiently aroused to make him ask of one of the chief mourners, " Hei, who dis?"

"It old Cicero Bunk, for me dam ol' fader, Massa Domingo," replied the mourner, who was a female. "Him walk off dis morning at las; tought him never would a dead, de old wortless!"

"Is dat de way you peak of your 'ceased parient, you——?" chimed in another mourner, when the voice was drowned by a terrific volley of abuse. A female bearer had descried in the street some person with whom she was at enmity, whereupon she dropped her hold of the coffin, which was carried on, and halted to revile her foe. The latter was overcrowed in the first encounter, and could make no adequate resistance, it was plain, from the beginning. But this circumstance suggested no generous forbearance to the assailant, who lavished epithets of scornful abuse from an inexhaustible vocabulary, and made the streets ring with her screams and violence.

Five times did she allow her wrath to subside into low mutterings, after spitting and otherwise decorously intimating that contempt had overmastered every stronger feeling; and five times did she turn back from the track of the funeral, forced by the welling eloquence within to renew the attack. The extravagance of her gestures was unbounded, and the play of her countenance might have suggested bosses for a Gothic masterpiece, or humbled the pride of nightmares. Frequently, feeling unable to give expression to her rage, she flung herself prostrate in the street; then, springing up again with a stone in each hand, she clashed them together like cymbals to intensify her railing. Although the quarrels of shrews in general are far too ordinary occurrences to excite any remark, the achievement of this professor was too grand to be treated with indifference. A crowd collected to admire the gifted negress—inferior scolds attentive to catch an idea, and ineloquent timid females fascinated by terror; while the male audience — the married ones less successfully than the rest—affected the *nonchalance* of connoisseurs. Domingo, among the crowd, observed the proceedings with a smile, thinking probably that Calisto, with all her faults, had not reached the limits of feminine attainment, when the smart touch of a whip made him look round and behold his "massa," who, in impatient accents, demanded what he was doing there, and why he had not gone up with the dogs.

"Massa know," pleaded Domingo, by way of apology, "dat me hab de tootache moast terrible bad; nebber sleep dese tree night. How me is to carry up dese sabage dogs, den, except me go down to Granny Sally and get him charmed?"

But massa knew nothing of the kind; on the contrary, massa knew full well that the toothache was a lie invented for the occasion, whereupon Melhado, administering another cut of the whip and some unrepeatable language, commanded the truant to follow him home.

CHAPTER VII.

LIEUTENANT LORTON, the young officer who had entertained Mr Melhado at breakfast, wandered between his room and the verandah before it, awaiting Domingo's return with the dogs, that he might despatch an African to lead them up as he had promised. As might be expected, the creole negro is of very different character from the native African, from whom he springs. He possesses a slight, a very slight, advantage in point of skill and intelligence, but morally he is, we grieve to say, by far inferior. The natives who appear in our colonies now, chiefly when rescued from the slave-ships of other nations, and many of whom take service in our black corps, are patterns of gentleness, docility, honesty, candour, and good faith. For heathens and savages this is high praise; and to the white man, by whose society the creole negro has become what he is, it is a fearful reproach. Of course the Africans, being steeped in ignorance, have ideas and customs which may well make a Christian shudder. Among their failings is a disposition to suicide, which they sometimes indulge with great wantonness. A young man, known to have been cheerful and active, has suddenly destroyed himself by musket-shot, first putting on every article of clothing that he could wear at a time—for instance, two shirts, two suits of clothes, and a greatcoat; then quietly laying himself at length on the floor or ground, placing the muzzle under his chin, and pressing the trigger with his toe. On the other hand, to characterise the creole negro is to make a list of all vices, one perhaps excepted — namely, drunkenness. He is but feebly alive to the delights of ebriety; and though some advanced minds, like Chitty's, felt a dim appreciation of the alcoholic ecstasis, they but wandered about the outskirts of a great verity, and ignorantly worshipped that which was declared to only the favoured whites. It will be understood, from the above remarks, why, in the charge of valuable property, a native African could be much preferred to a creole black. And there is another reason why the creole is hardly fit to be intrusted with dogs—particularly with savage dogs. In the history of the Maroon wars we read that bloodhounds were used to hunt the brigands who skulked in the forests; and probably the use of dogs was not confined to this period. Be that as it may, the West Indian negro has an antipathy to, and horror of, a dog, to which, when fresh from Africa, he is insensible. Hence it was that Melhado desired to have for escort of the dogs a man recently landed from Africa.

Before we resume the thread of the story, it may be proper to state how it happened that Lieutenant Lorton had the services of an African at his disposal. This young officer, with whom we made a slight acquaintance during breakfast, was, to use his own language, " one of the unluckiest devils on God's earth." That is not precisely the way in which we would have described him. We would have preferred to say that he was a youth of superior abilities and attainments, but of a nervous temperament; who sailed gloriously before the wind, but to whom an adverse blast brought the phantom of despair. He had been on the staff of a former commander of the forces in Jamaica, and had been noted at that time as gay, sporting, adventurous, clever, and conceited. Far from considering himself then the victim of ill-fortune, he bore himself as though fortune was his slave; and without being either bad-hearted or unscrupulously selfish, the tide of success made him insolent and affected. Thus he was almost disliked where many a worse man with a stronger head would have made himself friends. He was, as has been said, good-looking; he dressed well, danced well, rode flat races well, and talked well—accomplishments which were all at a premium. At length there rose up amid all this sunshine a little cloud of care, at first no bigger than a man's hand, but which grew and grew, and which was magnified in his mind far more than it was in fact. His regiment was ordered home, which made it necessary either that he should return with it, relinquishing his appointment on the staff, or that he should effect an exchange into a regiment in the island. He was very unwilling to do either, but at length decided on the latter; and, as the affair required to be negotiated in haste, he made his offer of exchange where it was sure to be accepted—namely, to a subaltern of a West India regiment, a poor youth who, having made up his mind to broil out his days in the tropics, suddenly saw an opening for home service in a white regiment, and darted at it with the frantic delight of a hopeless prisoner who succeeds to affluence. To Lorton, who never saw his regiment, it mattered little at present in what corps he served. Thus he retained the run of the General's house, and still enjoyed his share of gaiety and distinction. Scarcely, however, had this difficulty been smoothed, when the General was taken ill, and obliged to return, on short notice, to England, and give up his command. This was a terrible blow. Lorton, who had but just lost the chance of going home with his old regiment, found himself removed from the staff, and literally compelled to do duty with black troops. The sick General promised to use his interest with his successor, but the latter officer had friends of his own on whom he chose to bestow his patronage. Lorton made large offers for another exchange, but hitherto without success. He contrived to get appointed to the command of a small detachment of his corps which was quartered in Up Park Camp to furnish postmen, orderlies, and so on, and thus avoided joining at headquarters, which were in another island. But the change to him was miserable. Those who had before been angry at his supercilious airs, failed not to make him feel the difference in his position; yet nothing that they could do equalled the sense of disappointment and despair within himself. He was the most ill-used man in the world: nobody before him had ever known what misfortune was. He took his grief to heart, secluded himself, and became bilious and hypochondriacal. Besides mourning over his present troubles, he conjured up all manner of possible ones, and said that nothing in the shape of ill-luck would surprise him. All the world seemed to his jaundiced eye in a conspiracy against him; he became fretful and humorous, and nothing but his good sense and superior education gave him any support against his desponding temperament. These did, however, operate advantageously. He saw at length the absurdity of his woe, and made efforts to disperse or control it. Again his prepossessing figure was seen in ball-rooms, again he yielded to the entreaties of those who hoped through his light seat and cunning hand to see their horses win cup or handicap, and to be themselves exalted to the gods, the lords of the universe.* It was just at this time, when his wounds were beginning to skin over, that the Sophia Brown landed her interesting passengers, and that Arthur Brune began to receive homage and to taste of celebrity. Lorton had not simply to reoccupy his abandoned ground; he had to contend for it with a formidable rival—a rival who, instead of railing at Lady Fortune in set terms, was not unlikely, after a rebuff or two, to lead the said Fortune captive, as the brave and constant know how. Brune, who could do a bit of everything, rode against Lorton at Kingston races, and beat him. After all, it was the horses and not the men who contended; nobody blamed Lorton because he rode a losing horse; on the contrary, he got great praise for the

* "Terrarum dominos evehit ad Deos."—HORACE.

place he took under the circumstances. But this by no means satisfied him. Brune's general reputation was a grievance at which he was exceeding wroth; and now that Brune had borne away the palm from himself, his irritation knew no bounds. His temper decided a competition which might have been otherwise a very even one. Brune's hearty, hopeful disposition bore him through easily, while with poor soured Lorton every failure produced many others. Just when the mind of the latter was thus smarting with the injuries received from Brune, from the world in general, and from Fortune in particular, he first saw Violet Arabin: for we have explained how he had listlessly secluded himself, and refused to hear the voice of those delights which formerly charmed him. His taste at once appreciated all Violet's advantages —her fresh and peculiar beauty, her winning grace, and the modern style of all her accomplishments. Six months ago he would have been a forward admirer—possibly an ardent lover; but now there was, in his dark mind, a great gulf fixed between anything so passing fair as Violet and a being forsaken of his tuetlary gods as he was. He saw in her not a sweet object for his soul to doat on, but a crowning glory for the lucky Brune; for the humility which shut out love had large capacity for envy. He detested and despised this feeling, but he kept and nourished it. The pretensions of Melhado, which he early detected, were a balm to his spirit. He at once became the partisan of this underbred dealer—a fellow whom he had before distinguished with his contempt and aversion. He accepted Melhado's ready acquaintance, made him confess his passion, and sustained and animated his hope.

That Providence to which men in ordinary parlance give the name of coincidence or chance, ordained that Lorton should receive from a female relative at Cork some sheets of condolence, silly advice, and gossip—the last preponderating. The epistle contained a rambling account of the scrapes and enormities of two military heroes who had set all Cork by the ears. Irish ambiguity and young lady's grammar made a sad hash of personals and relatives, and conspired to perplex the reader as to how the degrees of guilt or glory were partitioned between Knox and Brune, for they of course were the *dramatis personæ*. There had been dreadful trifling with a lady's heart, and frightful gambling with the lady's brother; then at last a duel, in which one subaltern was principal and the other second. *Between* them a noise had been made in the world. Now Lorton wished sincerely, spite of his better nature, that Brune might be principally to blame throughout. He communicated his intelligence to Melhado, who, without any delicacy, at once ascribed to Arthur the whole of the blame, and communicated to Christy Arabin his own views of the case as conclusive and authentic evidence. Christy, more biassed, perhaps, than he knew of by his wish to find an occasion against Brune, believed implicitly the whole of the story; and though he could not suppress an admiration which he felt for Brune personally, he congratulated himself on the escape which he might yet make from a wild unprincipled son-in-law, and on the broad and smooth way which was now open to the overtures of Mrs Melhado. The reader knows how this poison wrought, and how it promised to wreck the happiness of two individuals, and to gratify jealousy, avarice, and presumption.

Now, then, let us return to Lorton, who, with a throbbing head, and an aching back, and a flushed and shivering frame, is lying on the sofa awaiting Domingo's return. He had been upset by Melhado's behaviour in the morning; and reflection on Melhado's contemptible character made him blush for the intimacy which he had allowed to grow between them. It was one of his depressed periods, when better feelings generally gained the ascendant; and he saw in their own odious colours the ideas which he had indulged, and the acts to which they led. This remorse was much increased by information acquired from recent letters, which showed pretty plainly to those not wilfully blind that the share of the transactions at Cork, fairly attributable to Arthur Brune, was but little to his discredit. It was plain that more charity in the first instance would have prevented a great wrong, which he had been instrumental in producing, and which could not now be mended. He felt that, if Brune were then present, he could find relief in asking his forgiveness, and offering amends; but he knew, at the same time, from sad experience, how a slight praise of Brune, or allusion to his success, would recall all the dark passion, and render him as ungenerous as before. Then the thought of his own weakness and changing humour came upon him as a curse. He felt the torture of despair, and wept. Presently he heard Sampson's step in the verandah, and summoned him.

"Sampson," said he, "is that loitering rascal come with the dogs yet?"

"No come yet, massa," answered Sampson.

"Abominable brute!" Lorton said. "Sampson, tell Nero that I shall ride the black horse this afternoon. I want the air, but Peregrine is too fresh."

"Yas, massa. Massa hab leetle feebar?"

"I don't feet quite right," Lorton said; "but 'tis nothing, 'twill soon pass. You needn't stay."

"P'r'apsin if me was to make massa some nice

cool, cool sangree, it would sweet him?" suggested Sampson, lingering.

"What, you villain! you want more white wine, do you? Always one word for me, and two for yourself. Cool drink, indeed! I feel quite cold enough already; something warm would be more comfortable. Now go—do you hear, sir?—go!" the last monosyllable almost a shriek.

Sampson escaped, and Lorton lay down again to ponder and fret and be miserable.

In a few minutes he was disturbed by Sampson's reappearance, and, starting up, was about to vent his wrath, when he saw in the negro's hand a glass of warm sangree, such as he had desired. This disarmed his anger immediately. He sipped some of the grateful beverage. "Sampson," he said, "I fear that I am sometimes very unjust to you, eh? You try my temper so. This is very nice. Now, give me my cloak, and I daresay this nervous shivering will soon pass off. You may keep the rest of the bottle of wine."

"Yes, massa, tank you, sar," answered Sampson, in a tone which seemed to imply, "Thank you for nothing," for it had never been Sampson's intention to let any of the wine revert to his massa.

Lorton now attempted to compose himself, but was almost immediately disturbed by the announcement of Domingo with the dogs. Spite of the languor of his indisposition, he roused himself and went downstairs to look at the animals, of which he had heard such lavish praises. They were splendid creatures certainly, red in colour, and their skins hard and thick. Every movement bespoke strength and agility. Intelligent eyes, sharp noses, and cropped ears, distinguished their countenances, but the heads grew considerably wider towards the joints of the jaws. The muzzles which they wore prevented their formidable teeth from being seen. Being fresh and well fed, their natural ferocity was just now much abated, and they twisted and gambolled and snuffed the fresh air as kindly as pointers would have done.

"Dis one call *Echo*," said Domingo, pretending to be quite at his ease with the beasts, "and dis one *Crackadile*. Plendid brutes dem is. Hi, Crackadile, poor feller, make me troke you;" but as Crocodile, who happened to be in a genial humour, offered to return the caress, Domingo let go the chain of the muzzled dog, and made a fugitive movement, which quite justified the precaution of sending an African in his company.

A black soldier now appeared, answering to the name of Snowball Snooks,* into whose hands were

* These poor fellows are always enrolled under English names, which are given to them by some of the white people of the regi-

committed the dog-chains (which he secured to a waistbelt of rope), and in whose society Domingo proceeded home to the mountains. Lorton returned to his quarters. The shivering passed off after taking the sangree, but it was succeeded by a restless heat, and his head and back were still painful. Before the time came for his ride, he had sent for the doctor, who ordered him some medicine, and recommended him to go to bed instead of going abroad.

ments—often by the sergeants. The appellations are quite arbitrary, and some of them are very absurd. Snowball Snooks is a very mild example. We have known them to receive the names of the officers of their own regiment; but different fashions of nomenclature prevailed at different periods.

CHAPTER VIII.

MEANWHILE Domingo and private Snowball Snooks pursued their journey up the mountains. It is not surprising that, under Domingo's guidance, their course was somewhat erratic. Indeed, Domingo had no intention of getting back before dusk, and he would not have fixed that date for his return, but for the knowledge that the book-keeper to whom he was consigned took his supper and rum-and-water after sunset, and was wont to growl savagely, and eke to snap, if he dared, at those who disturbed him at his meal. Snooks's English vocabulary extended to about ten words, or, by a liberal estimate, to twenty; the verbal interchange of ideas between the travellers was therefore very limited. Negroes, however, can achieve a good deal of conversation by means of signs and inarticulate sounds, and in this way a brisk and interesting dialogue might have been sustained, but for the African's lamentable taciturnity, which refused to respond to the voice and gestures of the charmer.

Perceive them he did, and must; and, blessings on mother Nature! the very defect which is fatal to colloquy forms the staple of a good listener. Snowball was too polite and gentle not to *appear* to listen: whether he attended, or whether his thoughts were away by the banks of the far Bancaro, where

"Were his young barbarians all at play,
And there their *Congo* mother,"

while he, their sire, rescued from a slaver, and dressed in the uniform of his Britannic Majesty, was leading bloodhounds up the Port Royal mountains, pestered by a loquacious and lying nigger, who gave him not a moment of repose.

Domingo, after a few prefatory questions and observations, intended to test the power and quality of the instrument on which he was about to perform, took from behind his ear, where it had nestled deliciously ever since morning, the remnant of his stolen cigar, and, with an air of crushing civilisation, tendered it to the poor African, saying jauntily, at the same time, "Ob course you smoke, sar; you will find dis de real habanna."

Snooks said, "No, no;" and first puffing his cheeks, and then making a grimace, he indicated that the proffered dainty was not appreciated by him.

"Hah!" went on Domingo, "I obserbe all time,*

* Always.

de pribate soldier, both bukra and neger, smoke common pipe. Bery well. Me got nuttin' to say agin de pipe, only cigars is more genteeler, and dem doesn't poil de camplexian, and dem make you smell more pleasanter." We deduce from the last remark, and from our knowledge of what he was when he confined himself to cigars, that Domingo, after a yard of clay, was unapproachable.

He now began to draw Snowball's attention to the places and objects which they were passing, not by any means as pointing out beauties of the earth or skies, but associating each spot with something interesting to his own perceptions. Pointing his finger across a hollow of the mountain, the innermost recess of which, in almost black shadow, cooled you when you looked at it, and between whose opening arms floated a mist which grew lighter as the breadth increased, and which blushed with the hues of paradise, while patches of white rock, rising above and overshadowed by dark-green bamboos, showed an impenetrable refuge from the blazing sun, he said— "You see dat estate down dere, sar? dat de trash-house * jist ober de furdest bamboo. Well, sar, down dere dem get one of de finest number 'leven trees in de country."

* A shed to cover the *trash* or crushed canes which have passed through the mill. In some colonies the trash is called *megasse*.

The species of mangoes are distinguished by numbers, and number eleven is by far the best.

Soon after Domingo cautioned his companion against an estate which lay near their route, saying, " It quite worthless : de busha" (overseer) "no tief nuttin' hisself, and no allow nobody else for tief nuttin'. He too honest for true!"

It was but natural that the exercise and conversation should make them extremely thirsty. Domingo, feeling dry himself, ascertained that Snooks was similarly affected; therefore, leading his companion a little way into the bush, through which at the time their path wound, and stopping close to a large tree, from which depended a number of parasitical withes, he seized one of the latter, and divided it with his knife at the distance of a few feet from the ground. Grasping that portion which still hung from the tree, he placed the end of it in Snooks's mouth. Then, holding it upright, he made another section higher up, when a flow of delicious water, forced through the tubes of the plant by the atmospheric pressure, poured into poor Snowball's parched throat. Domingo afterwards refreshed himself by a similar process, and the travellers resumed their journey with new strength.

At another time, as they got higher up, Domingo expatiated upon the provision-grounds, now exhibiting great beauty and plenty.

"Dere, sar, you see dem yams and plantains? you see de cocos and de ackees, and all de bread kind! My king, it make for me mout water! You eber see such probision-ground as dat, sar?"

"Ye, ye," said Snooks, making a gesture of assent.

"Where you see dem, sar?" asked Domingo, much astonished.

The African noted the line of his shadow, and then, stretching his hand towards the sea, he slowly moved it along the horizon till it rested pointing to the east. In this attitude he remained for a moment. Then he smiled sadly, shook his head, and laid the hand upon his heart.

"Hei," said Domingo; "you tink dat better country nor dis?"

Snowball looked to heaven with glistening eyes, then clasped his hands, making the dog-chains rattle, and, forgetting to move forwards, seemed overcome by sad recollections.

"Chaw," remarked Domingo; "what trouble you dis way?"

Snowball waved his hand deprecatingly, but Domingo went on with an air of superiority.

"You is too apt to complain of for you troubles, sar; you don't take no count of de blessin' you hab!"

Only a sorrowful, inquiring look from Snowball.

"You no got Tablish Church an' faitful meenistars? You no got libberl law and constitooshin? You no free? Hei!"

Though Snowball did not understand much of this grave reproof, his passion was now abating, and he began once more to move on composedly, to the great satisfaction of his eloquent instructor.

"You got wife, den?" asked Domingo.

"Ye, ye!" answered Snowball, pointing eastwards again.

"You will see him again, you tink?"

Snowball pointed to his own breast, then to the ground; after that, describing an arch in the air, he pointed once more to the east, his face radiant with a smile.

"You means," interpreted Domingo, "dat you won't see him till you dead and berrid fust; den you go to your country?"

"Ye, ye, ye," said Snooks, delightedly.

"My fader, dis man mus a mad!" Domingo soliloquised.

Here was a man pretty safe never to behold his wife again in this world—a simple ignorant man, quite incapable of appreciating the release which had befallen him; while he, Domingo, enlightened, and capable of enjoying his life, who would have devoutly welcomed such a separation, was condemned to a lifelong cohabitation with Calisto. This thought was very aggravating; it even caused Domingo's tongue to slacken for a while. He rallied, however, and, apropos of his reflections, confided to Snowball his domestic troubles, revealed his appeal to Mr Grant that day, and its result, and intimated that if Calisto were happily in Congo, *he* would be inclined to point the finger of hope toward the far *west*. This led to metaphysical speculations concerning the route taken by departed spirits, and finally to the solemn subject of *Obi*, at the very mention of which, under the breath, both men halted suddenly, and uttered a short exclamation, so peculiar as to astonish the dogs, and call forth a sharp yelp from both Echo and Crocodile. Snowball became now rapidly more interested, as Domingo, in a low mysterious tone, revealed some of the local secrets of Obi, and the name of the most cunning Obeah man in the district—a patriarch originally from Congo, but now of great age and fame, and of surpassing power. As a mile or two, right or left, signified little to Domingo, it was at last agreed that they should pay a visit to this awful magician, so that Snooks might behold the person and witness the sorcery of his renowned countryman. Accordingly, late in the afternoon, the two pedestrians and the dogs made their appearance in front of some negro huts, shaded with tall cocoa-trees and thick tamarinds and bamboos, in front of which naked and filthy black children, and comparatively clean and sweet goats, were just waking up to the coolness of evening with a great squalling and bleating, which did not harmonise with the cackling of numerous erratic fowls, but rather formed with it an excruciating combination of sounds. A black girl, who leaned against a doorpost plying the everlasting chewstick, interrupted her labours to indicate, by a backward point over the shoulder, the whereabouts of the Magus. He was seated on a treestump under a banana shade. A cloud of mosquitoes veiled his venerable person, which was otherwise imperfectly covered; the fingers of one hand scratched viciously among his hoary wool, the other held an empty calabash, from which he had lately eaten his evening meal, tokens of which clung about his oracular mouth. At sight of the dogs he ceased the explorations on his scalp, and half scrambled to his feet in fright.

"Hei, what de debbil make you bring dem dam dog dis side? You want for eat we up?" demanded the old gentleman, half turning as if to flee if the answer should be unsatisfactory.

"Nebba fear, daddy," said Domingo; "dem all safe and muzzled. Dem no trouble you. See here for you countryman come see you."

Hereupon Snowball addressed to the sage a few words in the Congo tongue, to which the sage replied, and a fraternisation or rather affiliation ensued; and as the Obeah man could have no objection to exhibit the treasures of his science to so eligible a disciple, Snowball, after fastening the poor hungry dogs to the trunk of a tree with their heads together, and nothing to interrupt the *tête-à-tête* (for the small negroes gave them a wide berth), entered the awful hut accompanied by Domingo. The interior of this studio was decorated with symbols and natural products, such as would not have very powerfully impressed a European, but which seemed charged with weird meanings and unearthly influence to Snowball, who lifted his cap and thrice did obeisance on entering the sacred chamber, which, besides the daddy's bed, contained several shelves, on which were arranged rags and feathers, bones and teeth, worked into a hundred fantastic shapes. There were a few dried herbs, but the staple articles were cats' and alligators' teeth, bottles containing blood, earth from graves, egg-shells, skulls of cats stuffed with clay, so that the clay and bone together should form a sphere; balls of earth stuck with parrots' beaks, or with dogs' or even human teeth; claws of animals, glass beads, and a mucilage contained in egg-shells or broken bottles. There were likewise many little bags containing the above-mentioned ingredients in various proportions.

The Obeah man did not follow his guests into the hut, being at the moment called on to give audience to a person who had come to consult him on matters of state. This was no other than our friend Leander, at whose call the old gentleman withdrew to the middle of an overshadowed spot, and summoned a small urchin, who, being of too tender years to understand important secrets, sometimes enjoyed the privilege of brushing mosquitoes from the learned man's person, when the magnitude or delicacy of his negotiations made it desirable that he should be free from bodily irritation.

"Know'd dat you was comin', Leander," said the daddy; "heerd for you footstep mile off!"

"Dat is all nonsense," Leander replied; "I not b'lieve a word of your gammon. Remember, I bin in Englan', where de people knows better!"

"My king!" exclaimed the indignant sage, "you no 'fraid for speak dat-a-way to me? You no 'fraid me make you eat dirt—you no 'fraid Duppy come choke you—you no 'fraid you find for youself change to one lilly pig, squeakee, squeakee? You really mannish! hei, me nebber hear sich a ting!"

"Don't vex, daddy," replied Leander, good-humouredly; "you can't frighten me wid your nonsense

Why, I seen conjurers dat will show for sixpence sich tings as would make you die wid spite, and yet eberybody knows dey is all a cheat."

"Chaw!" said the daddy, his wrinkled countenance puckering into a pitying smile—" Chaw! what you talk to me 'bout sich wortless creature? What dem able for do? Chaw!" And the sage spat in contempt on the ground.

"Look yere, daddy," said Leander; "what you tink of dis? I see one of dem conjurer breathe fire, favour debil in h——. I see one of dem make we sit in a dark room, den he say, 'Look sharp now, you will see duppy.' Den dere a little 'peck· of light seemin' a tousan mile off. It come nearer and nearer, and grow big and bigger. When it close up among de company, it a terrible duppy 'pon a pale horse with a dart in his hand. Anoder conjurer swaller a long sword, and pull it up again; den he pat his tummick an' say, 'All right.'"

The daddy's expression of contempt and incredulity changed gradually to one of astonishment during this address. But, being a practised impostor, he did not too readily accept Leander's facts. He again said, "Chaw! tuff and nansense;" but Leander saw that he was moved, so he gave him another dose.

"Look yere, daddy; 'pan my soul, I see dem load a gun and fire two barrels at a conjurer—bang! He only laugh and catch de two ball in his two hand. Nuttin' couldn't hurt him. Den dey try to tab him, and he laugh again. Ha, boy, you no kill me! And de sword come out quite bright and dry."

Then, enticed beyond the confines of truth by the Obeah man's astonishment, he added, "I see a nyoung woman jump over de church tower. Anoder one walk trough a brick wall. I see a man swoller hisself, hei! Don't tink I is taken in wid your poor negar tricks. You can't cheat Leander."

"'Top, 'top," said the daddy; "de buckrah man pretend for do it, and he no do it. Me do it for true."

"Ah, well," replied Leander. "Now look here, daddy. I bring you lot of beads an' English feathers, most lovely, and I got two or tree little boxes dat make you do wonderful trick. You see, I gib you dis an' plenty more, only you mus' show me how you make de tunder and lightning."

The old man's countenance brightened again with triumph. "Ha, ha, you 'blige to come to me wid all for you clebberness—ha, ha, boy! ha, ha!"

"Dat right," Leander said, "laugh away; but you mus' show me dis; an' besides, I tell you sometin' else. Nick Chitty comin' to ax you for make Miss Rosabella lub him."

"How you like dat, boy?" asked the sorcerer.

Leander made a wry face.

"Ah, berry well," mused or pretended to muse the sage. "Massa Chitty most 'pectable man—*him* no laugh at the Obi. Make me see—mus' do sunting for he. 'Pose me gib lilly powder to put in Rosy's ochra-soup, eh? No, dat make him lub too 'trong, make him tease Massa Nick all de day long, make him foller Nick about, so dat him no able to mind him bisness, nor hab no peace—mustn't do dat."

"Look here, daddy," put in Leander.

"'Pose now me put drop of sunting 'pon Rosy chew-stick? Dat make him kiss too much, him slobber Massa Chitty too much. Chitty no like dat."

"Hei, daddy, I tell you."

"Ah! Now me got it, of coorse dat de ting! Charm for him pillow, make him 'top at home and dream an' tink all time 'bout Chitty, and long for see him: make him watch for Chitty footstep, make him run trow himself into Chitty's arm when him come. Dat is it! Make him hang about Chitty neck and tell him he lub him. Nick like dat."

"Daddy, you can't listen?" interrupted Leander.

"Den him not bear de sight of any oder man 'ceptin' Chitty, nyoung man or old man, him tell dem all to go to de debil, him want only de one Nick Chitty. Me see, me see!"

"Daddy, you mus a mad," screamed Leander, stamping his foot. "You can't hearken a minute?"

"Beg for you pardon," said the Obeah man; "me only tinkin' what a nice wife Miss Rosy make for Nick. Nick like de bright yeyes; he like de fine bussum; he like de rosy lips. My! how Nick will kiss dem! Hei, where you goin', Leander, eh? What make you 'tart off in dat passiony manner, eh? What trouble you, eh, boy?"

"You goin' listen at last?" said Leander, turning in a great pet. "I tell you, you mustn't give Nick no encouragement. You mus' tell him Obi set for him if he meddle wid Rosabella. He mustn't tink of her, hear'ee? Tell him there is oder things for him to think about besides making love to young women! Tell him de debil looking out for him."

"'Top, 'top," said the daddy, "how me is to do dis when me able for make de nyoung woman lub him—why is me to do dis? Massa Chitty berry good man—quite de gentleman. Him nebber come dis side widout plenty nyam and plantain. Sometimes him bring bottle of rum. Berry nice man. Why me is to do dat?"

"Daddy," said Leander, "I will give you all the things I tell you of, and I bring you a bag of cornmeal and two bottle of rum besides, if you tell Chitty what I wish."

"Couldn't do sich a ting," said the daddy: "when you goin' bring de meal?"

"Bring it to-morrow," answered Leander.

"Couldn't tink of it," said the old gentleman: "when you bring de rum?"

"Bring all to-morrow; will that do?"

"After Miss Rosy make him sich a 'plendid wife, and after he lub her so! No, no. De rum good?"

"I bring you the best that can be got," said Leander. "Come, now."

"Poor Chitty," said the sage; "him ought to hab Rosy. Me too fond of you, Leander, dat de trut! You make me do cruel tings: you don't got lilly bit of nice baccy for de old man?"

"Yes; I bring you some baccy too, daddy. Now, you understand?"

"Me 'blige to please you, boy: can't tell what make me lub you dis way; it reely 'trange. Come see me to-morrow, and me tell you someting praps, hear'ee?"

Leander grinned and nodded as he withdrew. We presume, though, that he succeeded in corrupting the vaticination delivered to Mr Chitty, for the latter gentleman left the Obeah man's house that evening heavy and disquieted; while Leander and Rosy, who watched his return home, had some joke which amused them extravagantly.

The daddy, after dismissing Leander, devoted a little of his valuable time to Snowball Snooks, until the latter, being hurried away by Domingo, untied the bloodhounds ánd departed towards the bookkeeper's house, leaving afar off the negro hamlet, as it lay under the dark mountain, dyed in the soft glory of sunset, and sheltered by the scarcely-stirring trees, a type of heavenly repose. There are gentle lowings and faint tinklings, and a lazy hum and a coming silence: it is a dream of childhood!

The Obeah man, of whom we have just had a glimpse, is, it is believed, a sample of his profession in general. The reader has already pronounced him and his art ridiculous and contemptible beyond patience. But things must be regarded according to their estimation and effects in places where they exist; and the power of Obi over the negro mind has worked many a social and political convulsion, and caused sufficient anxiety to lawgivers. The statutes of Jamaica direct the severest penalties against it; and probably the other West India islands were equally anxious for its suppression. Its secret has never been fathomed by white men. The tricks and apparatus of the art are, as far as we can detect, the very grossest species of impostures, palpable even to a negro mind. But the terror which it inspires sufficiently attests its grasp on the imagination, and forces respect from those who cannot control it, much as they may contemn the means which it uses. The word

Obi introduced in ordinary conversation will cause a black person to spring almost off the ground, and utter the "hi!" of reverence or terror. The negroes will undergo immense labour and privation at the dictation of the Obeah man; and, to break a spell give anything short of life, as, if unbroken, it will probably destroy life itself. The superstition works by external symbols, the meaning of which has never been ascertained. These are to be seen in all directions—in fields, gardens, lanes, and houses. A man on issuing from his house in the morning, recognises some token, which is without significance to the uninitiated, but which *he* knows to be a warning that *Obi is set for him;* whereupon terror takes possession of him, and he can see no hope except by propitiating the sorcerer who has wrought the spell, or by enlisting on his side a professor of superior power. Many a time the victim failing to do either has pined and died, so confirming the opinion of the irresistible power of Obi. Even where no animosity of race dictated the charms, and the intrigues related to internal affairs of the negroes themselves, Obi was a serious plague to the master, as killing and incapacitating his slaves.

There was another class of impostors calling themselves *Myallmen*, who asserted that they had the power of reanimating dead bodies, and who sometimes exercised their art to the astonishment and terror of many witnesses. Either the seeming dead were in collusion with the Myallmen, or the latter knew how to induce a temporary *coma* by means of drugs, or by a mesmeric process. It appears that great perplexity was once caused by the execution, for some capital offence, of a magician, who, up to the last, assured his friends and admirers that death had no power over him. Hanged in their sight he undoubtedly was ; but whether the evidence of their senses was strong enough to overpower belief in the supernatural, it is not so easy to determine.

" And they believe him ; oh ! the lover may
Distrust that look which steals his soul away ;
The babe may cease to think that it can play
With heaven's rainbow ; alchemists may doubt
The shining gold their crucible gives out :
But Faith, fanatic Faith, once wedded fast
To some dear falsehood, hugs it to the last.'

CHAPTER IX.

WE come now to the day on which Mr Arabin and his daughter are to sail to Port Henderson, and thence proceed to Spanish Town. Mrs Arabin, it seems, is not to be of the party. There has been a little hurricane blowing for a day or two at Crystal Mount, and all the leaves are ruffled, and the genius of domestic harmony has fled before it. Mrs Arabin is in disgrace—she sometimes is so : Violet is scarcely able to elude the storm; it requires all her little management, and all her great affection and grace, to escape its fury: Mr Arabin is dreadfully out of humour; he is the Æolus from whom proceeds the tempest. No wonder, then, that when his wife proposed to remain at home, Mr Arabin ungraciously agreed to the arrangement, and thought within himself that it was quite a lucky whim! So Mr Arabin and Violet are expected in Kingston by Melhado between ten and eleven in the morning; Leander and Rosy are ordered to go down on foot, and rendezvous at the boat-wharf in Port-Royal Street; and Mrs Arabin has numerous duties to attend to at Crystal Mount.

On a bright morning, before the sea-breeze has set in, the city of Kingston is anything but a cool place. Spite of the heat, though, it is in a wondrous bustle; for all of English race, true to their traditions and descent, persist in transplanting every possible custom that is English, and, reason and climate notwithstanding, adhere to the hours of labour and business which are prescribed at the London Docks and the Stock Exchange. Only to hint at the grateful *siesta* of the south of Europe, and the other simple adaptations by which a tropical climate may be made enjoyable, is to rouse the old Adam Bull, and bring down frightful comminations on Jews, Turks, infidels, and especially on Frenchmen. Better to say nothing about it, and take things as we find them—to sleep away the delicious hour of daybreak, bathe and breakfast in the blazing heat of eight or nine o'clock, swelter in the streets or the counting-house, the highway or the fields, till evening; get a hasty ride or drive, then dine at sunset, and go to bed when the moon and stars distil their heavenly influence, and the land-breeze gently agitates the air; swearing that the night-wind is the source of all disease, and that the only way to thwart its influence is to take plenty of stimulants before going to rest!

Kingston, then, is a busy place for at least three hours before and three hours after noon. In the stores and counting-houses, or bustling along the streets and piazzas, are to be seen faces of every shade, from the fair tint in which are set the Saxon azure eyes, to the deep jet of the African, all engaged in the service of Mammon; but, to do them justice, looking as if they were not always so employed, and not half so gaunt and careworn as we see men about the resorts of commerce in England. Three great square dark holes under a piazza in Harbour Street were the entrances to the store of Melhado, Huggins, and Bamboo, one of the most celebrated depots in the island. Near one of the doorways sat, in the American fashion, with his feet upon an inlaid cabinet which stood exposed for sale, a youth, descended from both Abraham and Canaan — deriving from the former patriarch his features and screwy ringlets, and from the latter his smutty complexion and the woolly texture of the curls. He was mastering the leading article of the 'Jamaica Despatch,' and refreshing himself with a cigar. Deeper in the store, which, when you got out of the glare, you found to be stocked with merchandise of all imaginable descriptions strangely huddled together, were seven or eight other youths, white and brown, supplying customers or attempting some arrangement of the miscellaneous wares, among which could now be distinguished furniture, iron and tin utensils, printed calico, Indian-corn, cheeses, wax-candles, watches, books, china, glazed ware, pianofortes, patent medicines, umbrellas, saddles, harness, salt-fish — we can't go on! There were several inner rooms, all stocked with goods, and one of them containing a dozen shoemakers working under a white foreman. It was observable that the customers to this establishment stood in very humble relation to the young gentlemen who dispensed its contents: black and brown people waited patiently until it should be the pleasure of these ingenuous youths to serve them, and did not dare to make remarks on price or quality: an old lady who was entitled to a quarter-dollar as change against a dollar stood expecting for ten minutes, and at the end of that time ventured to ask for it; whereupon the amiable attendant flung it with an oath across the store, and asked her why the devil she was so troublesome.

When any entered whom the shopboys deigned to look upon as equals, they shook hands with them, and had a little conversation concerning things in general before they transacted business. There was a horse, or a dance, or a lady to be discussed, or a complimentary exchange of cigars to be effected, or a bet to be booked, or possibly a bottle of porter to be

L

tasted, with much smacking of the lips and criticisms on its quality. But if such glorious independence characterised the inferior officers of this great establishment, what must be the estimation in which is held a partner in the grand concern—a great, nay, the greatest triumvir, beside whom Huggins and Bamboo hide their diminished heads! What must the effect have been on this very morning, when, from a little den enclosed by railings, issued in unusual glory and fashion the irresistible Manuel Melhado! The coloured purchasers stood and stared in utter abasement before the brilliant apparition; the white ones composed their features, and watched from beneath their eyelids if haply on them might fall one gracious glance from the glass of fashion and the mould of form; while the gentlemen vendors struggled hard to exhibit a demeanour which should do proper honour to their great principal without sullying their dignity in the eyes of inferior beholders. The semi-Hebrew youth alone, who was of a rash and presumptuous disposition, lifted up his eyes to those of Manuel Melhado, and said, in pretty firm accents, that the sea-breeze wasn't come, and it would be infernally hot outside; and we have the pleasure of recording that this act of gallantry was followed by no appalling consequences to Aaron Mendoza. Melhado, it is true, did not directly answer the remark of his servant, but he desired him to get out of the way and mind his business—not, however, curtly, but with a good many expletive and intensitive particles of speech. On the whole, it was apparent that this venture of the young Mendoza was considered a success, as having been answered by the head of the house; and Aaron's consideration in the establishment increased from that day forth.

Melhado, meanwhile, made his way to the wharf in Port-Royal Street, where he was to await and prepare for the arrival of the party from Crystal Mount. The hour of meeting approaches, and already at the highest end of the city the fair fresh face of Violet Arabin breaks like the rosy dawn on watchers of the night. How dark or sallow show all visages when she appears! No lady, however successful at other seasons, can abide comparison with this sweet girl: they withdraw from sight while they cannot but look and envy; and from behind the jalousies they fret at the approach of Superior Beauty. Miss Vermont, a *quasi* belle of a desponding turn, is not seen in public for a week after; while Harriet Hope, stimulated anew to master the secrets of fascination, returns once again to her oft-spurned cosmetics, and resolves to be admired or perish. How do men of all ages gaze and whisper and follow with their eyes the rolling carriage, occupations being suspended as she passes! Thus did

Kingston comport itself at the presence of Christy Arabin's fair daughter. "But," it may be asked of us by lips whose questions we love to hear, "what were the pretensions of this West Indian Violet? Was she short or slender—frank or shy? Where lay her particular attraction? Was it style or features —figure or complexion? Was she—was she—at all, you know, in *my* way?" By the zone of Venus, fair querists, we cannot tell. We did never tabulate her charms. We saw, and we bear record, that Violet Arabin was lovely, and that she received what she deserved—to wit, the homage of all hearts: this is the sum of our knowledge. One hint, however, we will and can give: when you are natural and gracious, when least you seek for admiration and triumph, when you are most feminine and most attractive, you are most like the Beauty of the Antilles!

They had hit the time exactly, and had not to wait. Canoes and wherries were rolling about and bumping against the jetty, showing that the breeze had come. Sometimes the aforesaid breeze breaks faith with the islands, and does not arrive till long after its appointed time, ruffling the patience of intending voyagers, and wearying many a poor delicate soul that is longing for its refreshing influence. Let him who has known the prostration of those climes recall the anxiety with which he placed every day his pale thin lips and nostrils against the jalousie-blades, and looked out to seaward for the *Doctor*—how he has watched every tint of the horizon, hoping to detect the *cat's paw* which is to harbinger the refreshing wind. After being again and again disappointed, he has seen at length the unmistakable sign. Old ocean rises now and shakes his mane. There is the line of foam, miles —who shall say how many miles?—away. But the health-giver travels fast; and there has been little more than time to secure papers and fasten doors ere he is sweeping through the house, making everybody aware of his presence. In the harbour, too, he creates a considerable revolution. The clear emerald surface which looked, during the calm, not a yard above the bottom, where could be seen the treasures of the deep as plainly as if it were a large aquarium, is corrugated into infinite little waves and breakers, and the distorted rays show rocks and star-fish and polypi and sea-weed monstrously transformed. The true depth also is now more apparent. The little white horses dance over the expanse, and there is motion everywhere. He who has never seen a Jamaica canoe can have but little notion of how a small shell can walk the waters. She does not sail, but fly with you, light and airy as a bird; and they to whom rapid motion is a joy, may in her luxuriate as they could do in no other craft. True it is that there is a risk of her being rotten, and of your foot or the boathook going through her; true, that her mast, tackle, blocks, and sails are equally treacherous with her hull; true, that, besides all this, her mere lightness renders her liable to capsize at a sudden puff; and then the harbour is full of sharks! These considerations, however, weigh but little with wilful youth and health in the pursuit of pleasure. Up gets the breeze and away go the canoes, studding the water like nautili, and darting like a glance of the mind. We do well remember our first approach to the island when running down in the deep water outside the Palisades, over whose low sandy breadth from the deck of our ship we could see the inner harbour. From out at sea shot suddenly athwart our gaze a canoe—the first we had seen—with half-a-dozen negroes on board. Before we could collect our ideas, and settle what this fleet object might be, they had run her on shore on the Palisades and leaped to the land. There in another moment they lifted the light shallop on their shoulders, and carried her rapidly across the isthmus, from whose other shore they launched her again and shot into distance, the whole sight passing quicker than we can relate it.

Again, the sea-breeze is in Kingston harbour a "sojer's wind," *i. e.*, you can sail both up and down with it. Jack, we fear, in bestowing the epithet, wished to evince profound scorn for the character of the land forces as equivocal and shifty, compared with his own, which prompts him to go right in, and never contemplate coming out again, except with an enemy's ship in tow. Whether this etymology is just or not, certain we are that sailors as well as soldiers acknowledge here the blessing of the oblique wind which enables them to pass with the least exertion, the greatest rapidity, and the coolest temperature, from point to point of the harbour. The newest comer is aware that his chance of navigating the little bay is dependent on the coming of the sea-breeze ; but woe to the yahoo or Johnny Raw who, confiding in his prudence and the well-conned maxims of his friends, ventures among the sooty amphibii whose yells and jargon vex eternally that sunny strand! There is a most exciting competition for the possession of the yahoo, and a free pulling hither and thither of his person, for as yet he knows not that the flourish of a switch will scare the rascals as the crack of a hunting-whip a pack of dogs. Even when, after these tribulations, he is fairly seated in a canoe, they cease not to warn him of the demerits of the one he has selected, and the surpassing qualities each of his own barky. On this subject no two voices agree, but when he alludes to the sea-breeze, there is a sudden and miraculous unanimity. "Him come, massa; him blow quite 'trong outside; him bin dere dis hour," are vociferated from all sides. The yahoo is satisfied, surrenders himself to his boatman, and suffers himself to be paddled a little way into the harbour, beyond the possibility of his leaping on shore. Then he perceives the surface of the sea to be like glass—not a breath stirring; and a vertical sun is scorching him up as he floats motionless. He upbraids the deceitful boatman, and demands where is the sea-breeze, of whose propinquity he has been assured. In reply he is told, "Me no God, massa; me can't make de breeze blow." We earnestly hope that every yahoo feels as properly as we ourselves did under these trying circumstances—that is, that he forgives and yearns to embrace the man and brother who sits baking face to face, to whom the rays are not disagreeable, and who intends to charge by the hour.

The bark prepared by Melhado to carry fair Violet and her fortunes was of the class called "wherries" —very different boats from those which bear that name on the hoary Thames. The Jamaica wherry is properly a commodious barge, and this one had been fitted with cushions and awnings. They sail well, though, of course, not with the lightning speed of the canoe. After a greeting on the wharf, the embarkation was rapidly effected. Leander and Rosy posted themselves forward with the baggage and commissariat. The latter was considered indispensable by Christy, though the voyage would not last two hours: it included a carefully packed ice-pail, that the senator might not lack a cool drink. Violet, her sire, and lover were reclined beneath the awning; Christy taking a whole side to himself, that he might lie at length and blow his smoke away to leeward. Melhado seats himself by Violet's side—takes carelessly, and as of right, a place for which any other youth in the island would have fought, or knelt, or dared adventure perilous! Her presence alone would have subdued a generous nature, and a belief that she regarded him with favour should have made a man worship her! Such are the freaks of Hymen. Loveliness and lovingness, and all the gentle excellencies of woman withered by a barbarian who knows not what nor why he blights! Well, Melhado intends to be agreeable, but it is necessary to show that he feels elegantly tranquil, and politic perhaps, now that matrimony is so near, to let it be guessed that he will hold his own. The savage! The atmosphere, even at a short distance from land, is by comparison fresh enough to yield a most grateful sensation. Violet's tresses are moved about, and she slightly resigns herself to the pleasant languor, her eyes soft and downcast, and her accents low. "By George, she is a dainty one, and no mistake!" thought the young Melhado; "how she'll distract the men with admiration and the women with envy! 'twill be devilish pleasant to have her spoken of and addressed as Mrs Melhado!" Then, in the magnitude of his devotion, Manuel thought how he would adorn this beauty to make it shine its brightest; how he would ransack earth to deck her person; and how he would entertain sumptuously the world of fashion, that they might view his prize and envy him, the possessor. But, faithful to his breeding, his mind began, even now, amid the enthusiasm of admiration and the dreams of happiness, unconsciously, as it were, to consider the cost. "It's of no use desiring things that you've no chance of getting; therefore, Manuel, before you allow yourself to think about 'em, consider whether you're likely to be able to buy 'em, or to procure 'em in any other manner!" was a maxim of old Mrs Melhado, which her son had so well drunk in that he couldn't break it if he would. His dreams were always associated with estimates. The amazing splendour which he had now called up would be realised, he perceived, only at a heavy outlay; and yet the generous fellow did not determine to forego it. He only thought how much it would assist such meditations if he knew actually the utmost that, in the present or the future, he might expect to get from old Christy. Totally unconscious of the speculation he was exciting, that old gentleman had fallen asleep, though he smoked still. People breathe, don't they, in their sleep! and to Christy smoking was rather more necessary than breathing. Christy slept, considerate old fellow! Now, then, what a glorious opportunity to whisper impassioned nothings, and perhaps, under the guise of nothings, manage two or three important matters!

"Only that I want to talk to you, Violet, I could wish you to go to sleep, you look so handsome in that sleepy humour," said Manuel.

"I am not inclined to sleep," Violet answered; "but this pleasant languor makes one pensive ; don't you feel it?" and she sighed gently.

"Makes one sigh too, don't it?" said Manuel. "I wonder now what these pretty sad thoughts are about, eh?"

"There is not the least mystery about them!" she replied. "I was thinking of my mother at home, now alone, and of what a different home it must be to her, poor dear, when—when——"

"Yes, I know!" said Manuel, archly ; "well, I daresay it will ; but shall I tell you, now, what I was thinking of? I was thinking of all the delightful things we shall have by-and-by, and the style we'll do 'em in. I should like you, you know, to be the most brilliant person in the island—to have your house, and dress, and equipage, and entertainments on a scale of unprecedented magnificence: won't it be glorious!"

"I thank you much," answered Violet, "for proposing to gratify me at such trouble and cost; but I assure you that it is a glory which I should hardly appreciate, and for which, certainly, I do not think myself suited."

"By Jove, I know better, though," said Melhado, briskly; "you've more of the right stuff in you than you know of. You'll come out as a splendid woman of fashion. I'm sure of it."

"I cannot agree with you," Violet replied. "I do not at all mean that I wish to lead a life of seclusion or inertion; but that may be avoided by many methods preferable to becoming the slave of fashion."

"Well," said Manuel, "I don't know anything that you could do better when you've got the station and the means. Poor devils mustn't try it, of course; but for you, who may eclipse the whole of them, what can be more attractive?"

"I should think that some noble or useful motive would animate more enduringly than a passion for display. I can understand," said Violet, fixing her gaze upon the waters, and thinking, we fear, not exclusively of Melhado—"I can understand a woman's energies being aroused by duty and affection: I can understand her devoting herself to the solace and support of a generous mind, enduring privation, partaking danger, supporting pain, relinquishing accustomed delights, or roaming the world; but these are not fashionable ideas."

"All right," Melhado said. "It always takes a romantic turn at first, and a pity it shouldn't. A little enthusiasm makes people look so captivating sometimes. But then it always ends in silks and diamonds and that sort of thing. You'll come all right at last, and, I say, won't we be a stunner when we do break out! What lace and satins we'll have, what parties we'll give, what horses we'll drive, and how we'll astonish the world, our little self amazing 'em more than all the rest! *By* Jove!"

Manuel spoke with much enthusiasm, and poor Violet, believing that it proceeded from devotion to her, upbraided herself with the ungrateful return which alone she could make for such generosity. If Manuel could not win her love, did he not deserve something better than deceit? She had done him injustice.

Such compunctious reflections were not long allowed to distress her, for the gallant Manuel, eager to satisfy his curiosity, persisted in conversing.

"The worst of doing things in this style," said he, "is, that it takes such a confounded lot of money;

and though we shall be pretty well off, I fancy, yet a trifle won't suffice for all that I meditate."

"You have stated an excellent reason for leaving it undone, then," said Violet, smiling.

"Well, that depends," pursued Manuel; "when there are expectations, you see, people needn't be too chary of their present means. Everything will come our way, I suppose, eh? Do you happen to know how it's settled?"

"Settled! what?" said Violet; "I don't understand."

Melhado nodded at Christy's sleeping figure with a meaning look. "Must come to an end some time," he said; "not in any hurry—hope it'll be a long time first; but you ought to see that it's all left without reserve: no tying up. And you should be a pretty good judge of the figure, too, eh?"

His meaning struck upon the affectionate girl's heart like the touch of winter: it actually froze her blood. She could not reply, but sat paralysed with horror and disgust. Manuel, however, thinking that some silly hesitation kept her silent, prepared his most potent blandishments to follow up the inquiry. Heaven knows to what indignant utterance he might have driven poor Violet, had not the subject of his solicitude suddenly stretched and turned himself, declaring that it was cursedly hot, and he must have a drink. While Leander was ministering to the old gentleman's wants, Violet subdued her feelings, but quite acquitted herself of injustice towards Manuel.

They were about midway between Kingston and Port Henderson. The wherry shot along deliciously, and Christy Arabin, having refreshed his inner man with his favourite drink of brandy and iced water, thought he had slept enough. The problem was how to pass the rest of the voyage. He would continue to smoke, of course, but he didn't want to meditate, and all the shores of the harbour were as familiar to him as the pattern on his pocket-handkerchiefs, of which he had a liberal stock all alike. He took credit for much good taste and delicacy of feeling in not requiring Violet and Manuel to amuse him, and so at last he said he would go forward and have a talk with the Commodore—one of the black boatmen, and a personage of whom we shall presently have more to say.

Melhado saw at length that he had given offence. He did not exactly know how, but somehow he had clearly gone wrong. This must be rectified immediately. He must change the conversation forthwith, and strive doubly to be agreeable. Violet's resentment subsided into contempt. She perceived, after a short reflection, that the man's intention had been harmless, and that his nature only was to blame.

Her manner was no longer what it had been before, yet it evinced a quiet tolerance which persuaded Manuel that he would soon fix the loose screw, wherever it was, and make all go smooth again. He became assiduously attentive, pressed refreshment upon Violet, and was certain that she was faint and ill from the want of it. She took a little wine to put an end to his importunity—construing which act into a sign of returning favour, the magnanimous youth once more gave a loose to his fascinating conversation.

"I ain't a bad-tempered fellow, you see," said Manuel. "Can stand caprices capitally: they never put me out: shall be just the same hereafter, too, you'll see, however whimsical *you* may be. By George! I rather like to see you pettish; it becomes you—does, 'pon my soul. No, we shall never disagree about that, nor about any little feminine tricks: only, you know, you must never try to make me jealous—couldn't stand that on any account. Tease me in other ways as much as you like—in reason, that is —only in return I must have all those bright smiles to myself—must, by Jove, you little tormentor."

It was such a relief to Violet to find how thoroughly despicable this man was, that she felt disposed to be merry, and she laughed at this sally, to the great delight of Melhado.

"I am afraid you are a tyrant," said she.

"Not at all, not at all. I'm sure I'm quite right, only ask your mother. 'Twould never do, you know, to have a parcel of dancing and singing men about the house, paying you attentions after you are married."

"I don't think there is the least danger of that," said Violet, still smiling and amused.

"Oh, by Jove, I don't know," her lover replied; "there are many of these military fellows whom it won't do to break with altogether, and who are yet forward presuming coxcombs that require to be kept in order."

"Why," said Violet, "I thought the military officers were your chief and approved associates!"

"So they are. I don't mean by any means to exclude them; they're too much in the fashion for that. I only want to keep 'em from getting saucy, as I know they will when they're allowed. There are one or two in particular that I should caution you against."

"Indeed!" Violet said; "you must tell me their names."

"Well, in particular," replied Manuel, "there's that fellow Brune; one of the most conceited, offensive pretenders among them."

"You don't think well of Mr Brune, then?"

"No; certainly not. He goes everywhere, and

therefore people are obliged to know him till his character is better understood. But I shall have my eye particularly on that fellow, and I trust that you will always keep him on respectful terms. I shouldn't at all like to have to kick him out of the house."

"No; I am sure you would not," Violet said.

There was something real or fancied in the last quiet observation which disconcerted Manuel, and brought the colour into his cheeks.

"No, certainly not," he said; "and I'm sure, when you know my opinion of him, there'll be no occasion for it. 'Tis just as well we mentioned the matter. You remember he used to be a good deal about Crystal Mount, until he saw that his attentions were not relished, and that some of his doings began to be smoked. No doubt he would be delighted to make a lounge of our house, if he were allowed, for he's a sly, sneaking puppy."

Violet's eye flashed, and her lip quivered. It was with difficulty that she could control her feelings; but she thought again of Manuel's utter baseness, and summoned scorn to her aid.

"I have seen him *do* things," she said, "which would entitle any man to be spoken of in different terms from those you have used. 'Twould have been more like the character you describe, if, instead of acting, he had boasted of what he intended to do, and boasted to *women.*"

This was getting decidedly disagreeable, Manuel thought. 'Twas very hard too, for he had intended to be unusually complaisant, and had expected a most delightful sentimental voyage. Well, he had done his best, and couldn't help it if he failed. Women are so full of humours. "Perhaps, too," mused the profound Manuel, "she thinks it necessary to display her power. Well, let her; my turn will come, I promise her!" And, thinking thus, he saw without regret the shore not far ahead, and old Christy returning aft, that the boatmen might be free to attend to the landing. Christy had been hearing some nautical reminiscences from the Commodore, who claimed to have once sailed in the British fleet, and under Britain's greatest admiral. When Christy went forward, the Commodore, who had been holding an animated conversation with Leander, turned to him and said—

" I jis' tellin' dis gentleman I glad to find him bin in England. Dat is de way to make a man sensible, trabel about; 'top at home, you no sabby nutting! sar."

"Very true," said Christy; "experience like yours is not to be picked up without going a long way to look for it."

"Yes, sar," replied the Commodore, "me hab plenty of experience, and me is able to 'pin a yarn or two widout telling lie."

"Of course you can," said Christy. "Now then, Commodore, if you want a glass of rum, let's have one of your best."

"'Top, massa, make me see," said the Commodore. "You ebber hear 'bout de French frigate we chase off Teneriffe?"

"Yes, I know all that," said Christy: "the devil came and took her in tow, and got her off just as you were within range: that won't do."

"Hei! well, me will tell you ob de fight me hab wid de shark to leeward ob de great Cayman?"

"Heard that fifty times," said Christy, "and how you cut off the French admiral's pigtail, and your marriage to your twenty-fourth wife at Havannah, and the loss of the ship with all your prize-money aboard in a hurricane, which prevented your owning half the island: none of those will do."

"Chaw! massa know ebberyting," fretted the Commodore, much perplexed: "what can me tell him?"

"Let's have some fighting," said Christy; "a good engagement now, and the glass of rum shall be stiff."

"Dat de berry ting," replied the Commodore, slapping his trousers; "me will tell you ob a great engagement between Nelson and Boney. You see, we bin cruisin' some time 'pon de coast of 'Pain; nebber go into harbour, becausin, you see, Nelson hab a most lubly nyoung woman aboord, dem call Lady sunting or 'nother, me can't rightly tell de name. Well, after we keep de blue sea till de water stink faber jackfruit, and de bisket walk about de table, we begin to tink, 'Dis here no fun. Why de debil him no take we into port to get some fresh probishun, and hab a dance wid de gals?' De people beginnin' to get dam obstropolous, I can tell you, and it impossible to say what de dooce might hab come ob it, only one forenoon dem report a French frigate in sight. One of our frigates clear for action directly, and get under way to go out and meet her, when it seem she coming up quite friendly wid a flag ob truce. De lads forget all about de prog and de gals, and begin to wonder what make de Frenchman come dis side. Berry soon we hear what in de wind. Nelson pacing de quarterdeck, 'tamping him great foot, and raising him great voice, and cussin' faber madman. My, how dat man swear! Lad Gad, what you tink! de impedince ob dat Boney! Him send for tell Nelson him mus' hab de nyoung woman and carry him to France, and Nelson better gib him up quietly, and no gib Boney de trouble for come and fatch him away. Ob course Nelson send him back a dam 'pirited answer, and tell him he quite ready whenever Boney liked to come, and he gib him coco for yam. But de passion dat man in, me nebber see sich a ting! him flog half de ship's company, and crack de gunner's cocoa-nut* wid a rammer-head. Nobody didn't dare to go near him, and when de signal hofficer go up to do him dooty, and report de French fleet in sight, Nelson fly at him faber wild-cat, and he say, says he (terrible 'trong voice Nelson had), "You infernal cussed

. . . . . .

. . . . . .

. . . . . .

. (*desunt asperrima verba*)

. . . . . .

. . . . . .

. . . . . .

what de debil make you come 'peak to me dis-a-way? Eh, sar.' De leeftenant try again for do him dooty, and report de hennemy's sail, when Nelson square up to him wid both hands, and swear to Garamighty he knock him into next week if him no pull foot and be off. 'Knock away, admiral,' says de brabe nyoung hofficer, 'but I tell you de French fleet comin' for all dat?' 'Hei, what?' Nelson say; 'de debil! dat quite anoder ting. Ax for you pardon, sar; glad to

* Skull.

see you to dinner and grog after we sink dese damnable French 'coundrels.' Den he pass de word for get all ready, and by de time Boney come, we hab someting warm waiting for him. You see for me dooty keep me down below, and me no see what go on when dem fust go into axion, only me hear de row and see de smoke. After lilly bit ebbery ting quiet, all de noise 'top, we can't tink how dem make sich dam short work ob it. So me run up to see, and anoder gentleman ob color, who likewise come up to look about him, infarm me dat Nelson bin and boarded Boney ship, an' all about it. When de boarders 'cramble on deck, he tell me Nelson sing out, 'Where dat lubber Boney, eh? Make me see him; me 'mash him bl—y brains out. Hah, boy, you dere, eh? Come on.' 'How de debil you know me?' Boney say; 'you ebber see me before, eh?' 'Know you, sar, by de cut ob your infernal jib,' says Nelson. 'No more nonsense; bear a hand, now. Make me 'mash you.' 'Two can play dat game,' Boney say; 'now den, come on, boy.' When dem see Nelson and Boney goin' fight, ebberybody 'top firing and hollering, and come to deir ship's side to see de battle same as me is doin' myself. In two minutes Nelson and Boney draw off 'pon de quarter-deck, and down heads. Ebberybody hold him breat', when dey run at one anoder. My fader! cr-r-r-r-ack.

What a whop!* Berry well, dem shake deirself and draw off again. Hei! 'noder crack, terrible hard! Boney 'tagger lilly bit dis time, but him no capsized yet. Him 'tand anoder knock. But, my king! it a pounder faber fifty-pound shot. Nelson's yeyes flash fire, and he grind him teet' horrid. Den he rush 'pon Boney, and fell him as de cook's mate knack down a bullock. Boney, nearly killed and no able for get up, rub him head and say, he fight again anoder day; dat he bin come out widout him breekfiss dat morning, and sich kind ob pretence. But Nelson sing out sharp, 'Belay dat jaw; me will teach you to sarve out sarce to a better man dan yourself. Now, lads, seize up dat light-libbered lubber; put he in irons and gag him, den chuck him in a rum cask and carry him home to King George.' When dem see Boney walloped, de French fleet 'trike and de English

---

* For the benefit of those readers who have not studied the natural history of the Commodore's countrymen, we beg permission to explain that a negro duel, when it comes to blows, is conducted very much like a contest between two rams, except that the excitement and clamour of the bystanders belong more properly to ghouls and satyrs than to sheep. The combatants lower their heads and run at each other, meeting with a great shock. The heads are uncommonly hard, and sometimes a succession of encounters is required before one of the heroes drops or declines a further trial. In most cases the tongue is the weapon employed, and there is a prodigal expenditure of words and elevating sentiments.

cheer. King George send Boney to pick oakum in Santeleny, and he make Nelson a prince ob de blood. What you tink ob dat, sar?"

"Very good indeed," said Christy, "and worth a dollar; here it is. I thought, though, that you were on quite familiar terms with Nelson; haven't I heard you say so?"

"Me couldn't say dat, massa, becausin it was not de fack, and massa know me always 'peak de trut'. Me hab berry little personal 'quaintance wid Nelson—berry little. De last time me see him was at de Gun at Deal wid a 'plendid nyoung lady. Dem jist bin dancin' when me come in, and Nelson's pipe gone out while him dance. 'Hillo, messmate,' sing out Nelson, 'shibber my timbers, gib us a light and be d—— to you.' So ob course I hand him a light, and him say, 'What will you drink, old ship—glass o' rum?' 'No, admiral,' me say, 'rum is a common liquor; any low nigger can drink rum: me prefers brandy.' 'Two glasses ob de bes' brandy,' sing out Nelson. 'Your healt', sar,' he say. 'Your good healt', admiral,' me say, and so we pull foot and part. 'Who is de coloured gentleman I take brandy wid?' I hear Nelson say jes' after. Dat de last time I see him, but I b'lieve him is generally lounging about the Point in de summer mont'; but in winter him shut up, becausin it cold dere, and you see him gettin' dam elderly;

besides dat, him drink hard and bin a debilish sly feller."

After these interesting anecdotes, so characteristic of our renowned sailor, the Commodore's conversation became less worthy of repetition, and in a short time he was obliged to discontinue it altogether as they neared the land, and to request Christy to go aft, that the lightened bows might slide well on to the beach, and allow of a pleasant landing.

A few minutes saw Violet and Christy seated in their carriage, and starting for Spanish Town; while Manuel, by no means the happier for his long draught of love, prepared to return home in the wherry.

We watch our Violet along the dusty road, catch the flutter of her veil, and wave a sad adieu as the carriage turns out of sight; then away again to ruder scenes.

Pause we one moment, though, to make a startling revelation. We hear that on this day a note passed from Crystal Mount to Stony Hill; that Arthur Brune was again at the former place, and closeted with Mrs Arabin; that Mr Chitty was highly scandalised and much disturbed. The report is almost incredible, and yet subsequent events did not contradict it.

CHAPTER X.

One day, a short time after noon, a tandem was scientifically pulled up at the door of the same pavilion in which Lieuteuant Lorton lived. On the box sat Tom Gervaise in great state, with his luscious hat and double-thonged whip; beside him was Arthur Brune.

"Mr Knox at home, bo?" inquired Brune, descending.

"Yes, massa; he upstairs keeping de passover," replied a spare pensive young negro who stood on the steps.

"The devil!" exclaimed both gentlemen, who appeared to entertain a particular objection to that festival.

Keeping the passover was, however, only a phrase at that time in vogue in Jamaica, to denote a very simple domestic precaution. It meant spreading out one's kit or stock of clothes for the purpose of airing them; an operation which requires to be frequently performed in hot climates. Its etymology was this: Of yore the phrase had been, *Holding a Rag Fair*, or *a Monmouth Street*, the displays being much like those of the children of Israel. One day, however, it flashed across the brain of an officer, who was a profound Orientalist, that there was some historical connection between the passover and old clothes. Whereupon, without waiting to refer to his Josephus or Strabo, he applied the name at hap-hazard and on the spot; for, as Sir John says, a quick wit will make use of anything. The *jeu d'esprit* had a tremendous success, and was immediately adopted into the vocabulary of men of spirit, the discarded epithet of Monmouth Street descending to slow quartermasters and commissaries, or to subalterns who came in rearward of the fashion, and digested wit like boas, taking six months to a *bon mot*.

Lieutenant Knox, then, was keeping the passover, and was discovered by our two gentlemen in his verandah reclining in a rocking-chair, a cigar in his mouth, a volume of 'Tom Jones' on his knee, and a tumbler of brandy-and-water beside him. Over and about him hung festoons of cord laden with apparel, and open doors and windows showed within his apartment a continuation of the garlands exposed to a thorough draught. Flannel and linen formed the bulk of the wardrobe, but there were cloth uniforms seldom used, and plain cloth clothes very musty, and with traces of moth; while in a corner—how fallen from the consideration which they enjoyed in England!—slunk some greatcoats and cloaks, conveying a bitter moral to those who persist in going where none has need of them. Some worsted stockings and mufflers, which had been overlooked at the last passover, appeared now in a lamentable state of decomposition, and did not outlive the present feast. Besides preventing the ravages of moth, it was necessary to remove all sorts of grubs and insects, which, with no evil intention, crawled among and stuck to the clothes; and to dissipate the souvenir which cockroaches leave behind them.

As old Tom came thumping along the verandah with his stick, "Hollo!" shouted he to the proprietor of this miscellany; "what the deuce are you keeping passover for? Why didn't you choose some other day?"

"By Jove, old Tom!" responded Knox, ducking and shouldering aside the pendant garments, as Roderick Random was wont to do among the sick hammocks, "how do, old boy? And Brune too! devilish glad to see you," as the latter gentleman followed in Tom's wake, bearing the tandem whip as a gillie carries the pipes when the piper is not performing.

"The devil take your passover!" repeated Tom Gervaise.

"Amen," answered Knox, reverentially; "we'll put it off. Here, Gonsalvo, down with this rag-shop, and let's have some second breakfast."

"Massa goin' to 'top de passover?" asked Gonsalvo, who had had some trouble in arranging the hangings.

"Yes, and be hanged to you! we'll have it next week," decreed Knox, in utter defiance of Gregorian Calendar and Council of Nice. "Shut shop, do you hear? Skip, jump, and make a clearance in the crushing of a mosquito."

Gonsalvo de Cordova (for Knox's domestic bore the name of the great captain), after taking order for the supply of some food, proceeded to remove the display of woollens, muttering as he did so—

"Now, now, now, now, now, now, now! Did anybody ebber hear of sich a ting! Tree mortal hours me bin preparing dis dam passover dis mornin'; massa mus a mad. It really too wort'less. Wish dis Cap'n Gerbis did dead. Hei!"

"Well, Knox, how do you get on, old fellow?" inquired Brune. "How's old Clutterbuck? We must take care to congratulate him before we go back."

"We'll have him in to second breakfast," said Knox, "and probably another well-disposed person or two. He's going to give a devil of a dinner. You are coming down, of course?"

"Of course not," said Tom Gervaise; "what the devil do you take me for, that you expect me to join your debauchery? I shall spend that evening in meditation, with Blair's Sermons, or the 'Pilgrim's Progress.'"

"If you get drunk early, you will probably enjoy some very heavenly imaginings during the entertainment," replied Knox. "Now then, boys, what's brought you down here—anything particular?"

"That I will tell you more of before we part," said Brune. "I want you to lend me a hand in a small adventure."

"You may always command Edward Knox, you know, Arthur."

"Sure of that, old fellow; more anon. Here come more company."

Captain Clutterbuck, who has kindly lent his name to this narrative, now entered, and received the hearty felicitations of Brune and old Tom. Poor old Clut was overjoyed, and could hardly believe in his accession of rank. He nailed them both for his dinner, and declared he would have every officer in the island—the General included, if he could get him —and drown the whole in champagne.

"I'll tell you one man you won't get," said Knox, "and that's Lorton. Got a devilish sharp fever."

"Don't know anybody whose absence I should have less regretted," said Tom. "Now then, is this second breakfast coming, or not?"

"Here in a minute, my old file," said Knox. "Suppose you season your impatience by mixing some porter-cup?"

"Ah!" said Tom, "when I can be doing anything to benefit my fellow-creatures, I'm never impatient. Hand us the jorum."

Clutterbuck's excitement had not yet subsided, and it made him awfully hot. This was unfortunate, as, being a gentlemanly commonplace man, he shunned anything remarkable. If he had a coxcombry, however, 'twas an affectation of appearing cool. His wristbands were turned up, and his collar turned down, to a remarkable extent. The ribbon round his neck was scarcely more than a thread. His face was shaven almost bare, and his hair cut very close. All his clothes were well made, and on every other occasion of his life he looked cool and placid.

One or two idle men lounged in, and the second breakfast took place. This meal, which has different names in different countries, is in England denominated luncheon. The second breakfast, though, is rather heavier and wetter than the lunch, showing either that physiologists are mistaken in their dietetic theories for warm climates, or that creoles are very imprudent.

"Nobody 'll dispute my right to the first pull at the porter-cup, I suppose, as I mixed it," said Tom Gervaise, drawing the cuff of his jacket across his lips, and grasping the jorum's stem with his other hand.

"Oh, no!" said a smart ensign; "that would be a useless dispute; we only hope you'll let us have a little after you've done."

Gervaise did not allow the remark to interrupt his draught, which was on this occasion profound; but after he had drunk and passed the glass, with a river running down its inside, to his neighbour, his trusty stick was heard to make a *spiritual* noise against the ensign's shin-bone.

"Hillo, by Jove, what's that?" exclaimed the youth.

"That your leg?" said Tom; "how badly it rings!"

"Does it? I don't like that fun, though, I can tell you."

"They come out from England so devilish thin-skinned!" said Gervaise, addressing Brune. "Just look at his hands, Arthur, a mass of mosquito-bites! his neck on fire with prickly heat, and his leg, you see, can't stand a pat; must be carious."

"I don't despair of him, though," said Arthur. "If he listens to the teachers who are ready to form him, he may rival some friends of mine, and sport a face with bubuckles and whelks and knobs and flames of fire, like Bardolph."

"I pity you for having such tender shins, though," Gervaise said. "When I used to suffer from that infirmity, the prescription I followed was, extreme politeness to men who carried thick sticks."

"No use to offer you pine-apple, Tom?" said Knox, half-inquiringly, while he wrenched the tuft off a beautiful Ripley that a duke would have been proud to produce in England.

"No, I never eat Jamaica turnip," was Gervaise's reply; and the same indifference seemed to be felt by the whole party. The delicious fruit became afterwards the perquisite of Gonsalvo de Cordova, to whose morbid mind, however, it gave small satisfaction, for he said, as he slobbered it gloomily, and the juice ran out at both sides of his mouth, "S'pose now me mus' eat dis pine; it sure to make me bad. Dat is de way wid ebberyting in dis world; if you hab de pleasure, you hab de pain too. De lubliest mornin' end in 'torm and tunder, and de number 'leven mango give de 'tummick-ache. Heigh-ho!"

A heavy tread was now heard outside, and a voice sent before the new-comer pronounced in a fine Irish brogue, "God save all here." Nearly every man in the party exclaimed, "Pat Shane, by Jove!" as a jolly bronzed figure, the owner of the voice, strode into the room and commenced shaking hands. "How do, Knox? How do, Arthur, me boy?" and so on. When he arrived within reach of Tom Gervaise's stick he received a thrust under the fifth rib, accompanied by the salutation, " D—— your eyes," to which attentions he did not reply till he had grappled with the two men who intervened. Then he stood behind Gervaise, and, getting into either hand the nether lock of Tom's great whiskers, playfully seesawed his head, saying at the same time, "Tom, y' incorr'g'ble ould sinner, why don't ye die?" Refinement combines the closest familiarity with perfect decorum.

"Now then, boys, where d'ye think I've come from? Walked up in the hate of the sun from Rock Fort. If that doesn't desarve a drink, let no man do well in the hope of reward henceforth. Tom, rache the jor'm, me son. No dry fodder, Knox; couldn't ate if the loife depinded on it. Deloighted that I hit the moment for brandy-and-water and cigars. Another tumbler, Julius Sasar, or whatever name belongs to that beatific countenance ye've got."

Brune and Knox, at the head of the table, were engaged in a dialogue which appeared to become more and more interesting. At first they occasionally interrupted their colloquy, and joined in the general conversation; but they became by degrees more absorbed in their subject, and would scarcely attend, when appealed to, to corroborate a story of old Tom, who was affirming that he had one night heard two parrots on a tree conversing like human beings.

"Didn't I hear them, Arthur, as I was riding home from a dinner at old Taylor's?" asked Tom.

"I've often heard you say so," replied Arthur; "so I suppose it must be true."

"It must be," said Pat Shane. "Of course, Tom, ye were as sober as a church at the toime!"

"As sober as a small cathedral," answered Tom, modestly declining comparison with St Paul's or York Minster.

"D'ye mind what they said, Tom?" inquired Pat Shane.

"One of them remarked [here Tom tried his tongue at the brogue], 'Isn't Pat Shane a mortial ould riprobate?' to which the other replied, 'True for you, Poll; begorra, ye're roight this time.'"

"I persave," remarked Pat, "that they were imps incited by the divil to slander virtuous men. That being their mission, of coorse they didn't mention yerself, Tom."

Brune and Knox were now so earnestly engaged

that they withdrew into Knox's bedroom to avoid further interruptions. The eyes of most of the company followed them to the door, then there was a slight pause and an exchange of meaning glances, after which Clutterbuck observed—

"Our friend Arthur is decidedly down in the mouth; he has hardly spoken during second breakfast, and he ate next to nothing."

"Ye've not tould the worst yet," Pat Shane said: "he was very shy of his liquor too, and a man can't neglect that with impunity anywhere, more especially in this wearing climate."

Clutterbuck, who was a very moderate man in most things, ventured to remark that he thought fellows in general would do better if they had a little more of the shyness of which Pat complained; to which Pat replied—

"Then how the divil is it that, when a man gets shaky and queer, and stupid people begin nodding their heads and saying he's gone it too hard—how is it, I say, that the doctors, who ought to know best, always order wine, and, if the case is bad, brandy? Tell me that. If liquor's the *disase*, how can it be the rimidy? In my last rigimint, where they drank like fishes, we'd an assistant-surgeon from the county Kerry, a very larned man, and a beautiful *ecarté* player; and when he'd see a man lying on his bed, wake and pale and narvus, he'd say, 'Cheer up, me man, we'll give ye something to support the system and corrict this deprission.' Then maybe the patient 'ud say, 'Oh, doctor dear, but it's upsot entirely that I am—so *wake* and *spacheless!*' And the doctor 'ud ask him, 'D'ye see tadpouls?' And if he said he didn't, he'd get a drink of brandy, and soon be better. But he was sure to be asked, 'D'ye see tadpouls?' and if he said he did, they'd send for the priest to make his sowl, but he'd get the brandy all the same. Now, would a dying man get brandy if it wasn't good for his health? And could it be good for his health if it was the cause of his *decease*, I'd like to know?"

And Pat, in triumph, paused for a reply. No man ventured to question such an overwhelming argument, and Tom Gervaise's nod of approval ought to have quite rewarded Pat for his effort in exhibiting it.

"Well," continued Clutterbuck, "without intending to prescribe the quantity that any man should take, I should like to see Brune a little heartier. All the fun and the energy have left him. He never thanked me for the seal I sent him—not, I am sure, from indifference to the gift, but from distraction and blue-devils."

"I was wanst crossed in love," said Pat Shane, "but it didn't make me stroike off a tumbler; if anything, the contrary."

"What! has Brune had a disappointment?" screamed out one of the youngsters. There was a sudden hush. Arthur had managed to make himself respected among them; and though he was beyond earshot, his name and affairs claimed the low cautious tone in which men speak of those whom they look up to. The voices and manner of some of the party, and the stick of Gervaise, admonished the last speaker to be prudent.

"I wonder now," said Pat, thinking aloud—"I wonder whether, if that hucksterin' robber Melhado was to lave the field, Arthur's success would be certain."

"That's a useless speculation," Gervaise said. "Melhado's young and strong and saucy, and not likely to get out of the way."

"He might be politely requested to stip aside," responded Shane, "and he'd not stop the road again if he got hit."

"I daresay Brune'll pull his nose for him some day," pursued Tom, mysteriously; "you may all be sure that, if he doesn't do it now, he knows 'tisn't the right time."

"I know a man," replied Pat, "that'll think it the right time whenever he can get a colourable quarr'l with the dirty daler."

"Why, Pat, one would think you were his rival," said Tom.

" "I'm no man's rival, the heavens be praised, but a Christian gintleman, at pace with all mankind, and the mortal inimy of this presuming pup," answered Pat. "Ye don't know how well he desarves my distinguished detestation, but I'll tell ye.

"Ye see, he's been scraping up a wonderful acquaintance wid that disagreeable fellow Lorton, who's got a bitter tongue; but thin he's a gintleman, and knows when and where to give a taste of it. Be me sowl, but it's made me laugh sometimes when I heard him scarifying some poor unready divil, who could feel the points sticking in him, but didn't know how to parry them—ha, ha! Well, then, this gineral merchant—this Mister Melhado—thinks he must imitate Lorton's bitin' impident humour, though he hasn't got Lorton's taste and dissarnmint to show him when he's got hould of a fair subject. He tried it, I'm tould, once or twice, quite in Lorton's worst style, and was pretty successful in his hits: the men were taken aback, and didn't know what to make of it. But what does the thunderin' oaf do then, but think he's a proficient in the sat'r'cal line, and begin to make his thrusts indiscriminately, when, bedad! he falls foul of a tartar, if there's one in Christendom, so he does. If ye'll believe me, the low, dirty, money-getting vagabone thinks proper to take his fling at an Irish gintleman, of a family that's been cilibrated since the building of Babel. The Shanes comminced about that time. Yes, boys, may I niver see glory if the baste didn't try his indacent jistin' upon meself—be the powers he did! and this was the way of it. They'd the Gineral dining at the mess at Fort Augusta, and I was there, and so was this unmannerly robber. And, sis the Gineral, sis he, 'What's the news that's come by the packet, for I've been so busy wid despatches that I couldn't read it yet? What is there stirrin', Mr Melhado?' Now, ye see, Melhado and me niver took kindly to one another, and we'd been sparr'n' a little that evening, and so he says to the Gineral, takin' care that I should hear, 'There's no news at all of any importance, sir: two or three Irish blackguards hanged, that's all.' Presently I asked him, 'Might I inquire why you applied the term *Irish blackguards* to the persons that ye said was ixicuted?' 'I called them Irish,' sis he, 'because they wor born and hanged in Ireland; and I called them blackguards because they wor convicted of a diabolical outrage.' But I wasn't to be put off that way; and so I went on, 'You coupled the words together in an objectionable way, sir; I'd have you to know that I, as an Irishman, don't fancy hearing you spake that way of "*Irish blackguards.*"' 'You do quite right,' sis he, 'to stand up for your order. I wish I'd spoken more respectfully of these unfortunate men.' Well, I knew the whelp was troiflin' with me, but, for the loife of me, I couldn't tell how to meet him at the moment, his manner seemed so quiet and sincere. I caught a twinkle in the Gineral's eye, too, as he looked across the table at one of the staff. First I thought of sending a decanter at Melhado's head, but that wouldn't have done, of course; and so I said quietly to meself, 'Make much of your joke, me flower of the forest, for your laugh won't last long. Pat Shane owes ye one, and he'll pay to the last pinnyweight;' and so I will, divil take me if I don't."

"Serve him right too," said in concert two or three of the juniors, with whom Shane was an oracle in matters of honour.

"Gervaise," said Clutterbuck, who wished to change the subject, "I knew a brother of yours, called James, many years ago. We travelled in France together. Where is he now?"

Tom, when this question was asked, was transferring his cigar, which was very dull, from between his fingers to his mouth. As soon as his lips had a fast hold of it, he turned his forefinger vertically downwards, looking at the same time at Clutterbuck who understood from the pantomime that James Gervaise, his *quondam* acquaintance, had been gathered to his fathers, and that his disconsolate brother

Thomas was unable to answer articulately, either from emotion at the mention of the name, or from the risk of letting his light out. Then Clutterbuck, seeing that Tom was for the present silent, turned to Shane and asked him whether he was aware that Lorton, of whom he had lately spoken, was seriously ill.

"I heard," said Pat, "that he'd a slight fever."

"Quite correct," answered Clut; "the fever has never been violent, the doctors say, but it hangs upon him and wears him sadly. He's been in a low nervous condition for some time, and that keeps up the complaint. They would send him home if he could be patched up sufficiently to be put on board, but he's too weak at present."

"He'll come to no harm," said one of the party; "he's too disagreeable for that. It's only your good fellows that are taken off, like poor Simpson, and Hillyer, and Drysdale."

"I don't feel sure of that," Clutterbuck replied; "the doctors are puzzled, and shake their heads. Ordinary treatment appears to have failed, and when it comes to that, there's ground for apprehension."

"Then, by this and by that, Tom, ye must pray for him as ye did for the corporal at Hutton's Lodge. You're the boy for healin' when the faculty breaks down."

Seeing a look of great astonishment appear, after this observation, on the countenances of the younger guests who had not been in the island at the time of the occurrence to which Pat alluded, he offered to enlighten them concerning it; but as Pat was not remarkable for condensation, we will tell his story in our own words:—

Tom once lay at an outpost in charge of a small detachment, one of whom was, on a sudden, taken alarmingly ill. The nearest surgeon was sent for, and he declared that the patient could not live two hours. It was the spiritual physician who was now required in haste; but, alas! the whole dreary district boasted no such comforter. In this extremity, Tom, though all unused to religious exercise, determined that his dying brother should not lack such assistance as he, Tom, could afford. Accordingly he appeared, prayer-book in hand, beside the bed of suffering, and, opening the volume, read impressively that portion of our beautiful liturgy which supplicates spiritual aid "as for this kingdom in general, so especially for the High Court of Parliament." Whether the man's almost miraculous recovery was the direct result of Tom s ministry (as hath by some been affirmed), is a point which we presume not to decide. We leave it to be judged of by every man as his conscience shall prompt, believing that course to accord best with the interests of truth and the principles of religious toleration for which this realm hath long been famous.

Tom growled surlily when Pat narrated this anecdote, and shook his stick at those who laughed. He wouldn't, however, be decoyed into conversation, and the whole company seemed to feel the effect of their meal, and to sink into a sleepy, smoky condition. So, finding them such stupid company, we propose to follow Knox and Brune, and to find out what their important conference was about.

"Did I rightly understand your hint, Arthur?" asked Knox, when they had got clear of the din. " Have you really determined to attempt it on Clutterbuck's night?"

"I have determined!" said Arthur. "It must depend now on others whether I shall be able to carry out my scheme. Gervaise is to be charioteer from the mountain's foot. Mr Grant, who considers that matrimony is, at any price and under any circumstances, to be encouraged among the blacks and the military, has promised his assistance. I go this afternoon to get the important parchment from the Governor, and I have taken means for the success of the attempt on the high ground. We must now see how Melhado and Mr Arabin can be detained in camp till daylight after Clutterbuck's entertainment."

"Depend on me," said Knox, "to aid in any

scheme you may devise. My invention's not so good as yours. How do you propose to manage it?"

"I've thought," said Arthur, "of making them tipsy, or of crippling their chaise, or both."

"Both very uncertain devices," said Knox; "we must do something surer than that. What think you of a quarrel?"

"I have rejected that plan," said Brune, "because I would allow no man wantonly to endanger his own life or another's for my gratification."

"Leave it to me, then," said Knox; "I think I see how to manage it, and we'll risk no lives, but have some fun. We'll keep them here, if we have to lock them up. In the last resort I would advise some of our lads (who will by that time be full of champagne) of what's afoot, and I don't think they would allow sport to be spoiled."

"One word more, then, before I disturb Gervaise from his grog. They tell me, my dear fellow, that you've been playing deeply lately. For heaven's sake stop while it's not too late. Anything that my small means can do you may command. Think of your mother—do, Knox; and if they have any play after Clut's dinner, as they probably will, refrain."

"I assure you, Brune," said Knox, "that I am perfectly disgusted with play, and have formed a resolution, which I think will hold, to give it up entirely."

This resolution, though, was formed with a proviso and exception which Master Knox thought proper to keep in reserve. He was most sincere at that moment in his contrition, and wished with all his soul that he had never touched card or die; for he had been playing deeply, as Arthur had heard, and so great was his embarrassment that the sale of his commission alone could extricate him. About half its value was already lost, and he had determined to risk the other half in the attempt to retrieve his affairs. After Clutterbuck's dinner, he determined to have cards or hazard in his room, and it was in connection with this plan that he proposed to bring about the detention of Melhado and Christy. He was obliged to reserve himself for the great *coup* which he meditated at play, but he thought Pat Shane might be wrought into a humour to do the quarrelling. Accordingly, after Tom Gervaise had been got under way, and the tandem *en route* far Spanish Town, Knox sued for a private interview with Pat, which Pat graciously accorded, merely guarding his honour by stipulating that he was to hear no proposal concerning mutiny, or coining, or making away with the mess sherry, which was a widely celebrated wine.

Having reassured him on these points, Knox proceeded to inquire if it would give him any pleasure to serve Arthur Brune, to which query Pat Shane replied by a series of questions to the following effect:

"Does a game-cock like foitin'? does a turtle-dove love billin' and cooin'? does a mortherin' lawyer love fingerin' the fees? They do. Well then, what they'd do for either of them deloights, I'd do for Arthur Brune, d'ye see? Now then, go on, Knox, me boy."

"Certain reasons make it desirable that Melhado and his party should not leave this too early after Clutterbuck's dinner. I can't enter into particulars."

Shane compressed his lips till his mouth nearly disappeared, and executed a series of short double nods indicative of entire comprehension of an ineffable mystery; then he repeated, in business-like tones,

"Go on, Knox, me boy."

"We thought, perhaps, that the surest cause of detention might be the settlement of some misunderstanding—always a longish affair; and that if you didn't mind——"

"That's it; be me sowl, you've hit it. That's the card, Knox. Consider 't settled from this time. He'll not go home till mornin', ye may take your dying davy, and perhaps he'll not *go* then; he may be carr'ed. Ah, go to the divil wid ye!"

Saying which, he smote Knox playfully on the ribs so as to render him inarticulate, and was walking off, highly satisfied with the result of the interview, when the other seized his arm and held him till he recovered breath enough to speak again.

"Stop a moment, Pat—(gasp)—you—(gasp)—you—(gasp)—haven't quite—(gasp)—understood me."

"Haven't I? the divil! but I have, though! I have yer meaning as true as gospel, and when that's the case, the less said the better. If a casualty should occur, there's censorious persons always ready to pervert a gentleman's spache, and insinuate that he thought of doin' it beforehand. Oh, bother, don't let's talk."

"But, Pat, you *don't* understand, I assure you. I never thought of anything serious. A little sham sparring, just to prevent their seeing how time flies, and then an amicable arrangement, you know, and a breakfast here, or something of that sort——"

"Mr Knox," said Pat, drawing himself up, "is it me, of the blood of the Shanes, that ye mane to insult?"

"Am I a likely man to insult you, Pat?"

"Maybe not. We've been ould friends these seven years, but may I starve if I can construe yer last remarks otherwise than dishonourably!"

"My dear Pat, can't you understand a bit of fun?"

"Fun! on proper subjects, of coorse I can. If it's cardin' a proctor, or boultin' a turnpike, or takin' a funky rider over some damnable raspers, or any other harmless divarsion, I've not the laste objection. But to be throiflin' with matters of honor! Is't a Shane ye're asking? Bathershin!"

"Why, what could be the harm of it? only a little joke."

"Harm!—joke!"

"Yes; what harm?"

"A purty commotion there'd be in Ballyshane the day they heard of it! Can't I fancy Father O'Rourke, with the big hat on him, and the heavy whip in his hand, bidding them keep their tempers and bear the dispensation with patience, and foaming himself at the mouth with rage and shame! And Tim Brallaghan and the rest of them turning up their eyes and cryin', 'Who'd have thought it of Pat Shane—a boy that would never crack a joke on a piper, because a piper once played before Moses?—and to find *him* making a jest of serious things;' and Mike Duffy, the villain! that I bate out of shape for rudeness to Mary Higgins, with the heart's black drop welling over at the eyes of him; while he pretinds to be tinder and sorry for poor Pat's disgrace—the desateful Judas! And one says this of me, and one says that; and at last comes by a little black-eyed divil with the purtiest feet in the world, and she says—God bless her!—says she, 'What's that ye're saying about Misther Shane?' says she. 'Which of ye is there that would dare to tell him to his face that black's the white of his eye, or the smallest spick on it? Shane's sarving his country,' says she; 'and I'll be bail for him he never done a thing the likes o' yees should despise him for. Oh, that the Vargin 'ud give me a man's strength this hour, and I'd write *Slanderer* upon the forehead of the first that dared to slight him, ye calumniating villains!' She'd say this, but she'd be wrong—she'd have to own afterwards that 'twas heaven's own truth—and she'd hide her darlin' head for shame. And—oh, blood and turf!—can a mortial man bear this thought? Knox, me boy, ye're an old frind and a true, but before Pat Shane'll troifle with his honor, or make a sport of sacr'd instichusions, he'll be caught robbin' a church or flinchin' at the second tumbler!"

Thoroughly overcome by this burst of eloquence, Pat allowed himself to be posted in a chair, and wiped his face at considerable length with a cotton handkerchief, whose home was in the crown of his hat, where it performed the office of a sun-screen when not on active duty.

Knox began to despair of obtaining Pat's consent to a quarrel of convenience; at any rate, he thought it prudent not to push the point further just now. He had secured his Irish friend's co-operation to a certain extent, and he would find a more favourable opportunity, or perhaps corrupt Pat's second; for the same love of combination which made him confident with the pasteboard and bones, made him take a pride in mastering this difficulty.

So Knox sat down to ruminate—a process to which he was at all times prone, whether he had any business requiring consideration or not. With a little more of the active, and a little less of the reflective element in his composition, he might possibly have run a more honourable career than he has achieved, or is ever likely to achieve. For dreamy desultory reflection is a dangerous and unprofitable, though a seductive habit. Knox, who is still alive, does not consider that the pleasures of imagination have compensated him for the consciousness that his life has hitherto been of little use: he has seen visions and dreamed dreams, but he has contributed nothing to the great mass of human work; the next generation will be neither the better nor the worse for his existence: he fears that he has lived in vain. Yet 'tis a strong mind that, having learned the spell, can refrain from using it: he who possesses the golden key is evermore drawn toward the enchanted garden. He will clothe the arid desert with bubbling fountains and fresh mossy banks; on the tented field he hears the voices of children and the songs of youth and home; he roams delighted through the mouldering Past, and dares to frame a forethought of the awful Future. But to the striving, active present, what does he contribute? And whenever Knox thus searched his own nature, he would see in envied contrast the character of his friend Arthur Brune. Arthur could think too, but he usually thought with a purpose in view; he could take a rapid survey and form an irrevocable decision: then his bodily energies took up the matter and wrought it to its end; he realised and conformed to the actual present, all other thought excluded for the time; and as it was with his gun or in the race so was it afterwards amid the din of battle; he drew his sword from its scabbard with a determined arm, and until it returned thither again, after an eventful encounter, his mind was with it. And the fortunes of the two men have been such as their dispositions might have led one to predict.

This, however, is not hastening to the event, according to the maxim of our friend Quintus Horatius Flaccus.* Wherefore we interrupt these reflections, and take up the relation of events from the line where we writ that Knox sat down to ruminate. Between scheming and dreaming, he was very happy in his rocking-chair, but there we must leave him or disobey Horace, and possibly exhaust the patience of

* "Semper ad eventum festinat."—HOR.

the courteous reader. The substance of what Knox thought will appear by-and-by, and we have nothing more at present to say of him or his establishment, except that Gonsalvo de Cordova, after clearing the tables of the second breakfast, made a melancholy meal in the verandah, standing up as he ate, after the manner of negroes, and mingling on his plate pork chops, rice pudding, lobster salad, and apple-sauce; after which sad repast he felt in some degree prepared for the duties of the afternoon, which consisted of sitting on the back door-step and scratching his head.

CHAPTER XI.

"YAH-I-EPP!" shouted old Tom, as he put his team in motion, making his voice perform the office of the guard's horn; whereupon orderlies and stray non-commissioned officers faced inwards and saluted as the tandem passed, and niggers, with broad grins on their faces, scampered out of the road, crying, with their peculiar chuckle, "Hei, Massa Gervaise!" and one or two of them got tickled by Tom's lash, to the unbounded amusement of the rest. At the sound of wheels, half-a-dozen dogs rushed frantically from the different buildings to bark, but, perceiving the unerring hand that wielded the whip, they suddenly altered their minds and retreated, many of them, though unscathed, emitting faint yelps from agreeable associations.

We have incidentally mentioned that Gervaise and Brune were bound for Spanish Town. They were going to wait on no less a personage than his Excellency the Governor; that is, Brune was going to beg an audience with the great man, and Tom Gervaise went to pass the time, and on the probability of getting up a jollification at a strange mess.

The Government was, in those days, still a very high appointment. The importance of the island was waning, but she still boasted herself the brightest jewel in the British crown. Soon after, she ceased to boast, or to give any other sign of self-esteem. Her complacency, if she retained any, became reflective and visionary, turning evermore silently back to the days of her glory. It has amused us sometimes, while lounging listlessly in a hammock, and surveying through the half-opened jalousies the laughing mountains and the teeming plain, to recall her past history, and conceive a parallel between her vicissitudes and those of the mother country.

There have been four epochs in the history of Jamaica suggestive of, if not answering to, the radical points of English history.

It had its savage aborigines, a less warlike race than the Britons, and to whom the fierce Charaibes, inhabitants of the Western Antilles, acted the terrific part of the Picts and Scots.

Then came the haughty Spaniard, so far resembling the Roman that he introduced science and the arts of life. But in his treatment of the harmless and ignorant natives, how far did the proud champion of the Cross sink below the Pagan! At the time of the Spanish conquest, the island contained 60,000 inhabitants; and fifty years after, hardly one representative remained of these wretched Arowauks. Their wholesale destruction was accomplished by the invaders with circumstances of wanton cruelty too horrible to relate, or even to reflect upon. The marvel is, how human beings could be guilty of such atrocity; and the human beings here upon the scene professed to be the most devout sons of the Church—her missionaries, God save the mark!!

Anon, the third race of conquerors not only corresponded to the Saxons, but were the veritable sons of Hengist's and Horsa's host. In 1655, Heaven, by the agency of Oliver Cromwell, answered the cry of vengeance that had gone up from the slaughtered Indians. An English force landed on the island in May, and smote the cruel Spaniards to the uttermost parts thereof, annexing Jamaica thenceforth to the British Empire.

To complete the historical parallel, something important is wanting. We have matched our Britons, our Romans, and our Saxons; but how to find an antitype to the glorious Normans? Bare facts will not do it for us; but if we look at the results of those facts, we may yet light upon something that burns with the flame of chivalry. It is true that no knights and warriors came in pomp and panoply to dispossess, and then unite with the Anglo-Saxon, for the next immigration tells of chains and degradation, and the horrors of the middle passage. Soon after our conquest began the regular introduction of African negroes* to the West Indies—a race whose miserable beginnings and servile condition gave no warning that their weakness should one day agitate nations and penetrate the hearts of kings. These were not Normans; no! but were lance and mail ever associated with a more sublime enthusiasm than that which impelled Christian Europe to the succour of the slave? Was the rescue of His sepulchre or the deliverance of His creatures the grander achievement of the soldiers of Christ? Hermit and paladin, and most Christian prince, and most holy father, though their zeal was ardent and their courage boiled, can vie with crusaders of these latter days only as the host of Israel may be compared with the universal Church; the former but a type of the latter. Yea, the intermingling of the sable race with the bright children of the Saxon *has* given rise to a school of chivalry the highest and the most powerful that the world has ever seen,—the highest, because its aims and its rewards are beyond the earth; the mightiest, forasmuch as it has triumphed over nations and gov-

* James I. chartered the slave-trade in 1618.

ernments and monarchs in the Old World, and is now about to shake terribly the New World of the West!

At the date of our story, the Negro question was creating its very fiercest contentions. Jamaica was being torn and ruined by excited factions. The planting interest, after years of domination, found itself suddenly overborne and trampled on, while upon its forehead were branded all the sins of oppression committed since the world began. The triumphant abolitionists, as if the sacredness of their grand object absolved them from all blame as to the means they might use, conducted themselves with a vindictiveness and rancour which disgraced their profession, and soon were blinded to the difference between truth and falsehood, right and wrong. The weak Government at home, unable to control the torrent, lent itself to the iniquity with which emancipation was carried out, so that every official appointed by the Crown, from the Governor downwards, was forced into the position of a partisan, instead of holding the scales and controlling the fury of the factions. Confounded by, and indignant at, the injustice with which they conceived themselves to be treated, the planters nevertheless exhibited their ancient independence, and showed once more the bold front which had before now successfully resisted Imperial aggression. But this time the opposition was vain and ruinous;

it served only to stimulate the hatred of their irresistible foes. The battle was not yet fought out at the date of our tale: the island legislature was as yet vigorous and hopeful, and breasted manfully the waves that were destined to overwhelm it; but it often, in its indignation and despair, lost sight of dignity and prudence. The local government, reduced to be the leaders of a violent faction, appeared to no more advantage than the legislative body. The Governor was said to be "a fine old fellow, who would stand no nonsense." The Council and Assembly likewise contained several fine old fellows who would stand no nonsense. Nonsense, therefore, seemed to have but a bad chance, and yet the proceedings on both sides were marked by the folly and petulance of childhood. Had it been the fortune of the island at this critical time to be governed by a man of temper and discretion, instead of by a fine old fellow who would stand no nonsense, or had the colonists appreciated the magnitude of the opposing force, and bent before instead of resisting it, she might, like Barbadoes, have passed comparatively uninjured through the ordeal of emancipation. But that was not to happen.

The state of dissension of course afforded openings for loud-mouthed agitators and demagogues to exhibit their stump-oratory, and to grasp at places and gains. Crowds of these appeared, all with liberal and philanthropic sentiments on their lips, but the lives of many of them characterised by greed and hate. Like Judas, they were eloquent concerning the claims of the poor, not that they cared for the poor. And in the very front of the political agitators stood the religious sects,* the preachers acting as the leaders, and instilling their secular doctrines, and inciting to deceit and dishonesty from their pulpits. The clergymen of the Establishment, for the most part, sided with the planters, and shared the odium levelled at them. They were, therefore, of little use. But there were a few young and enthusiastic ministers, like our friend Mr Grant, who endeavoured, amid the roar of factions, to gain a few ears for the voice of true religion. They were nearly all young and inexperienced; most of them, going right as far as they could see, were unable to realise in their minds the state of things, and many of them had a zeal which outran discretion.

All of us are aware of the wreck in which these things resulted; but many who know the result may not know the elements from which it proceeded. We have ventured, therefore, on these few words of explanation.

And now we have to be taken rapidly over the

---

* We except the Wesleyan Methodists, who were said strictly to confine themselves to spiritual concerns.

thirteen miles that separate Up Park from Spanish Town. Old Tom is the very person to do us that service. We rattle along, each person absorbed in his own reflections, and noticing nothing—not even the immense cotton-tree on the right of the road, beneath which sits an elderly negro retailing the milk of young cocoa-nuts for the refreshment of parched travellers, hewing off the outer husks with a weapon that might, for its form, have hung by the side of Haroun al Raschid, and converting the nut itself into a cup. 'Tis a simple draught rudely prepared; but if the old tree be there, and an old vendor beneath it when you go that way, our life on it, reader, you will halt and drink! He found no customers in Arthur and Tom that day. They passed silently along, first a warm horse stepping smartly and tossing his head, then another ditto, ditto, then two travellers abreast in their chariot, then two little streams of smoke.

Now, it naturally enough happened that his Excellency the Governor, being, as has been said, a fine old fellow, held a favourable opinion of a fine young fellow like Arthur Brune. But fine old fellows then had a way of showing their goodwill which we should in this day think objectionable. His Excellency gave Arthur a reception, whose warmth, as indicated by the oaths he used, was intense. He had just then a little leisure, which he kindly devoted to the entertainment of his young friend, to whom he addressed a sprightly conversation, strongly spiced with *doubles entendres*, and illustrated with anecdotes, from which the chaste Maga, even though approaching her fiftieth year, would avert her eyes with indignant majesty. That was the way in which fine old fellows condescended to those whom it was their pleasure to honour. Arthur for a long time bore with his Excellency's humour, and laughed at his jokes, longing to speak of the business which brought him thither, but not finding an opportunity, so continuous was the flow of his Excellency's conversation. At length the great man looked at his watch, interrupted his discourse, and was about to dismiss his young friend graciously, when Arthur besought an extension of five minutes, saying that he had a favour to ask.

"Well, my boy, what can I do for you?" said his Excellency. "Name something in reason, and you may command me."

"I want a licence to marry," said Arthur, firmly; "and I beg of your Excellency the favour that you will for a short time keep the granting it a profound secret."

"Licence to marry!" repeated the Governor in amazement. "Why, what the devil! Marry! Why, you can't be serious."

"Quite serious, sir," Arthur said.

"Why, I really thought now you were one of the fellows that will take the places of us old cocks when we go our ways. I took you for a soldier, every inch of you. Marry! By Jove!"

"I have not the least intention, sir," said Arthur, "of giving up the service; and if I know myself at all, I shall not be less worthy of his Majesty's commission after marriage than I am now."

"Pooh, pooh!" said his Excellency; "wait till you're a field-officer at least. Marriage is a mistake in a young officer; fellows never worth a farthing after. Takes all the dash out of him. And a married subaltern! damme, you must be joking! Eh? Can't mean it. All humbug. Mustn't think of such thing. Rather sign a death-warrant for you!"

Arthur made a suitable acknowledgment for this mark of regard, but persisted that he was quite in earnest, and had well considered the step he was about to take.

"Then I can only say I'm infernally sorry," said the Governor. "Mark my words! You'll live to repent it. Fine young fellow like you throwing yourself away! Besides, I thought you were rather soft about that girl Melhado's going to marry—devilish delightful girl she is too—splendid bust—cursed deal too good for that fellow;—thought you were a little moonish in that direction, which seemed a capital thing, as it would keep you single. I say, Brune, whoever it is, you haven't got anything to match old Arabin's daughter, I'll take my oath!"

"Miss Arabin's," said Brune, steadily, "is the other name which I wish to be inserted in the licence."

His Excellency looked hard at Arthur to examine whether his eye showed symptoms of insanity; failing to perceive which, and at the same time recollecting Arthur's demand of secrecy, the representative of majesty began to perceive how matters stood.

"The devil it is!" then said the Governor. "May I ask what Mr and Mrs Arabin and Mr Melhado say to the arrangement?"

"I grieve to say, sir," answered Arthur, "that the marriage, if you give me the means of effecting it, will be clandestine."

"After which will come duels, actions at law, courts-martial, and I don't know what pleasures beside?" said his Excellency, inquiringly.

"I think not, sir," replied Arthur. "I have weighed well the consequences of what I meditate."

"You think you can do it neatly?" asked the great man.

"I have every hope of carrying out my design."

Here his Excellency was so overpowered by his feelings, that after a suppressed chuckle or two he

P

burst into a fit of hearty laughter, which brought tears out of his eyes.

"Capital!" said his Excellency, when he regained command of his voice; "only do it well, and I'll forgive you for marrying."

"Don't you," continued he again, unable to control explosions of delight—"don't you feel great remorse at the trick you're going to play that excellent young man, Melhado?"

"I do," said Arthur; "I wish I could avoid it."

Whereupon his Excellency made a grotesque face, which said, as plainly as a grimace could do, "I see you're a wag as well as a sly dog; but I have some fun in me too, and we understand each other," and then he pursued his remarks with intervals of laughter.

"By ——, it'll set the whole island by the ears. Why, what an audacious young scamp you are, eh! Arabin won't have *bo* to throw to a goose for the next twelvemonth; and as for Melhado, oh, 'pon my soul, it's too bad. Well, she ought to marry a redcoat, I'll be —— if she oughtn't; 'twould be a slur upon the cloth to let a civilian have her. But the sell it'll be for them is best of all. Oh, by Jove, it's capital!"

In fine, so great was the Governor's glee that he promised to have the necessary parchment prepared that evening with great secrecy, and desired Arthur to dine at the King's House that he might receive it. And Arthur having incidentally mentioned that Gervaise had travelled with him, his Excellency graciously extended his invitation to that officer, who was somewhat embarrassed at receipt of it, seeing that he had come over unprovided with a red jacket, without which it was as bad taste to appear at King's House, as for a Jew to go to a marriage without a wedding garment. The difficulty was eventually got over; but as Tom was both tall and stout, there was some trouble in fitting him. They applied at last to a captain of the St Jago Militia, who was sufficiently stout, but who being of small stature, Thomas presented himself at the viceregal board with six inches of ragged shirt visible round his waist. The hiatus did not spoil his dinner, and his Excellency was so delighted with the coming elopement that there was little ceremony. It would have given us great pleasure to repeat some very excellent anecdotes and *jeux d'esprit* to which the Governor gave voice on this occasion; but we have so altered in only a quarter of an age, that the conversation of men who enjoyed fame and rank, and who were of mature age at that time, is objectionable in the present day.

CHAPTER XII.

IT is quite true that Lorton lay very sick while the[se] things were passing. He had a bad nervous fever—one of the most difficult diseases that doctors de[al] with in that climate; it is so hard to treat it in an[y] way. Often to support the patient is to increase th[e] disease, while to lower the fever is to kill the ma[n.] People don't think of going to sea till they get ver[y] ill; and when they are very ill, they are not fit to b[e] embarked. Once launched on the Atlantic, they soo[n] revive; the difficulty is to get them there. If poo[r] Lorton, when he clasped together, as he often di[d,] his thin hands, on which still hung the trinkets whic[h] he had worn in happier days, a world too wide fo[r] his shrunk fingers—if, we say, he had by this act un[-] wittingly invoked a colossal genius, who said, "[I] am ready to obey you as your slave; I, and th[e] other slaves of that ring," he would have replied, lik[e] Aladdin, "Whoever you are, take me out of thi[s] place;" and he would have added, "Place me in a[

English ship five hundred miles from hence, with her head toward that pleasant country; let the fresh winds course upon my hot parched face, let the salt breath of the sea bring life and hope to my soul. I would be riding away on the billow, and hear the mariners sing the songs of my native land." Such imaginations sound childish, and well they may, for healthy childhood is a state of mental energy and clearness compared with the weak yearnings and fancies of the fever-tossed in a tropic land. There is the worn, racked body and the shattered mind, the strong will reduced to plaintive whinings, and the understanding leagued with deceit and despair.

"Give me some drink, Titinius!
As a sick girl,"

cried mighty Julius, quelled by fever's power. And worse than the pain of body and the failing mind is the sense of desolation which overwhelms the poor sick soldier away from home, thrown in his helplessness on strangers and hirelings. The nurses are proverbially skilful and attentive in Jamaica, medical attendants accompany every regiment, and comrades are generally kind and sympathising; but these do not, by the bed of sickness, compensate for some low sweet voice which is longed for there.

To Lorton his attack was truly a bitter visitation.

In the silence and frequent solitude, his old grievances, magnified by disease tenfold, tortured him from hour to hour. He was bidden to expect recovery, but what comfort was there in that! To recover health would be to be once more buffeted by Fortune—to be alone in misery amid a smiling, happy world. The sickbed or the grave seemed fitter for one so persecuted. Yet his mood would change to Hope sometimes; bright visions and lofty aspirations would visit him again, and he would pant for health and vigour that he might realise his dream. He was restricted entirely to the recumbent position, but lifted by day from his bed to the sofa, where he lay propped up with pillows. The doctor had insisted on the attendance of a nurse; and accordingly there sat near him the grandly-developed form of Miss Malvina Mac-Glashin, her dark wool concealed by a cotton handkerchief, which was knotted across the nape of her neck, with two enormous mosaic drops in her ears, a triple chin, a chintz wrapper of a florid design, and reaching a little below her knees, and a pair of morocco slippers, the heels whereof were well trodden down, and the toes pointing inwards like those of a parrot. Miss Malvina was a lady of colour, somewhere about quadroon in blood, and tolerably light-brown. Her age was between forty and fifty; she inclined decidedly to embonpoint; a fine bridge on her nose was the charter by which she claimed kindred with the MacGlashin, and a pair of lips about two inches thick conspired with hair and skin to indicate the other source of her hybrid existence.

"Isn't it nearly time for the medicine, Malvina?" inquired the sufferer, who has been restless for some little while.

The brown lady rose, and with a motion which we should esteem neither light nor graceful on this side the Atlantic, lifted Lorton's watch and showed it to him, for the revelations of the timepiece were foolishness to Miss Malvina.

"Wants ten minutes," Lorton said, "but that doesn't signify; I can take it now."

"My chile," replied Miss Malvina, with a whining drawl, "when de dactar say a ting, it is praper to do it; so you mus' wait till de tree hour is up, and den I will give you de draff."

"I expect Mr Knox here to see me directly," pleaded the patient, "and we may as well get the medicine over before he comes."

"Very well, my chile," said Miss MacGlashin, "it is near de time now, and if you promise me not to talk too much to Meesta Knox, you shall have it. See now, only dis half glass of de mixture, and den dis nice piece of pink shaddock. Dere now, he really take it good; now den, pop in de shaddock, and the nassy taste will soon gone; so, so, dat is it. Now, let we make de room look leetle bit neat and tidy before de visitor come in. Where dat creature Sampson?"

Miss Malvina knew her work too well to call or knock in a sick-room for the assistance she required. She stepped into the verandah herself for the purpose of sending down a message by the first passenger; and in so doing she caught sight of Sampson rolling in the grass below, whom she forthwith summoned to the upper chamber by the title of "lazy, wort'less hangman." It was wonderful the gentleness with which they both moved about and arranged the room. Plates, glasses, and bottles quickly disappeared; table-covers were smoothed, and chairs set in their places. Lorton had a clean shirt put on him, and his hair carefully and gently dressed; then he and his apartment were perfumed with eau-de-Cologne.

"Ah, that's nice!" he said; "I really think I feel a little better!"

"Yes; only keep quiet, and do as you is told, and you will soon be better, my chile. De fus' young man I ever nus, he very much in de same way as you is, and I bring him round. Nice young man! he come court me before he sick: I used to pretty den; dat is a long time ago. He most my fus' sweetheart. Chaw! how I lub him! Those times was different from now. De officers more attentive to de young ladies, and de sailor officers bring in prize-money, and make we handsome presents. My! how de doubloons fly about! never see dem now. And de beautiful horses and de kittureens! I shall never see de like again. Hei! What dat you have dere?" suddenly said she in a loud whisper to Sampson, who was retreating through the door with sundry articles which he had been desired to clean. "What is dis?" repeated Miss Malvina, following him into the verandah, and seizing a black bottle from under his arm. It was three parts full of madeira.

"I tink it did turn bad," said Sampson.

"Take it back," said Miss Malvina, not deigning to notice the lame excuse. Sampson obeyed, muttering to himself as he did so, "Dis brown lady too bad, cubbich* as a 'tar-apple tree. Massa nebber do so."

We by no means wish to create an impression that poor little Sampson was an incorrigible thief. He had his own notions of what his merits entitled him to, and took care that he was not neglected. When Lorton was well and in his better humours, he was generally very considerate, and then Samp-

* Probably a corruption of "*covetous*," but used in the sense of *parsimonious* or *illiberal*. The star-apple tree does not cast its fruit, however ripe; hence it is emblematic of a close-fisted person.

son was content with what was given to him; but when Lorton was in his tantrums, and the rates were not duly paid, then Sampson considered it proper to distrain. Of course, when his massa was weak and sick it would have been a cruelty to trouble him about such matters, and therefore a quiet process was the best that could be adopted. It was most officious in Miss Malvina to interfere thus between an upright domestic and his lawful perquisites.

Miss Malvina looked towards the window, and nodded in reply to a sign from Knox, who had made a quiet reconnaissance to ascertain whether the patient was awake and prepared to receive him. A flush overspread Lorton's wan face as he shook hands and answered the usual interrogatories. Even this little excitement tried him, it was clear; seeing which, Knox addressed his conversation for a while to Miss Malvina.

"A little feverish still, Malvina—pulse variable," said he; "we must still be careful to avoid excitement."

"He will do very well, sar," replied Miss Malvina, using the severity which is proper when unprofessional people attempt to talk scientifically to an adept. "Can you tell me what is de hour?"

"Just gone three. Didn't you hear the bugle, old girl?"

"I am not an old gal, Meesta Knax. You will be good enough to recolleck dat you is talking to a leady."

"Of course," Knox said, "but your figure and face are so girlish that one forgets. Let's see, you must be quite a woman now; yes, of course!"

"I am afraid dat you is making fun, sar," remarked Miss MacGlashin, composedly.

"There was a gentleman of your name at mess last night, Lawyer Macglashin. Is he any relation?"

"He is my broder, sar."

"Indeed! I was not aware of that."

"My *white* brother, dat is. He wouldn't tell you so. They is not bery proud of their coloured relations. They can't wash out the MacGlashin blood for all dat. It is here;" and Miss Malvina placed her hand on the magnificent region above her heart.

"He ought to feel flattered," said Knox, "at having so lovely and accomplished a relation."

"Ah, sar," sighed Malvina, "you is not so prejudice as dese creole whites. You cannot understan' deir silly pride. I often say I will go home to Scotland, where they will not be ashamed of the MacGlashin blood, whatever is the skin it run under. De heart of dat people is warm, sar!"

"But their country is devilish cold," said Knox.

"What does de cold matter to me, sar?" said

Malvina, loftily: "if I have de blood I have de spirit too, and I can bear de cold like de res' of my relations."

"You'll have to wear a kilt."

"Whatever is de proper dress, sar."

"And to live upon whisky and oatmeal."

"Of course, sar."

"And talk Gaelic."

"Yes, sar."

"And play the bagpipe."

"Whatever oder leadies does, sar."

Malvina, it is clear, dreamed of a land that was very far off, where the MacGlashin was lord, and where she would be welcomed as a sister, and sit in honour a MacGlashin among MacGlashins. Poor soul! and yet let us not too hastily lavish on the brown woman our complacent pity. Which of us does not secretly cherish a vision no less absurd than Malvina's idea of the misty heather—unattainable, untrue, and which, if it could be realised and won, is unsuited to our nature?

"Malvina," said Lorton, who was composed again now, "oblige me by seeing what they are about with my broth. I think Sampson will not prepare it nicely without your directions."

"De wort'less!" said Miss Malvina, drawing her robe around her and sailing off, while the dragging of her slippers along the boards of the verandah could be heard for many a yard.

"Come close to me, Knox," said Lorton, "that I may speak low, and husband my strength for what I have to say. You are Brune's friend. I fear that I may have assisted in doing Brune a grievous wrong. I would speak of the matter to you, and, if there be cause, try to make amends to him. There is a belief in Mr Arabin's family that Brune is a gambler and a bully; that he cruelly crushed the affections of an Irish lady, shot her brother, and decamped. The story was carried to them by Mr Melhado; Melhado got it from me. I have here the account which furnished it, written by an Irish female cousin. Making all allowance for gossip and exaggeration, the whole thing is very bad; but, you see, the language is ambiguous—there appears to have been another officer concerned, to whom may belong part of the odium. His name is not mentioned, but Brune's is, the reason being that I, from this country, made inquiries concerning Brune when he first came out, and people were talking of him so much. I have often—oh, how often, lately!—examined into my feelings at that time, and cannot hide from myself that I greedily believed what was said to Brune's prejudice, and that I neither suggested nor sought for palliating explanations—indeed, that I wished for none. The blow was not aimed openly; the poison wrought underground: the effects, I know, have been most serious. Tell me, Knox—tell a weak, miserable man—did Brune do that which has been laid to his charge?"

Lorton's chest heaved, his hands shook, his lips quivered, drops stood on his brow, and his eyes were suffused with tears. Knox, without answering, looked at him for a minute, partly observing his emotion, partly revolving smarting thoughts within.

"Speak," said the sick man; "speak to me, Knox. I cannot wait."

Knox took hold of the thin, quivering hand, and as he pressed it, said, "Lorton, Brune has been cruelly slandered. May God forgive those who wronged him!"

There were sobs now and choking sighs from the sofa. Lorton was in an agony of remorse, and Knox, astonished at his condition, knew not at the moment how to allay it, or what he should do.

Suddenly Lorton sprang upright on the couch, the light of fever gleaming from his eyes, his hands clenched, and his whole frame supernaturally braced.

"Take me to him!" he shrieked; "I will tell him all. I will beg his pardon on my knees. I will do all—give all to atone."

Knox held him fast now, and with some trouble

got him into the recumbent position again. The transient flash of energy disappeared, and was succeeded by a passion of tears. Knox saw that this matter must be disposed of now. However trying it might be, it was better it should be ended than that it should lie festering and fretting, under the delusion that it might be better borne hereafter, so he said, " Listen to me, Lorton. If you will compose yourself you shall hear the story of this affair. Nobody, I am sorry to say, can tell it you more truly than I. There, now, be calm, and turn your face this way. An explanation to Brune will do him not the least good at the present time, and will do you much harm. When you are stronger I shall be very glad to know that you have made it. This, now, is the outline of what passed at Cork, and you shall judge how far Brune deserved what has been said of him. *He* did not play high at Cork, but there was another young officer there, belonging to the depôt, who was less discreet. He had won some tolerably large sums from a Mr O'Flaherty, who, it seems, was not quite prepared to pay. The score had been going on some weeks without the Irishman clearing any part of his debt—indeed, he rather increased it ; but, in the mean time, he had hit upon an expedient for not only getting easy treatment, but for doing a little family business. He introduced his creditor to his sister, a wild, handsome, clever girl; and the silly fellow at first took the bait, and thought himself desperately in love. If the young lady had been left to play him skilfully and patiently, he would possibly have sealed his ruin by marrying her; but O'Flaherty, fearing lest so promising a plan should miscarry by delay, attempted to precipitate matters, and called upon the young officer to speak out like a man, and not to trifle with his sister's young affections. This entirely uncalled-for interference caused the lover to consider his conduct and his situation, and to perceive that he was getting within the meshes of a very ugly net, to extricate himself from which, however promptly he might act, would require some discretion. Fortunately he took Brune for his counsellor, who soon saw through and exposed the whole affair, and who speedily made it known to Mr O'Flaherty on his friend's behalf that, before making any demands in his fraternal character, it would be desirable that he should pay his debt, otherwise the singleness of his motive might be suspected. Imagining therefrom that the youth was intimidated by his bluster, and that he had only to press on and succeed, O'Flaherty sent a challenge, which Brune peremptorily refused to let his friend accept until the money had been paid. But Brune intimated that he himself was ready at once to fight if O'Flaherty must have a victim. This did not at all harmonise with the programme. O'Flaherty insisted that his quarrel was with the man who was trifling with his sister; and by some means or other he managed to procure the money, and paid it; whereupon he was informed that the duel might take place whenever he wished. He seemed, however, to have cooled in his warlike intentions, and some days elapsed without a repetition of the challenge; consequently he received a hostile message, to which he replied that he could not meet a person who, having been called out, had declined the encounter. Mr O'Flaherty was immediately after this horsewhipped in the street by the man whom he had selected for his brother-in-law, Brune and many others witnessing the chastisement. The matter excited much scandal, and was, with many colourings, reported in the papers. The account followed by your lady-cousin may very likely have been one of those circulated, but the true one is that which I have just given."

"But may you not have been imposed upon as well as she?" asked Lorton, feebly.

"Not easily," was the reply, spoken in a hoarse voice and with averted head. "The name of the lover, gambler, and brawler, is *Edward Knox*."

Malvina's horror, when she returned with the broth and found her patient tossed and exhausted, may be imagined. She dismissed Knox, darkened the windows, moved her poor charge back to his bed, which was now well cooled and aired, and resorted to the many soothing expedients which her long practice showed her to be proper.

"Malvina, you are everything that is kind and gentle," whispered Lorton; "but what—what would I not give to see my mother's face bending over me as yours is!"

"Be patient, my chile," answered Malvina; "please God, we will have you well again soon, and your moder shall bend over you in ol' England!"

The result justified the opinion which induced Knox to go through with the discussion of Lorton's trouble in reference to Brune when it was once begun. The sick man was evidently soothed by being disburdened of this matter, and Malvina owned the next day that no evil effects of the scene appeared to remain. For a day or two Lorton even seemed to rally, but such a mind was not long in calling up others of its many cares to file and wear the miserable body. Still he dragged on, apparently not worse, but of course losing strength by confinement.

At home, sickness seems the natural result of fogs, frosts, and constant changes; but in the tropics its appearance is less comprehensible. Everything without is associated with life and joy and beauty. Newcomers rejoicing in the brightness, the warmth, and the loveliness which are everywhere manifest, are apt to think the visitations of disease but bugbears to frighten children. Up to the time of being attacked, people generally preserve their spirits and their energy. "Disease," say they, fondly, "is afar off, where winter shakes in melancholy halls." But no; it is even at the door!

Thus, probably, must it ever be. Where Earth is most fit to be enjoyed, there must come the most startling warnings that Earth is not our resting-place. We say, Lo, here is Paradise! lo there! But a dread Teacher is near to claim our whole hearts, and forbid undue affection for created things. 'Tis the same lesson read under every sky. "Whither shall I go, then, from thy Spirit? or whither shall I go, then, from thy presence? If I climb up into heaven, thou art there; if I go down to hell, thou art there also. If I take the wings of the morning, and remain in the uttermost parts of the sea, even there also shall thy hand lead me, and thy right hand shall hold me."

CHAPTER XIII.

As will have been perceived, Arthur and Violet were in Spanish Town at the same time. They did not, however, meet there. It was not Brune's wish that they should, and it was much better for all parties that they did not; for Melhado, anxious to efface the recollection of that disagreeable day on the water, had joined Mr Arabin and his daughter.

Having effected the purpose for which he went thither, Arthur was anxious to return from Spanish Town to Stony Hill. He therefore, on the morning after they dined with the Governor, got Tom Gervaise out of bed as early as he could, and urged him to go back. Tom had, however, by no means fulfilled the little scheme of enjoyment which he had sketched out, and fought hard against going—indeed positively refused to go. Brune, having exhausted his exhortations in vain, bethought himself of a lure which had the desired effect. He promised to send on a runner to order a dinner, of which turtle-soup and stewed eels were to be components, at the Ferry House Tavern, half-way between Spanish Town and Kingston, if Tom would only get them thither by the appointed time to eat it. Thus he not only induced his frail ally to go, but caused him to start punctually, which he would hardly have done had there not been a risk of spoiling dinner.

They rattled back to the Ferry, and were informed that everything would be ready in ten minutes, so that Arthur had just time to wash before dinner was announced. During this interval, Tom Gervaise loitered outside a little room where the dinner was being dished, and took in odours that might create an appetite under the ribs of an alderman who has passed the chair.

The dining-room looked very nice—spacious, cool, and shady. The table was set in the midst, with a bright tureen and capital dinner-service. Fine limes for the turtle-soup were piled in a little glass dish by themselves, and two or three peppers, of various shapes and colours, rested on the top of each salt-cellar. A black bottle of claret in a wet bag stood on a slide between the dishes. Indeed, everything looked complete to a common observer; but Tom Gervaise was not, on such occasions, a common observer; and, scanning curiously the arrangements of the table, he asked sternly where the punch was.

"It ready dereckly, sar," answered the waiter. "Missy bery sorry it oberlook at fus, but it soon come; dem making it."

"Forget the punch! Turtle-soup without punch! Arthur, do you hear? the villains have forgot the punch!" and Tom waxed wroth, and spake great swelling words, and bound himself under a curse, saying that he would neither eat nor drink till the punch should appear. "And look here, bo," he added; "tell her to put in a little extra spirit; that's the only way to prevent my pulling the house down and making dogs' meat of the whole brood of ye."

As there would thus be a few minutes of self-imposed expectation highly trying to Tom, Arthur suggested that it might pass the time if he would go and wash his hands. Tom was glad to escape the tedium even at the expense of ablution; and it is written in the chronicles of the house of Gervaise that he called for water, soap, and towels; and that, without constraint, bodily fear, or delusion of any kind, he did then and there of his own free will wash, clean, and entirely purify his hands, and afterwards did dry and wipe them, the hands aforesaid, and that he returned to Arthur Brune buttoning his left wrist-band (the right had no button) just as the punch was ready.

And Tom did eat and drink; and his heart expanded under the influence of the good cheer; and he laughed and spake pleasant words, and was satisfied exceedingly. A little child might have played with him!

Their dinner ended, it was arranged that they should continue their journey in about an hour, by which time it would be cool. Meanwhile, that he might not sit by and see Arthur discharge a bill of which he ought to have borne his share, Tom said he would stroll out and smoke a cigar. Accordingly he dragged himself very leisurely out from the back of the Ferry House, and so along some enclosures which groaned with plenty of the sweet cane, till he got to a cool shady field of guinea-grass, through which ran a little stream. Just in front of him were two negroes intently watching something in the grass.

"Wha you got dere, eh, you sars?" inquired Tom, who thought himself a proficient in the negro dialect.

"It is one crab, massa," replied one of the men; and Tom on coming up saw between the roots of the plant a solitary land-crab,* which appeared to have

---

* Bryan Edwards, quoting Du Tertre, writes thus of the land-crabs:—"These animals live not only in a kind of orderly society in their retreats in the mountains, but regularly once a-year march down to the sea-side in a body of some millions at a time. As they multiply in great numbers, they choose the months of April or May to begin their expedition; and then sally out from the stumps of hollow trees, from the clefts of rocks, and from the holes which

lagged behind his kindred in their annual migration, and to be endeavouring to overtake them by travelling at unwonted hours.

"Devilish fine one too," said Tom; "that fellow would eat remarkably well."

they dig for themselves under the surface of the earth. At that time the whole ground is covered with this band of adventurers; there is no setting down one's foot without treading upon them. The sea is their place of destination, and to that they direct their march with right-lined precision. No geometrician could send them to their destined station by a shorter course; they neither turn to the right nor to the left, whatever obstacles intervene; and even if they meet with a house, they will attempt to scale the walls to keep the unbroken tenor of their way. But though this be the general order of their route, they upon other occasions are compelled to conform to the face of the country; and if it be intersected by rivers, they are seen to wind along the course of the streams. The procession sets forward from the mountains with the regularity of an army under the guidance of an experienced commander. They are commonly divided into battalions, of which the first consists of the strongest and boldest males, that, like pioneers, march forward to clear the route, and face the greatest dangers. The night is their chief time of proceeding, but if it rains by day, they do not fail to profit by the occasion, and they continue to move forward in their slow uniform manner. When the sun shines and is hot upon the surface of the ground, they make a universal halt, and wait till the cool of the evening. When they are terrified, they march back in a confused disorderly manner, holding up their nippers, with which they sometimes tear off a piece of the skin, and leave the weapon where they inflicted the wound.

" When, after a fatiguing march, and escaping a thousand dangers—for they are sometimes three months in getting to the shore —they have arrived at their destined port, they prepare to cast

"Yes, massa," one of the blacks said, "him will bery nice; make massa a sweet supper. Supposin' massa goin' home, it quite wort' him while to carry him dere. Do take him, my massa."

The consequence of following this generous advice

their spawn. For this purpose the crab has no sooner reached the shore than it eagerly goes to the edge of the water, and lets the waves wash over its body two or three times to wash off the spawn. The eggs are hatched under the sand; and soon after millions at a time of the new-born crabs are seen quitting the shore, and slowly travelling up to the mountains."

He goes on to quote Brown's 'History of Jamaica':—"The old crabs, having disburdened themselves [as above], generally regain their habitations in the mountains by the latter end of June. In August they begin to fatten, and prepare for moulting, filling up their burrows with dry grass, leaves, and abundance of other materials. When the proper period comes, each retires to his hole, shuts up the passage, and remains quite inactive till he gets rid of his old shell, and is fully provided with a new one. How long they continue in this state is uncertain, but the shell is first observed to burst at the back and the sides, to give a passage to the body, and the animal extracts its limbs from all the other parts gradually afterwards. At this time the flesh is in the richest state, and covered only with a tender membranous skin, variegated with a multitude of reddish veins; but this hardens gradually, and soon becomes a perfect shell, like the former. It is, however, remarkable that, during this change, there are some stony concretions always formed in the bag, which waste and dissolve as the creature forms and perfects its new crust."

"To these full and particular accounts," says Edwards, "I will add, of my own knowledge, that many people, in order to eat of this singular animal in the highest perfection, cause them to be dug out of the earth in the moulting state; but they are usually taken from the time they begin to move of themselves till they would have been, that Tom's hand would have been clasped acutely by the crab's nippers. It was a cruel joke to try upon any one: it was an impudent joke for a negro to play on a buckrah gentleman: but these phases of it were nought beside the presumption which selected him, the intelligent Tom Gervaise, as its subject—Tom Gervaise, who supposed himself to know the ways of the island so well that he had a sort of property in them!—Tom Gervaise, who considered his right infringed if any other person in his hearing ventured to tell a native story, or to explain a custom or tradition of the colony!—Tom Gervaise, who was accustomed to pour fresh instruction o'er the minds of yahoos by inducing them to the very act to which he had just been incited!—it was a sin ranking close behind apostasy and blasphemy. Mercy there could be none; and Tom's stick visited the calves of the offender's legs with power. Lucky that the man's position was not such as would have put his shins more in the stick's path, or those tender parts * would have known tri-

---

reach the sea, as already related. During all this time they are in spawn, and if my testimony can add weight to that of all who have written, and all who have feasted, on the subject, I pronounce them, without doubt, one of the choicest morsels in nature."

* You may pound a nigger's head till you have tired yourself, and broken your knuckles, without affecting *him;* but to touch bulation. The unhappy criminal sent up a yell of agony and terror as this judgment overtook him, and executed the first movements of a very lively *pas seul;* but seeing a second blow about to descend, he abruptly terminated the dance, and rushed of .t the top of his speed. The stroke missed, but its force overbalanced him who dealt it, and Tom Gervaise staggered repeatedly ere he could regain his equilibrium. During these reelings the other negro made his escape, or he would surely have suffered for the transgression of his comrade. Had Tom's ability equalled his great revenge, he would have given chase; but the niggers were off like young roes, and his crazy old machine might as well have tried to scale the heavens as to catch them. On his turning a corner, however, an unexpected chance hove in sight; for there, upon a high rocky bank, stood Arthur Brune with a telescope in his hand, looking seaward and landward, and into the many-coloured woods, and adown the long straight Spanish Town road over which they had lately driven.

"Hollo, Arthur! stop that black rascal," shouted Tom. If Tom's lungs had been as good as they were twenty years ago, instead of a wheezy, dilapidated old bellows, Brune could not have heard. Tom

him across his shins, even with a slight switch, is to discover the mainspring of his system. It drives him frantic.

fancied, though, that he had roared with pristine vigour, when he saw Arthur throw himself suddenly from his eminence and rush across the field. Already he clutched his stick with a humane grasp, and limped towards the prey like an old lion whose jackall is in certain cry, when, to his surprise and indignation, he perceived that Arthur's course would not cut off the escape of the negro, but that it was directed to some other object. Undoubtedly it was so. Arthur had neither heard Tom's shout nor seen his pursuit, nor been thinking of Tom's quarrel, or anything that was his. He had walked abroad, restless with checkered thoughts, and taken a glass from the inn, that the sights of external nature might, if they could, quell the tumult of his hope and difficulty, and joy and fear. And as he curiously scanned the long line of road, and watched the passengers, there came in sight a carriage driven with furious speed—so fast that it fairly riveted his vagrant attention. Was the driver mad, or drunk, or helpless? He must be one or other, for the son of Nimshi never drave like this. Rapidly the outlines became more distinct. There were two horses before the flying vehicle, and two persons within it. Yes; and now there is the streaming of a light garment and a fluttering veil: one of them is a woman. Another instant, and his heart seems to recognise the dress—

the figure—the very features! Merciful heaven! Violet herself!! And, like a demigod, Arthur bounded to the rescue.

He shot across the field, he leapt the fence, and cleared the yard, and tore down the rickety gate and the rickety gate-post fast locked to it, and stood in the road while yet the reeling car was several yards off. It was a curricle; the reins and whip still in the hands of Melhado, who, white and wild, seemed to clutch them convulsively, but to have lost all sense and nerves and motion. A sharp jar behind Arthur told that the toll-man had shut-to the gate (for a difficult wooden bridge had superseded the old ferry). Arthur waved his hat to show that the danger was understood, and Violet knew at once who made that gesture. The sight of the strong and daring young man gave her confidence; her lover's presence made her scorn the danger. Her eye was true, her brain was clear; she comprehended Brune's signs, for the mind and heart of that man, were they not her heart and mind? and she rose without trepidation or confusion, and, clearing her clothes from her feet, and from the side of the carriage, stood for a few moments calm and steady as the frantic coursers dashed towards him. Then she cast herself, without faltering, into the arms of Arthur Brune, who, strong and active as he was, staggered and fell with the shock, but not till he had broken the fall and shielded Violet from serious harm. Scratched and bruised, he was up again in a second, and Violet in the same time was in charge of the "leady" of the house. But before that second had elapsed the mad steeds had swerved at the gate, and, turning sharply, flung out poor Melhado into the deep mud of the creek; then they continued their course on to the filthy swamp that skirts the sea, where, amid mangrove stumps and mud, their career was stopped, and they tore, and fretted, and kicked at the handsome curricle.

The toll-man and the two negroes of the crab adventure fished out, after some little time, the wretched Melhado, his gay clothes covered with black mud, his hat gone, and his hair—nay, his very eyes and nose—filled with the soil of the creek. As they landed him, Tom Gervaise just came, blowing and fuming, on the scene; and at sight of that avenger the two blacks dropped their exhausted burden on the creek side and fled. Tom, being very much out of breath, and seeing pretty plainly what had happened, did not ask questions or make remarks, but quietly surveyed Melhado, as he leaned upon his stick and smoked. The sight seemed to give him satisfaction, for Tom, who knew of Manuel's shortcomings as a charioteer, and who was wroth at his costly turn-out, had often prophesied a "smash." Manuel, from exhaustion and suffocation, could not speak, and Tom, as we have said, would not; but the latter, after a minute or two, began to move slowly round the unlucky Phaëton, pausing at intervals in his revolutions, so as to ascertain the whole extent of the discomfiture. At one of these halts he espied a little spot below the coat collar which had by chance been left untouched by the mud, and upon this Tom carefully broke off the ashes of his weed, which, in his abstraction, he had allowed to grow half an inch long. Having at length assured himself of Manuel's utter humiliation, and noted all the circumstances of his plight to tell at mess, and for general conversation, he suggested to the toll-man that it would be better to pour a few buckets of water over the gentleman till he should be fit to touch, and then to get him taken into the house and put to bed. The fugitive blacks did not return, but the servants of Mr Arabin (who had by this time come up), and some people from the inn, came and lifted Manuel once more. Christy had of course gone to ascertain the condition of his daughter, and been inexpressibly relieved at finding her safe. He cordially thanked Arthur Brune. Then he went to see after his future son-in-law, and arrived just in time to take the direction of the case out of the hands of Tom Gervaise, and to see poor Manuel properly cared for. Tom, it will be remembered, knew nothing of Violet's accident, or even of her being there; therefore, when he surrendered Melhado to old Christy, his next object of interest was the curricle, up to the axles in mud, and before which the horses, hampered by the mire, were yet tugging and plunging, breaking the harness by degrees, but not yet clear. He privately admitted that the horses were admirable, — well bred, well matched, and beautifully formed; also that the equipage in general was unexceptionable. But he consoled himself for the admission by reflecting that the wealth which could command these treasures could not buy the skill to handle them. And so Tom went off to look after his own team and cart, which, if less showy, he flattered himself would be tooled home by the first practitioner in the island. While he was in the stable-yard Mr Arabin came in, after seeing his son-in-law stripped, and washed, and put to bed, to look at the miserable remains of Melhado's fine equipage and his pair of splendid horses, which had by this time been extricated from the mud.

"Lucky you came in," said Tom, "or that fellow would have rubbed a hole in your horse in another minute." The horse was in no danger of being rubbed through; on the contrary, he was getting the faintest possible shadow of a rubbing, though the coachman, stripped, and hissing through his teeth, made a great show of exertion. Tom therefore spoke in bitter irony, which caused Christy to appeal to the feelings of his servant by tender advice and hints of cowskin. After these the coachman hissed a good deal harder, showing that he was accessible to gentle reproof.

Then they smoked for some time over the wreck, when Tom broke silence by saying, "Devilish clever business!" Christy shrugged his shoulders. "Shocking, shocking," said he; "but I can't grieve over the horses and trap when I think of the escape my daughter had. I expected to find her maimed, or even killed. Thank God!" after which unusual ejaculation Christy wiped his brow; then he added, "Remarkable clever active young man, that Brune, and no mistake about it. Owe him Violet's life; glad to find he is not much hurt."

Gervaise, not being cognisant of the events alluded to, asked Mr Arabin to explain his dark sayings, and thereupon Christy repeated as it had been told to him the perilous adventure, winding up again with a hearty commendation of Arthur.

"Humph!" grunted Tom, "you should have laid those remarks to heart before. Nobody 'll dispute with you that Arthur's a devilish fine fellow. We fancied once that you admired him as much as any-

R

body; thought *he* would have been your son-in-law, instead of that miserable, disagreeable spoon!" and Tom pointed his thumb over his shoulder towards the room where poor Manuel lay, holding the cigar between the middle fingers of the same hand.

"Ah, did they indeed?" answered Christy. The remark made him very angry, as he called up plaguy old ideas, which he hadn't half set to sleep; moreover, the facts of the last hour seemed to din in his ears the same doctrine. Christy was a tolerably free-and-easy fellow, and could stand a good deal, but yet we think that such a remark just then would have induced him to quarrel with many men. It was, however, perfectly useless to have a row with Tom Gervaise. The shrewd old senator knew this, and therefore he held his peace and smoked gloomily away.

"Wasn't it rather rash," asked Tom, after a short interval, "to let your daughter travel in a carriage drawn by such wild cattle?"

"Wild!" answered Christy; "there were never quieter or better-tempered horses."

"Not broke to double harness then, probably?" suggested Tom.

"Perfectly broke, sir; a baby might drive them."

"Then I suppose some infernal accident set 'em off?"

"Accident!" repeated Christy, now recurring to the origin of the disaster, and forgetting everything else, "there was not the shadow of an accident. Damme, sir, a pair of pet lambs would have been turned into hyenas by such handling. The poor brutes showed immense docility by only running away; I wonder they didn't——" Then catching on Tom's face a look of well-satisfied contempt, Christy became aware of his indiscretion, and concluded by saying, "Well, it's of no use talking about it now; the thing's over, and I'm thankful it was no worse."

"Always said it would come to this," said Tom, who was so delighted at the fulfilment of his prediction, that, having occasion to take a fresh cigar from his case, he offered one to Christy, an honour which he seldom conferred on anybody.

"No, thank 'ee," said Christy; "I always like my own better than any other; suppose you try one, and see what you think of it."

Tom Gervaise took two, whereof he lighted one and put the other into his case, returning at the same time that which he had first intended to consume. The tobacco re-established amicable relations, as if they had been a couple of red Indians. Tom guessed that he was helping Arthur Brune by keeping old Christy outside, and so he discussed the points of the horses, the build of the carriage, and the method of shoeing, at length; he also made some valuable remarks concerning bearing-reins, which amused the councillor, and detained him a good while.

Meanwhile the lady of the house, in her own apartment, gave a vent to her feelings on the late occurrences.

"My! dat buckrah is reelly a noble young man! And it is a sweet nyoung leady, too. How he catch her!—so. My king! it must have sweet * her to be save dat way. When I have been catched in a nyoung man's arms, I find it very pleasant. It is quite de ting to make people love one another!"

"Dat won't do, Miss French," said Christy's coachman, who happened to come into the room; "she goin' to marry de gentleman dat come out of de creek."

"No matter for dat, my good sir," pursued Miss French; "she love dis handsome buckrah, if I know anything about sich matters. I obserbe her look. Chaw! don't tell me! And as for dat Meesta Melhado, he no good. I know'd his fader well. He stop often at dis house when he was a member of de Assembly. He drink nuttin' but brandy, and he bring his own bottle. Chaw!"

Arthur, we may be sure, made use of the opportunity thus afforded him. Violet had really suffered

* Delighted.

nothing more than fright; and when they had taken her into the house, laid her on the sofa, and given her some smelling-salts, she declared that she felt steadier, and would soon be composed again. The landlady ordered in for her a glass of raw brandy, which, not being desired by Violet, was mingled with some cold water and swallowed by her parent. Christy was soon satisfied by her assurances and by her good spirits that Violet had sustained no injury; and therefore, when he heard of Melhado's plight, he went off to examine it for himself.

"Dearest Violet," said Arthur, when they were alone, "this opportunity is most valuable; but as it may be interrupted at any moment, let me, without preface, speak of some weighty matters. My plan is being matured rapidly. Everything seems propitious. My journey to Spanish Town has been attended with complete success; for, see, here is a document which charters for us both, let us trust, long years of happiness. Nay, dearest, I cannot allow myself the pleasure of seeing you read its contents; the time may not permit; but I will tell you what it is;" and he whispered, "A marriage licence: you guess, I presume, the names of the parties."

Violet's face, which had been pale from her accident, for a moment blushed like the delicate lining of a shell which happy Nereids love to make their car; but as a mortal dream of those fair beings, the colour fled and blanched her beauty like the lily. She did not change nor falter in her decision; but yet the sight of such a document might well send back the blood to her heart. What before had been indefinite and uncertain, seemed now confirmed by the seal of destiny. A hundred thoughts rose up within her, each claiming attention, when none could receive any. Oh that she could have wept! but no, Arthur has words that crowd into that span of time, and Violet must listen now, and reflect, and, it may be, weep, when he is gone. And clearly and rapidly did Brune then detail a scheme which we do not give in his words, because the course of our story will develop it. With scarcely beating heart she heard him to an end. When he had ceased she was a few moments silent. Then a low voice, coming as it were from the depths of her heart, murmured—"Be it so, Arthur: I consent."

"Bless you for that," said Arthur; "I cannot thank you as I would in this almost public room. An indiscretion might subvert our whole design. Therefore I behave like an ordinary acquaintance now, that hereafter I may be acknowledged as your choice before all the world." And Brune refrained himself, and sat at a distance, and spoke of matters indifferent till the entrance of Mr Arabin and Tom

Gervaise, which soon took place. Christy, having ascertained that Violet continued to retain her self-possession, turned to Arthur Brune.

"And you, Mr Brune, how do you feel now?"

"Oh," said Arthur, "I had quite forgotten that I am hurt. A little sore, thank you, but nothing worse."

"Allow me to order in some champagne," said Christy; "we shall all be the better for it—don't you think so?"

"None for me, papa," said Violet; "I do not require it."

"And I," said Brune, "had been taking good things of all sorts in plenty before you came up; so I had rather have nothing more."

Christy now looked at Tom Gervaise, who, on principle, said he would not mind a glass with Mr Arabin; accordingly those two seasoned vessels imbibed a little more wet.

"I say, Gervaise," observed Arthur, "remember you are to drive me home. Don't take any more, or you'll upset us."

"Not I," said Tom; "I don't deal in upsets. As long as I can see, or even feel, I can drive straight. Only your jimmy-jessamy conceited muffs that go to smash and endanger ladies' lives!" Tom looked sternly at Violet as he spoke, intending to convey to her that contrition alone, and an entire change of conduct, could win his forgiveness for ever encouraging Melhado.

There was nothing now to prevent their departure, so Tom and Arthur set off, leaving Christy and Violet to follow; while Melhado, who was ascertained to be uninjured, was to remain in bed, and have clothes and a carriage sent for him next morning.

"I'll be hanged," said Tom, in excess of admiration, "if I couldn't marry that girl myself!"

"Could you, old boy?" said Arthur.

"That is, if I were a marrying man," explained Tom, careful even in his enthusiasm.

Arthur was too much excited to converse. His pulse beat strong, for the events of the afternoon had brought him unexpected aid, and the sight of Violet, and the opportunity of preserving her, wrought his spirit to its highest mood. Long his thoughts fermented within him; at last, when they were far on their way, the fire kindled for a moment into utterance, and he burst forth—

"By Aphrodite and her mischievous son, the Fates, it seems, will have it so. Be propitious, ye powers, but a little longer, and I win the fairest bride since Helen!"

Tom nodded assent, but did not commit himself to words, having dropped his acquaintance with mythological personages, except a malignant power presiding over men's eyes with whom he maintained a constant intercourse, and on whose favour he greatly presumed, insomuch that the whole time of the divinity must have been occupied by the frequent, and, it might be said, wanton requisitions which he made on his own and his neighbours' account.

Tom, too, had his pleasant meditations, and evidently felt that the accidents just passed were in harmony with his own ideas of the eternal fitness of things. He, also, could not at one time forbear to speak his satisfaction.

"A counter-jumping snob! I sent him word that I'd upset him the first time I met him on the road, but I needn't have intended the trouble. Such a whelp is sure to smash himself. If old Arabin hadn't come out, I'd have had him under the pump, as sure as his name's Melhado. Serve him right too, the conceited ass!"

CHAPTER XIV.

AT length arrived the evening which was to witness the delightful ceremony of *wetting* Captain Clutterbuck's commission. The event had created a great sensation. Clutterbuck had asked as many guests, civil and military, as the room would hold. The messman had made unheard-of preparations. Fortunately an American ice-ship was in the harbour, and that there might be no failure of this luxury, a quantity which must have weighed several tons had been purchased, and piled up at one end of the room in blocks like a grotto or fernery, creating in that neighbourhood a radiation of sharp cold which might have been expected to cause serious illness to those who were placed within its influence. It is not, however, recorded that any of that jovial party suffered even inconvenience. At the cold end they drank plenty of wine to keep up the steam, and at the warm end they employed the same remedy against the heat and relaxation. Old Clut had seen to the cooling of the wine and other liquors himself, and lived in a nervous, excited state all day, having never before been the hero of such an entertainment. Half an hour before dinner-time he was in the mess-verandah in the very coolest arrangement of costume, but no more cool than a salamander would be if he had his shell-jacket carefully turned down, and wore a waistcoat and trousers of a material not much thicker than cambric. He fidgeted through the half-hour at last, and then the company began to arrive, on foot and on horseback, and in gigs and top-chaises and waggons. In the lower storey under the verandah three or four white mess-servants marshalled a staff of negro waiters in white suits; these received an augmentation at the arrival of nearly every guest, by his domestic joining their ranks.

Such a clatter there was in the verandah above, after a dozen or two had come in and given old Clut each a torrid shake of the hand, which is not the pleasantest thing in life, though never dispensed with here! Besides soldiers and sailors, there were lawyers and clergymen, and planters and dealers. Christy Arabin's conveyance disgorged its owner and Melhado for the upper regions, and Mr Chitty and another gentleman of colour for the black ranks underneath, where Mr C. at first assumed the airs of a pampered menial, but was speedily reduced to order by the white waiters. This check rendered him externally sulky, and inwardly determined to double the amount of pillage in the way of wine, fruits, sweets, &c., which he had previously intended to carry off. The Rev. Mr Grant was there, and an acting judge who held a lower permanent appointment—a functionary of Irish extraction, heavy embarrassments, and a social turn. Bitters were handed about in liqueur-glasses to provoke appetite. It was with reference to these preparations that Tom Gervaise performed, on this occasion, his solitary act of self-denial. He firmly refused to take any bitters, feeling bound to reserve every cranny for the feast that was at hand, and to take the edge off his thirst with the iced punch that was to follow the turtle. Tom was in great feather. There were some yahoos, or Johnny Raws, belonging to the last reinforcement, and only a few days on the island. These young gentlemen were in a state of pleasing distraction at finding out the entire incorrectness of the ideas which, before and during the voyage, they had formed of Jamaica. The lowering atmosphere, fœtid with miasmata and mist, the arid plains marked only by gravestones, the sickly miserable population, of which they had dreamed—where were all these? At present they are simply dizzy with the agreeable disappointment: by-and-by they will vote the whole account a bugbear, become foolhardy, and pay for this temerity with their health or lives. During the dawn of reaction on the minds of unsophisticated youth like these, it was one of the benevolent pleasures of the excellent Gervaise to caution or to reassure them as to the phenomena of the island. One after another they approached the corner where Tom was standing, and hung upon the accents of his kind experience. It was only now and then that Tom's lore was audible amid the babel, but a few gems were overheard and recorded. For instance, he said to an open-mouthed weedy youngster:—

"Earthquakes, my dear friend! they're so common that we think nothing about 'em. Just look at my shirt that was shivered by one as I drove down to dinner from Stony Hill;" and Tom drew attention to his best shirt, the bosom of which had been plaited, but was now split into ribbons.

Soon after he was heard saying, "Fever be hanged! you only get fever through funking. Live like a man; take your liquor heartily, and eat the country peppers —you'll never have fever then. Daresay your mother told you to be temperate, and avoid the night air. All women are fools."

And, just before dinner was announced, Tom told them, "If a yam is at all large, it comes out of the ground with its roots scorched: they don't dare to dig foundations for the houses; that's the reason they are all on piers: in fact, it's well known that there's only a sheet of brown paper between this and h— f—."

As he pronounced the last words, whatever they were, Tom saw the archdeacon looking at him from the other end of the gallery far beyond earshot, whereupon he cast down his eyes and muttered, "You be hanged," as if rehearsing a convincing and exculpatory answer to a supposed rebuke of the dignitary.

Dinner is served at last, and, after a short scramble, the multitude is arranged in order around the board, Clutterbuck in the chair as governor of the feast, supported by a clergyman and a colonial officer of state. The army and navy distributed themselves among the plain coats, the archdeacon said grace, and the feast began. If that party wasn't in spirits, outward and visible signs are a mockery, a delusion, and a snare. Reserve or affectation there was none: the jokes were a little broad, perhaps, and some of them a thought personal and glass-papery, but the laughs had the genuine ring, and the appetites did credit to the bitters. The colonel of the regiment sat between Arabin and Melhado, doing honour to Christy as a member of Council and leading colonist, and to the other as a person about to form a great connection, and wed the belle of the island. Melhado, who had never before been treated with such distinction, was immensely pleased with it, and wished that his mother could only look in upon the dinner. Those about him expressed great regret for his misfortune at the Ferry, and did not hint at any fault on his part. Brune had withdrawn himself among a slow set on the same side of the table as, but remote from, Tom Gervaise, lest his voice or neighbourhood should tempt Thomas into incautious candour when the bands of his discretion should be loosed by the champagne. Pat Shane, in a noisy corner of the table, effected a rapid interchange of ideas with some choice spirits, who had apparently determined not only to dispel care and sorrow for a few short hours, but to push hilarity to the extremes of decorum. On Gervaise's left hand sat one of his juvenile friends, who, fascinated by his conversation, had almost jostled a civilian to procure the place; his right was occupied by a fine, old, hard-baked planter, who had been forty years in the colony, and never in that time flinched from food or drink. This gentleman's habits being eminently practical, he had no energy left for conversation. Tom, nevertheless, liked his society, feeling the propinquity of so indomitable a reveller to be a great moral support.

Immediately after the turtle and punch commenced the challenging in champagne, and men did not cease to dare each other to that refreshing encounter till land-crabs and cheese brought malt liquor once more to a premium, and that beverage blew off its indignation, engendered by previous undeserved neglect, in vicious and frequent pops. Pat Shane's party went very recklessly at the long-necks, not considering the work that lay before them.

"What the devil," said Pat Shane, "is the use of taking thimblefuls of champagne with one another—a glass with you and a glass with you, in that tadious way? Why not drink from tumblers, and all together?" This suggestion was acted upon as 'soon as made.

"Look at that hangdog haberdasher, Melhado, now," said Pat in a high voice, under the influence of these improved draughts. "Oi hate him, so I do. There's a fellow to be faysted like a big-wig, and to be sitting cheek by jowl with the colonel! Tom, you must tell us again of the figure he cut when they drew him out of the creek, the baste! It's a new way of boultin' a pike, first to boult to the right, then to go boult into the creek, and then to boult six quarts of mud: there's a sintince for ye with as many *boults* in it as there are in the ironmongery department of the villain's own store, or on Tim Whelan's door at Sligo, who fastened nineteen on th' outside of it, to show what a dale of treasure was within. To handle a whip nately comes close after a good finger for a hair-trigger or a strong head for liquids in the scale of blessings and graces, but to be murtherin' a lovely crayther, and destroying a curricle, and taking a mud bath, isn't any grace at all, but a *dis*grace intirely. Be me sowl, if that darlint girl was of my mind, sorrow a touch she'd let the crummugeon feel of her dilicate hand. This is to her health; I wish 'twas whisky, and she'd know the ginuineness of my devotion. There's truth in wine, they say; but there's Scripture trust in the mountain dew. The people that made that saying about the wine was ignorant haythens, unacquainted with the Bible and poteen. He's not married yet, and there's many a slip betwixt the cup and the lip."

No consideration was strong enough to prevent Tom Gervaise calling across the table:—

"He little thinks what's in store for him to-night, Pat."

"Indeed he does not," said Shane, imagining that Gervaise alluded to the fight that had been arranged.

Another person had been listening to the conversation: that was Mr Chitty, who had been busy in assisting Shane and his friends to champagne, and passing bottles three parts full to accomplices in the verandah. When Nick heard Gervaise's remark, a suspicion of some treachery rushed across him, insomuch that he involuntarily gave utterance to a "Hei!"

"Now then, Julius Sasar," said Pat Shane, using his generic term for all negroes with whom he was not personally acquainted—"now then, don't be making use of haythen interjections behind a Christian gintleman's chair; but fill moi tumbler—don't you see it's impty? I can't see for the loife of me why we shouldn't have a dozen or so of bottles on the table, or within reach, instid of being depindint upon divils like you. 'Tisn't the fashion to use your own hands for anything. By-and-by a man won't be able to shave himself or commit suicide without somebody to do it for him!"

"Soaker," called Tom Gervaise to a fiery-faced officer who sat opposite, with vacant, staring eyes, "a glass of champagne with you. What's become of Lofthouse of yours? don't see him here."

"Oh, he can't come. There's somebody sick: his wife, or one of his children, or something of that sort."

"Your health! The deuce take women and children!" said Tom, draining his glass.

The sot opposite bowed too, and raised his wine, but set it down again untasted when he heard the last part of Tom's toast. He thought of a little, motherless, neglected girl, made over to the care of strangers in England, and was conscience-stricken and unhappy for five minutes: at the end of which time he called for a glass of brandy, and proceeded to drink himself blind.

Poor Arthur all this time was not enjoying himself. He sat nearly opposite to Melhado, the sight and voice of whom did not tend to soothe the excitement he was suffering. Had he not well considered the step he was about to take, and assured himself that it was, under all the circumstances, his duty to take it, his manly nature could not have endured to sit at the same board in seeming charity and good-fellowship with one whom he was plotting to disappoint so grievously. Few men, we fancy, would have entertained such scruples, and many a man would have laughed in his sleeve at the thought of outwitting a treacherous and ungenerous rival. Nevertheless it required Brune's recollection of that *other* happiness that was at stake besides his own to prevent his renouncing his plan. He sat near Mr Grant, with whom he endeavoured to keep up a conversation that was to banish for a time the thought of the adventure arranged for the coming night. To Mr Grant this was comparatively easy, as he got on his hobby of marrying all the negroes to regenerate them, but to

Arthur it was not congenial work. He was not a man, either, to be allowed to keep in the background. Usually one of the merriest companions, with a wit which, if not always scintillating, did not stoop to abortive jokes, but gave out something to tickle when it *did* speak—a referee on all sporting matters—the best-read military man and the truest soldier among them, and noted for sound discretion, though by no means for presumption, in the conduct of worldly affairs; being, above all, of a kind and affable disposition, nis notice was challenged by all sorts and conditions of men. "Brune, a glass of champagne?" "Brune, we've not taken wine!" were continually the invitations addressed to him. Christy Arabin, now relieved of the dread of having him for a son-in-law, and grateful for his late rescue of Violet, indulged his predilection for Arthur, and made overtures to converse with him.

"Fine young man that," said old Christy, in a low voice, to his neighbour the colonel, after failing for the third or fourth time to provoke Brune's conversation.

"The most promising I know, in the regiment or out of it. If he escapes the perils of this place and this society—as I believe he will, for he has sense and firmness—his name will be better known than it is now."

"No, none of that stuff," said Gervaise to a servant who offered him curry—"none of that; I've got a very pretty thirst on me without." But Tom immediately repented of his forbearance, and called after the man, "Hollo! come back here; it looks amazingly good—I'll have a little;" and so it was with everything presented to him.

Clutterbuck tried to look cool, and to do the honours in a manner becoming the occasion. In the first endeavour he was not successful; in the second he succeeded as long as his faculties lasted. Imagining it to be his duty to set a great ensample of making merry (where, indeed, no man required either practice or precept to prompt him), he was incessant in his invitations to take champagne, and the number of glasses he got through was astonishing, considering what a sober and regular man he was. Pat Shane remarked, that "if mere instinct could do so much, what might not such a man achieve if liberally educated! But, then, Clut had no proper ambition, and would not cultivate his talent." The task which he had set himself for this exceptional occasion was certainly herculean, and Clut's gallantry succumbed at last. After he ceased to bow and talk, he rested his head on his hand, and continued his bland smile of hospitality, though rather less expressively than before.

The most delightful ceremonies must conclude, and Clutterbuck's dinner,—after wending its glorious way through turtle and mulligatawney, thence to callipever, mountain mullet, and flying-fish; then again to ragouts of turtle, alligators' eggs, fricasseed iguana, and other native *entrées;* next culminating in saddle and sirloin as at home, subsiding into wild guinea-fowl and wood-pigeons, and winding up with mango tarts, shaddock fritters, pine-apple jelly, and creams and sweets *ad infinitum,*—came to an end. The grace was said, the cloth withdrawn, the mess mahogany shone out well rubbed for the occasion, and the decanters and dessert took their turn. Christy Arabin himself, in a neat speech, proposed Captain Clutterbuck's health, and long life to him, after enumerating his many virtues and illustrious achievements. Clutterbuck expended his last effort of will in keeping his legs for three minutes, and giving vent to a flow of oratory remarkable rather for the fusion of its words and the repetition of its phrases than for force or originality. Nevertheless, it must certainly have possessed merit of some kind, for, as Clutterbuck sank once more into his chair, the cheering was vociferous, and the rapping and rattling could hardly be induced to stop.

As Tom Gervaise became now less busy than he had been for the last hour and a half, he once more delighted the admiring ensign with his affability, and sought to illuminate the tyro's mind.

"Is that archdeacon a clever man, Captain Gervaise?" asked the lad.

"Wonderfully so," replied Tom.

"He doesn't look it, though he has a good appetite and takes his wine kindly. What's his line?"

"Sermons and general science," said Tom.

"Ah, I don't read that sort much, but I read lots of advertisements, and don't recollect his name. Do you remember any recent production?"

Gervaise paused to examine his memory, and then said, "He is bringing out an interesting treatise on the digestibility of land-crabs, and their pretensions as an article of food. Didn't you observe him at dinner practising what he preaches, and tucking them in one after another?"

"Didn't he! But why is it necessary to write about them? I suppose people here know perfectly well whether land-crabs agree with them or not without a clergyman's voucher!"

"The book is supposed," said Tom, "to be a reply to his wife, who won't let him eat them (though he doats on 'em), because they killed his predecessor. He doesn't dare to contradict her to her face."

"The deuce! what a spoon! Is she an Amazon?"

"That little delicate woman you were talking to the other night at old Lopez's, with her dress so terribly scanty at both ends!"

"That his wife! why, she's as gentle as a dove; and such spicy ankles! By Jove, Captain! you don't mean to say he's afraid of such a little duck as that!"

"You should see," said Tom, "the milliners' bills that he has to pay to soothe her. It costs three-fourths of his income to keep her indecent."

"I thought her the very picture of neatness. Hasn't she nice feet, though, and ankles, and, for the matter of that——"

"For shame, young man!" said Tom Gervaise.

The ensign coloured scarlet, and rapidly changed the subject.

"And who's that vivacious little squinting man in spectacles, Captain?"

"That; oh, that's Lawyer Blake, now acting judge —a broth of a boy."

"Very learned, I daresay?"

"In a cockpit or at picquet you can't match him, especially after midnight. He knows a good many things, but law isn't one of them."

"How did he get a government appointment, then?"

"Because he was bankrupt in pocket and reputation, and just the sort of reprobate that unscrupulous ministers send out to draw colonial salaries and degrade colonial courts: not a bad fellow, though," said Tom. "Listen; he is going to sing."

And Acting Judge Blake, whose mercury now stood at an exceedingly genial and large-hearted temperature, sang with much expression and no voice a popular Irish melody, which appeared to give the greatest satisfaction. The learned gentleman then, in right of his melodious achievement, called upon Captain Clutterbuck to sing himself in, making a very humorous speech in humble imitation of Counsellor Curran. But, far from being able to sing, Clut could scarcely articulate; and two or three of his friends, of whom Arthur Brune was foremost, having requested Mr Knox to take the chair, escorted the new-made captain to his quarters, where they carefully undressed him and placed him in bed, setting a light near, and a glass of weak brandy-and-water within his reach; and Arthur Brune threatened Clut's domestic with very dreadful pains and penalties if he should defraud his unconscious massa of one drop of the mixture. Arthur did not return to the mess-table that night, and many of the graver guests likewise withdrew, leaving a numerous invincible phalanx, who resolutely closed their ranks towards the head of the table, and never allowed a blank chair to hint for an instant that the evening was growing old. Perfect enjoyment could not, however, be said to be attained until the colonel, having risen, invited some of the elder officers to take coffee at his house. He included Arabin and Melhado in his invitation; but these gentlemen, it appeared, were under engagement to play a game of cards in Mr Knox's rooms. Christy was just beginning to feel himself a boy again, and did not consider any man his friend who desired to take him home before morning. It was in those days the custom of every mess in Jamaica to allow the introduction of cigars and brandy-and-water after a certain hour in the evening. No sooner, therefore, had the colonel and his companions departed, than each man began to blow his cloud and to require a tumbler and some iced water. The singing recommenced with spirit, and became very hearty and humorous. It would be easy to name and publish several choice melodies which were performed on this occasion with unbounded applause. They are, however, suppressed, under the fear that they might be less palatable to the refined reader than they were to the jolly companions who heard them. The learned acting judge was frequently called upon, and never in vain. Pat Shane's canticles were remarkable rather for boisterousness than for prudery. Even old Christy, after his first tumbler, became infected with the spirit of harmony, and poured forth his soul in a ditty which did little credit to his taste and his grey hairs, but which delighted his hearers more than anything they heard from their contemporaries.

Captain Thomas Gervaise was not addicted to singing, and the advanced bacchanal next him seldom used his voice in any way after five o'clock in the afternoon. These two respected gentlemen were therefore understood to be excused from vocal obligations. But Pat Shane viewed their exemption with extreme disapprobation, and even railed at Tom for the honourable privilege which he enjoyed, saying, "Tom, y'unmelodious ould monument, how can ye remain silent when there's every incintive to harmony? Your face is loike the lion's head on a waterpipe, and gives out no sound but the gurgling and gulping of fluids. Here we've been piping to ye like them blessed babbies in the marketplace, without projuicing the desired effect. Ye must chant, Tom, me boy. I'll tell ye now; be the ghost of Moses, I'll give ye a clane new shirt if ye'll sing us a song!"

"You haven't got credit for a shirt in all Jamaica," said Tom; "you're obliged to send to Ireland for home-spun linen, or you'd go naked. You don't fancy I'd wear such stuff as that!"

"Calico houlds the dirt better, and so ye prefer it, I'm thinking," replied Pat; whereupon Tom showed the head of his stick above the table as a caution.

Mr Knox, from the chair of state, made proclamation that there should be one more song all round, and then an adjournment to his apartments to enjoy coffee and chicken-hazard, or any innocent recreation which gentlemen might prefer.

"Only one more!!" echoed several voices, discontentedly. "Remember he said *all round!*" put in Pat Shane, "and round things have no end; so clear your chanters and begin. Here's an ould cock that'll crow with any of ye yet," saying which he smote Christy Arabin smartly on the back; for in the various disturbances which had recently taken place in the symposial system, Pat's orbit had been erratic, and he had finally gravitated to Christy's elbow.

This last circuit of the muse was of course the most remarkable of the evening. Earlier efforts might have excelled in grace or sentiment, but in respect of massive power, unassisted by art or ornament, the palm was unquestionably due to the crowning round. Many of its songs required a chorus, and all the others obtained that support, whether they required it or not. Finally, in refutation of any censorious cynics who might insinuate that the orgies had been prolonged to exhaustion or excess, the whole band filed down the mess-room steps and on to Knox's rooms, raising a chant in praise of punch, as *fresh* as those Normans who advanced to Hastings fight singing the songs of Rollo!

CHAPTER XV.

IT is necessary now that we take note of Mr Chitty's movements. After descending from the mess-room, and after doing all that was in his heart as regarded the consumption and purloining of viands, Menelaus bethought him of that expression used by Tom Gervaise during dinner, which had unpleasantly affected his nerves, and which still, whenever he thought of it, caused an unaccountable misgiving. The fact was, that Nick's mind had been for some days much unsettled—indeed, since Brune's appearance at Crystal Mount. That appearance Nick conceived to bode no good to Christy's family arrangements; it was, moreover, associated with the pang arising out of a suspected understanding between Leander and Rosabella; so that, altogether, it excited a disagreeable foreboding, which various small incidents appreciable to Chitty's keen perception had augmented. Wine and feasting, as is generally the case in rancorous minds, far from dissipating, only intensified his apprehensions. He could extract no definite suspicion from the meagre evidence, and felt the need of counsel and confidence. How to get these was the question. To call Christy from the festive board to listen to a cock-and-bull story (as this would be, even when lavishly embellished with lies), would have no effect save to bring down anathemas on his head as an old idiot; to call on Melhado would bring blows in addition to abuse. In this dilemma he betook himself to a keener wit than either of theirs; and as soon as he could eat and drink no more, and had bestowed his movable plunder, he started off through the bush to Kingston, and stopped not till he arrived at the door of Melhado's house, where he craved an audience with that gentleman's mother.

The old lady was at that time seated on a rocking-chair in her saloon, which was lit by a number of wax-lights under brilliant glass shades.* Her spectacles were on, and the Rev. Laurence Sterne's 'Sentimental Journey' lay open before her; for she was a wilful old dame, and not to be deprived of the enjoyment of real wit and sentiment by nonsensical

---

* The reader who has not visited the tropics will reflect that, where windows and doors are open, and every breath of air is invited to enter, candles must speedily be blown out if not protected.

squeamishness. Show her any of your correct moderns who could write like him, and she would think your prejudice entitled to attention; but you knew very well you couldn't.

A young negress with a red handkerchief on her head, and wearing one solitary garment, the name of which we are not at liberty to communicate, but whose material was *osnaburgh*, brandished a flapper, with which she chased the mosquitoes from her "Missy," and controlled the frolics of moths, bats, crickets, fiddlers, cockroaches, and a host of winged insects which made a disagreeable humming and buzzing, and were continually dashing themselves against the glass shades in attempts to get at the lights: occasionally they took headers against the old lady's eyes and cheeks. As is the case with many strong-minded persons, Mrs Melhado was not gifted with extreme patience; and whenever a crawley-bob succeeded in charging her, she sharply chid her attendant. Sometimes she aimed a vicious blow, which the small obscurity generally evaded. The subtle plotter, who never ceased to keep a watch upon Brune, knew of his visits to Crystal Mount, and of the rescue at the Ferry. She felt sure that these things had a great significance, and was much disturbed in consequence, so that the child was experiencing a crosser time than usual.

"Bunchy, you little aggravating toad," said Mrs Melhado, "what did I tell you?"

"Missy say she 'mash for me wortless head de nex one dat touch she!"

"I did; and now come here: one nearly blinded me this minute, and there's another up my nose while I speak: come here."

"No, no, no, no! I beg you, my sweet Missy, I beg you!"

"Come when I tell you. It will be worse for you if I have to rise."

"Hi-yi-yi-yi!" howled Bunchy; "me goin' for get *fum-fum:* me will dead. Oh, my king! Oh, fader!"

"Very well, I must fetch you, then," said the old gentlewoman, preparing to rise; whereupon Bunchy raised the most dreadful squealing, and set her back and the palms of her hands against the wall, while she rapidly struck the floor with her alternate naked feet. On a sudden the squealing and dancing ceased, the head was raised attentively, and the small voice said—

"Hei, Missy! somebody comin' dis side; make I go see who dere." And Bunchy glided like a dark arrow from the presence of her mistress, to reappear in an instant, and announce that Mr Chitty was without, desiring to speak with her on "impartant bisnis."

T

"Now then, Nick, what brings you here at this time of night? I thought you were at camp with your master," said Mrs Melhado, sharply, as Mr Chitty entered and made his obeisance.

He explained that he had been at camp through the dinner, which *en passant* he characterised as a "'plendid ting of de kind, an' werry elegant in de legs of beef and custards;" that he had heard several dark hints which he understood to bode no good to either Miss Wiley or to nyoung massa; that he had considered the propriety of calling the attention of Mr Arabin or Mr Melhado to his suspicions, but in his discretion, under the circumstances of meat and drink, he had refrained from consulting those gentlemen, and thought it his duty to consult Mrs Melhado.

"Right, Nick," said the old lady; "you've got some gumption. I don't think either of them would have listened to your story if you had gone to them. Tell me, now, what was said, and I shall know if it signifies."

"You see, Missy," said Nick, "dem drink in de wine faba 'ponges. Where dem put it all, me can't rightly say: tink dem mus' be holler inside, de same as de rum puncheon. De more dem swaller, de more room dem seem to got. Dat ole Cap'n Gerbaise an' Massa Shane find at las' dat dem not able for drink fas' enough out of de long glass, and dey ax for tumbler. Den it go down more faster dan a water-'pout. Couldn't sarve dem fas' enough."

"But get on, Nick," interrupted the old lady. "I want to know what was said."

Mr Chitty, being well corned, was unusually loquacious, and not very clear. His perspicuity was further impaired by the conduct of small Bunchy, who, clambering noiselessly on to a writing-table behind her Missy's back, executed a series of dumb shows of an insubordinate and contemptuous character. The gleeful spirit of healthy childhood—Heaven's gift to white and black, to bond and free—broke forth, regardless of the risk of detection and of sharp vengeance. There stood the little imp mowing and grimacing, and mimicking the old lady, at every turn of whose head she flitted to the floor in silence, like the shadow of a bird, and then mounted and began again. Had Mr Chitty been alone with the child, he most assuredly would have inflicted condign chastisement for such liberties taken in his august presence; but the freemasonry of race deterred him from betraying her to the white lady.

Spite of his difficulties, Menelaus began again: "Missy mus' hab de goodness to wait lilly bit: me is talking as fas' as me can — me can't talk no faster. Well, you see, dem mus' hab someting running in for dem troats, and when the wine no run down, de talkee run out. De noise dem make, my! and de wine it make dem more wiciouser dan mules, and dem swear an' holler; mus' a mad. Den Massa Shane begin to cuss* nyoung Massa Manuel, and say he wish him head 'mash, an' Miss Wiley too good for him. Him say so, Missy, but him don't 'peak de trut'. Me allis say dat Massa Manuel de biggest buckrah gentleman in de place. Me allis 'tand up for massa when dem cuss him. Me say all time——"

"Do get on, Nick; what did they say?"

"Ax for you pardon, Missy. Me is not de soart of pusson to weaste time in talk. Ebberybody know dat Nick Chitty one berry silent man—berry circumspec: him see good many ting dat him not tell nobody, 'ceptin' to dose dat it consarn. Now, if Missy will please to listen, me will tell de 'tory in berry few words."

Nick then went back to the beginning. Mrs Melhado perceived that her only plan was to let him have his way; so she set herself resolutely, though not very patiently, to listen. The moment her attention became fixed, Bunchy's eccentricities assumed a more daring character. The small body, without creating a sound, writhed and gesticulated not alto-

* To *curse* often signifies no more than to *abuse*.

gether ungracefully. Standing on alternate feet, she kicked, or made believe to spring, at the old lady; or she threw herself into attitudes of mock defiance and scorn : then, flourishing her little weapon like a sword, she made sweeps and passes with it through the air, and finally delivered cut No. 7 towards Mrs Melhado's crown, as if the little hand and arm had belonged to Shaw, and the flapper had been the sabre of that redoubted life-guardsman. Mr Chitty contained himself admirably, and in due time picked up the thread of his discourse. Then he proceeded—

"Massa Pat Shane, him cuss nyoung massa, and say him no good enough for Miss Wiley; and ole Cap'n Gerbaise him say, 'Look out, boy, to-night; him will be sarve a trick dat he little tink of before de morning.' Den dem cock deir yeye, and nod deir head, an' tink all right."

"It may be only some nonsense, after all," said Mrs Melhado; "was there nothing more?"

"No nonsense, Missy, no nonsense," said Nick, eagerly. "You tink ole Nick no sabey when dem goin' to do de real wickedness? Me know dem not makin' fun."

The old lady mused: "Perhaps you are right," said she. "I think that this matter, though it may mean nothing at all, should be looked to. Take a mule from the stable, and go up now, with all speed, to Crystal Mount. Don't go to bed, but observe all that is going on in the premises. If you see the least cause for alarm, send down for your master at once—your *master*, mind: it won't be sufficient to acquaint Mrs Arabin. I have never felt easy since you told me of Mr Brune being up there lately. Here, take this: I always requite useful service. And now, be off!"

Having dismissed Nick Chitty, the old lady was much disquieted, and paced the room hurriedly, quite forgetting little Bunchy, who, squatting in a gloomy corner, did not even roll her eyes, lest the motion should attract attention, and the adjourned ceremony of *fum-fum* be consummated. Her mistress was, however, occupied with far other thoughts. Though she had been interrupted, and had inserted her spectacles at that pathetic page in the 'Sentimental Journey' where the fair and gushing Rambouliet temporarily retires from the scene, she did not resume her reading. She reflected with extreme anxiety that the success or failure of her plan might depend on the discretion and fidelity of Mr Nicholas Chitty. Mrs Melhado was too shrewd not to know the spite with which fate regards such compacts as her treaty with Christy Arabin. Smooth as everything looked, a false move, or an accident, or a counter-stroke, might upset the scheme. Ready and strong-willed herself, she recognised instinctively the same qualities in Brune, and felt an undefinable dread of him, such as she was accustomed to inspire in others. Scarcely knowing the young man by sight, she had learned his character and acknowledged its force. She did not dare to reckon on success till all should be accomplished; and she was haunted by a presentiment of mischance, which her self-command barely enabled her to conceal.

She slept not that night.

Mr Chitty emerged from Melhado's house with spirits much lightened by the largesse which his tidings had obtained, and by the prospect of occasioning a little disappointment and misery ere long.

' In the stable he found a spur, which he girded to one of his heels, and soon placed in close communication with the flank of his mule; the spurring of whom, mingled with administrations of supple-jack,* quite stayed his appetite for mischief, and caused him to gallop along pleasantly, and to think calmly over what he had to do. He soon decided that, in case of summoning old Christy home, he must employ a messenger in whom he could place some confidence. Now Leander Mr Chitty at once rejected in his mind. "Him no good, him wortless," thought he, and passed on to the consideration of other ser-

* A tough *withe*, used as a whip.

vants, among whom he found it difficult to make a satisfactory selection. For Nick was aware that, on the knowledge of Big Massa being out for a jovial night, and of many neighbouring Massas being similarly engaged, a great Obeah ceremonial had been arranged on the estate, and that the adorers of Mumbo Jumbo were expected to attend in large numbers from the whole neighbourhood. If, therefore, he could succeed in finding a messenger, he could by no means depend on the message being carried quickly, or at all. After revolving then all available emissaries, as we see the Cardinal Duke de Richelieu do in Sir Edward Bulwer Lytton's play, he, with the prompt decision of that minister, fixed on our friend Domingo, whom he had used on former occcasions, and whose loyalty and zeal he thought he might be sure of for the nonce. Accordingly he pulled up the panting mule at Domingo's hut, and desired him on no account to go abroad that night, as there might be work for him which would bring a rich reward. He likewise promised a particular intercession with the Obeah sage on Domingo's behalf; and this promise seemed warranted by the intimacy and consideration which he enjoyed with that distinguished person. Large numbers of the people, both male and female, were already about the fields and paths, but it was too early for any of the Obeah rites.

Mr Chitty's own mind on the subject of Obi could not be described as one and indivisible, for he wandered sometimes into extremes of superstition and of scepticism, and traversed all degrees between those states. By night, and in times of difficulty or affliction, his faith was more or less lively; but prosperity and daylight shook his affiance—yea, even to scoffing and reviling. He had on more than one occasion so far forgotten himself as to use very strong, contemptuous, and bad language touching the solemn meeting which was now assembling; and that notwithstanding his interest with the Obeah man, and his expectation of assistance from that source in his suit to Rosabella. The recollection of this profaneness crossed his mind as he saw his single-hearted brethren collecting; and the magnitude of the power which he had provoked, and the dire results which might follow, smote his craven conscience with staggering force. What if the Obeah man, while seemingly bland and respectful, had secret notice of his calumnies and impiety! What if the caution given him to beware of another professor was simply a mode of communicating a coming doom which he felt that he so justly deserved! As these thoughts gained strength Nick was getting on to a dark and legendary part of the road, where his heart stood still with terror. It is not recorded that his hair stood on end on this or any other occasion, but there were symptoms sufficient to confirm the fact of his pot-valiant bluster being thoroughly subdued, and of his mind being in such a nervous and superstitious condition as to account for the scene which soon followed. He tried to feel plucky on emerging into a more open road, faltered an oath or so, and essayed to whistle, but produced only a tremulous asthmatic hissing which must rather have amused the spirits whom he was braving. A little more light was un-questionably a relief though, and a pull at his rum flask was not without a reactionary effect. Helped by these stimuli, Nick contrived to get off the mule's saddle and bridle, and to turn him into a piece of guinea-grass as soon as he got home. Then he took his measures for observation and concealment. Two or three times he thought he heard footsteps behind, but persuaded himself that it was fancy. The moon was not up, but it was far from dark; and after re-connoitring the house and premises, he selected for his post a small building consisting of two rooms, one over the other; the upper being a gay little pavilion commanding a fine view, and the lower a homely garden-house, to whose height the building was screened by shrubs, except that the doorway was clear, and had a good view of two sides of the dwelling-house, and of the private road which connected the property with the public way. Down here he would be admirably placed. While exercising a sharp look-out, he would himself be in deep shadow, and the absence of openings in the wall behind him would insure both eyes and ears from distraction. Against all these recommendations Nick saw one disagreeable objection to the place. There were near it one or two tombs containing the ashes of former denizens of the place, such objects being by no means uncommon on estates. In his present frame of mind he would as lief have declined their neighbourhood; but the garden-house was so eligible that he gulped down some more rum and his fear together, and made with tolerable steadiness for his station. Was it his fancy? Yes, of course it was his fancy; he was always fanciful when he felt as he did now; but he could have sworn that he saw a duppy* glide from one of the tombs, and vanish in the very building he was approaching. This nonsense was of a piece with the footsteps which he had thought he heard dogging him at intervals for the last half-hour. With great resolution he walked to and entered the building, and then he laughed at his own fears as he seated himself on a box which he felt near the door, and collected his senses for keen observation. The rum and the excitement together raised a per-

* Spirit.

suasion that his watch would not be in vain; and, as he reflected, the charming idea gained strength that he might frustrate somebody's cherished hope that night; and he not only forgot his fears, but began to have a sense of enjoyment.

"Ha, boy!" chuckled old Nick to himself, "you tink you dam clebber. Berry well, perhapsin you is. You hab plenty brains: berry good. You savey ebberyting; you not like poor black negar; him don't savey nuttin', poor debil! You make capital plan; you nebber tink dat 'tupid ole Nick Chitty able for cheat you. Ole Nick, hah! No, I ax for you pardon, *Mennylaiss*—yes, *Mennylaiss*, I believe, is de name you is please to call dat ole feller!" And Mr Chitty ground his teeth together in a charitable manner, while his countenance in the dim light of the doorway exhibited that sort of benign expression which the wolf puts on when waiting impatiently for a lamb. There was a luxury in that silent half-hour which it would have been hard to part with at all, but which it was thrice and four times distressing to have disturbed, as was at last the case; for in the very height of his reverie Mr Chitty was startled by a hideous groan: then a sepulchral voice said—

"Hei, you ole raskil, debil come fetch you at las'. Here, duppies, one, two, tree of you, take up dis ole rogue. Carry him 'trait to h—: hear 'ee?"

"Oh fader, oh murder, oh my king!" groaned Nick, in excruciating terror, and conscience-stricken. "Me nebber meaned it; me was only joking; me allis lub de Obi; ax de daddy."

"Silence, sar; no 'peak a word: hoo-o-ooo!" roared the voice, and a clap of thunder shook the room, while Chitty was violently thrust from his seat and belaboured with blows from invisible hands and sticks.

"Oh, wurrah, wurrah, wurrah! Oh fader!" groaned he.

"You 'peak anoder word, s' 'elp me Gad, me kill you 'pon de 'pot," returned the voice.

"What mus' me do, sar?" sighed Nick, submissively; "me is 'greeable to do anyting."

"Hah, dat sound more properer," the dread one replied; "dat more righter. Now, den, if you don't want to be choke outright, put for you face upon de ground and listen."

Nick prostrated himself.

"Rub for you mout' and nose well in de dirt. Now den, sar, you is not to tell no libing soul anyting you see dis night. Dere is duppies an' debils flying about plenty, perhapsin you might see some of dem. If you does, no say a word, or you is a dead negar. Now, mind anoder ting; if you eber tinks of courting Miss Rosabella, de Obeah come kill you sure as a gun. Me know ebberyting you does; don't tink for cheat me, you dam black negar. Hei! what dat? Me mus' go. Mind what me tell you."

The celestial visitant ceased abruptly. Again the thunder resounded through the apartment. A foot was placed heavily upon Mr Chitty's body, and a weighty person was felt to jump over him. The jar upon his spine caused him involuntarily to disobey the injunction he had just heard, and to raise his head. A form which seemed gigantic had just cleared the doorway, and bounded along the path to where it joined the other path from the house. At the junction were two figures in light floating garments, evidently some of the duppies against whom Chitty had been cautioned. The three figures joined, and took the road leading from the property. Nick stood astonished, gazing after them till they disappeared, his heart going pit-a-pat, and his tongue cleaving to the roof of his mouth with terror. "Oh, lad-a-gad!" groaned Mr Chitty, chafing his bruised members, and wiping the cold perspiration from his face, "Duppy da come!" After a few moments of horror, he felt that the actual sight of duppies was more tolerable than the fear of their appearance. He had looked upon them, and still lived; nay, save in the matter of a bruise or two, he was none the worse. Nick had a tolerably quick brain, and he no sooner began to use it, than it set about clearing his bewilderment. Though he had been incapable of observing accurately at the time when he beheld the apparitions, there had been in the figure and gait of one of them something which called up the image of his beloved Miss Rosabella. The idea, after once presenting itself, grew rapidly stronger and stronger, until he perceived that, after all, it was more likely to have been his "'pring-flower" in the flesh than a disembodied spirit. Then came the thought of his rival Leander, and jealousy solved the whole riddle. The very design which he was there to frustrate had been effected before his eyes, and he knew it not. Fool, dolt, idiot that he was! he had been completely cozened. Of this he felt sure; and yet there lingered a shade of difficulty, which still seemed to link the affair with the supernatural. The deceit might have been easy enough if everything had been prepared for it, but his selection of the garden-house was unpremeditated, and his very presence on the estate was not designed by himself when last he left the premises. Therefore, supposing the whole thing a trick, the juggler must have divined his motives and intentions, which indicated something more than human ability. *We* could have relieved Mr Chitty's mind, as we will now do that of the reader, by observing, that negroes are accustomed to think aloud, and that Nick, rendered incautious by his potations and the wish to subdue his fear, had been, while disposing of the mule and reconnoitring the ground, most communicative to himself, as well as to another person who had watched him. Having thus destroyed the beauty of the mystery, we may as well complete our confidence, and say honestly, what we had rather not say —that two of the figures seen by Nick Chitty were Leander and Rosabella; while the third—how shall we name the third? The third was the sweetest being in the island—Violet Arabin! Thus the murder is out. Violet, in tiny thin shoes, and wrapped in a light shawl, had stolen from her father's roof in the night-watches. Whether her flight was confided or not to any other person in the house save her companion, we are unable to report. All we know is, that Leander, in after years, was accustomed to urge Rosy to confession on this point, while declaring that he saw a light in Mrs Arabin's room, and that between the window and the lamp he distinctly perceived a figure moving nervously about, and apparently watching the fugitives. But it is notorious that negroes talk a great deal of nonsense.

With a trembling and hurried step did Violet wend

her way to the entrance-gate, escorted by her companions. Having passed through into the public road, she cast about her an anxious glance, while Rosy ejaculated, "Hei, buckra no come!" The person they expected to meet there was of course Arthur Brune, a man not given to break tryste on any occasion, far less on one such as this! The difficulty of Violet's situation requires no description. A hasty consultation was held, in which both her companions counselled return. Rosy promised to remain on sentry at the gate, and to give notice of Brune's arrival. But Violet did not choose, after the step she had taken, to cross again that night the threshold of Crystal Mount. Her decision had cost her too much to be thus dallied with, and her faith in Arthur assured her that he could not be far away. Nick Chitty's presence in the garden, too, was a sufficient reason for not going back, nor halting in uncertainty at the gate. For some way down the mountain there was but one principal road, and she determined to take it. It was easy, at most places, to elude observation by retiring among the rocks or bushes, and Arthur was sure to be met before they had travelled far along it. It proved, however, that there were a great many black and coloured people about, as we have already seen. Some of these evinced a disposition to join company, and identify the party. Wherefore Leander soon persuaded Violet and her attendant to keep to a negro path that ran at a little distance, almost parallel with the road, while he himself, on the public way, kept a look-out for the tardy lover. In this way they had proceeded for some time, still without meeting the object of their search, when the question of return began to be agitated again by the brown lady. Violet, though determined to resist her solicitation, knew not, nevertheless, how to reply to Rosy's arguments. Her shoes were torn, her feet were sore, her voice was nearly lost through shame and disappointment. Overcome at length with emotion, the poor girl seated herself, with a sigh of despair, on a fallen tree; and, unable longer to control her agony, she bitterly wept. Rosabella, greatly affected, and getting frightened, leaned over her mistress, giving what consolation and encouragement she could, but urging her to retrace her steps. Suddenly was heard the sharp yelp of a dog, which made Rosy start according to the instinct of her race. The bark was repeated after a short interval; then again it followed, getting quicker.

"Hei!" shrieked Rosy, "de dogs come tear we—make we run."*

* Let us run.

Violet controlled her feelings, and, in her turn, soothed the alarm of her attendant.

"Nonsense, Rosabella," she said, "they are watch-dogs on some of the surrounding estates, perhaps miles off. You can hear them at a great distance on a night such as this."

"Dere, dere again! dem come nearer," sobbed Rosy. "Oh lad, what we is to do!"

It seemed certainly as if the dogs were coming nearer. Presently Leander joined them from the highroad. He, too, had been scared by the approaching animals. There was no further talk now of returning home; that would have been to meet the dreaded dogs. Violet, seeing them disposed to push forward, exerted herself to advance again, and despatched Leander back to the main road, promising that all would walk briskly abreast, or nearly so. Quickly as the party now moved, the dogs' voices gained on them. Leander was not long in once more rejoining his convoy, his fright being excessive. Both he and Rosy were past hearing reason, and, half leading, half carrying Violet, they struck off on a crosspath which led to a house at no great distance, where they might be within reach of shelter. Horrified, indeed, they were; but not so much so as will be the reader, when we state that the yelps and howls proceeded from our friends Echo and Crocodile, and that the gentle Violet Arabin, to whom all connected with her were so loving,

> "That they might not beteem the winds of heaven
> Visit her cheek too roughly"—

the delicate girl, for whom hundreds of one sex were at the time sighing, and whom hundreds of the other sex were envying — was literally being hunted by bloodhounds.

CHAPTER XVI.

THE book-keeper to whom, as we have seen, Echo and Crocodile had been consigned by Melhado, being a young man of enterprise, had, ever since their arrival, been burning with the desire to test their qualities. However, no opportunity of doing so presented itself until the great Obeah assemblage of which he had notice, as was stated some way back. Then he determined to astonish some of their deluded minds, and to create a summary dispersion; at least he did not plead guilty to any worse design, and it did not appear that Melhado's instructions pointed to anything more sanguinary. Accordingly he took the field in most approved style, mounted on his fleetest nag, with topboots and spurs on, and a wonderful hunting-whip in his hand. He had amused himself till past midnight with consuming cold rum-and-water, which, together with his sporting turn-out, so raised his spirits, that, when he had ordered the muzzles to be taken off, and he heard the brutes try their voices in low single yelps, he began to search his memory for hunting-terms of which he had read, and to crack his whip and cry " Yoicks !" in a very creditable and intelligent manner. His "Tally-ho !" gave evidence of considerable talent. He likewise incited the animals to " Hark forward ;" but that exhortation was unnecessary, seeing that they were already proceeding at a vigorous pace, and puzzled him to keep up with them, as he had to make several detours. At length, soon after crossing the main road, they began to raise their noses more frequently, and to give longer and louder notes; and finally, heedless of a caution to "hold hard," they ran completely out of sight in full cry. It is dreadful to contemplate the peril in which our sweet girl was placed, of being attacked and probably torn and mangled by these ferocious brutes! The shelter for which she and her escort were making was not very distant, but yet so far off that no human foot could reach it before being overtaken by the fleet pursuers. The dogs were in the same enclosure as our party, and might in daylight have seen it; and a catastrophe was imminent, which it sickens us to think of, and which would have given a page to the annals of the island interesting and harrowing in all time, when, by a providential intervention, the animals diverged suddenly from the track of our fugitives, and made off with increased zeal and redoubled howlings in an oblique direction. To explain the escape it is necessary to return to Mr Chitty.

We left that gentleman in all the pleasure of a dawning consciousness that he had been *done*. To do him justice, he did not, after this discovery, waste time in lamentations or oaths, but set himself energetically to work out what mischief might yet be in his power. He determined to bring Christy upon the scene in all haste, and to do what he could himself to arrest the fugitives. In fulfilment of both intentions he took the way to Domingo's hut, and having roused that individual from the side of his beloved Calisto, bade him hie with all speed to Up Park Camp, and tell Massa Arabin that he was wanted at home directly—something terrible had happened. He was to request Mr Arabin to look at his watch when the message was delivered; and, if it was within two hours from that time, Domingo would receive three dollars (a Jamaica pound). Having despatched his messenger, Nick went out among the people, who were collected in the fields, to get news of the runaways, and stop them.

"You is not clear off yet!" thought Menelaus. "Ole Nick no fool."

Domingo put his best leg foremost to win the pound, and started away at a great speed, which brought him at a fortunate moment across the track on which the bloodhounds had wellnigh run into our party. Either for old acquaintance' sake, or for his very superior bouquet, the dogs, after a short hesitation, ran decidedly on his trail. He soon discovered his horrid predicament with an agony that cannot be described; yet he exerted both skill and muscles to escape. The whole mountain-side was well known to him, and by some dexterous drops, jumps, and climbings, he gained every now and then a start on his pursuers. The danger was so imminent that he did not dare to lose time in seeking for a tree into which he could mount, otherwise he might have been secure, though his errand would have been left undone. Once, after running for some yards along the bed of a mountain stream, he knew by the cessation of the baying that his pursuers were at fault, and he halted to draw breath and dash the perspiration from his countenance. Alas, no! they are once more on his trail, and the race for life has yet to be run. Away again, and away: it were endless to narrate the shifts and doubles of the hunted man, or the fell instinct of the hounds. As long as his strength and wind were in fair condition, he ran with hope and sometimes with success; but when these were fast failing, and his feet were galled and cut, and full of thorns, and his clothes, and almost his whole person, torn and bloody from the passage through the thickets, the blackness of despair came over him. 'Twas for dear life though, and worth contesting to the last: wherefore he pushes on, blown and footsore, but as yet untaken. Lusty confident life is an awful power! It maintains the struggle with greedy death, and baffles sometimes the grisly king. Give the mind her due glory here, and forget not that she will survive when her present dwelling-place has returned to be the dust of the earth: but for all that, a sound deep chest and trusty sinews are a great possession—such as a man may lawfully rejoice in!

Some way down the mountain he knows of a ravine bestridden by a foot-bridge formed of the trunk of a not very thick tree, and made practicable by a light handrail which has been secured to it. The dogs might venture to follow across, but they must do so singly. He may be able, with a stone or a stake torn from the bridge, to stun them as they come over in succession, or possibly to strike them into the chasm below. He loses a few minutes in seeking right and left for the path which leads to the bridge; but it is time well expended. He is already on the tree-trunk while his pursuers are struggling and yelling down the steep in rear. The frail causeway bends and totters beneath him; but, courage! he is safe across. And now a thought strikes him. Cannot his arm, nerved by the fear of death, suffice to dislodge the structure? He will try. He does try; he makes a mighty effort. It creaks and vibrates. Another pull—hurrah! Listen to the echoes as the dismounted bridge crashes down the rocks below, and leaps and bounds as if in triumph too. But he has only a short regard for the tumbling log. On the opposite bank of the ravine four eyes shine now in the light of the risen moon. He can look at them as he recovers breath, and as the terrible throbbings of his heart subside a little. Between his deep-drawn sighs he can shake his fist and gasp a curse at the fiends. Softly, poor Domingo! you have done a bold and a clever thing, but you have not escaped Echo and Crocodile. They have learned their dreadful work in Cuba, trained by an indefatigable chasseur. They have been taught to meet such a difficulty; and, after a few cautious investigations to be sure of the case, they turn their noses up the ravine to double round its head. 'Tis nigh half a furlong up; can they, without scent, recover his trail? Perhaps not—there is one chance. If they do, they are thrown back by a disheartening interval —there is another chance. He has at any rate advantage of time enough to climb a tree. But there is no tree—nothing but rock and underwood and grass.

The voices are still. He knows not where the dogs may be. Perhaps they are running in a false direction; but they *may* discover the true one. 'Tis best to get forward, yet he can afford to go more gently. He swings along: all seems still and safe. Heavens! has he escaped? Dares he think that he has? Almost he hopes. Hope not, miserable man! there is the yelp again. They have recovered your trail. But cleverly avail yourself of the start which you have so gallantly won. The dogs' voices once more send the electric terror through his veins. He runs amain; and the dogs run. Do they gain on him? He can hardly tell; but he fears they do. Hah! there—there is a hut, and he can gain it. He is on the plain now, and scours along toward the refuge— a negro's house. How's this? The owner has gone to the Obeah meeting, and has fastened his door. Confusion! but Domingo can break in. He throws himself against the door, but it resists. Again. Why is it stronger than negro doors in general—why? But it is so: he cannot force it, and to lose time is to lose life—away! away!

. . . . . .

In the small hours of the morning a native of the county Tipperary was fulfilling his appointed duty as a sentinel in Up Park Camp, at the postern which faces the mountains, when the Enemy of Mankind, in bodily shape, was seen to scramble over the railings as no human being could have done it, and then to stagger forwards, with a diabolical wildness, across the sentry's beat. Hell-hounds at the same time filled the air with their cries, and struggled frantically to force themselves between the iron rails. Private Michael Muldoony was afterwards picked up insensible from the ground at his post—a thing that had happened before. On inspection, he was found to have been picked up sober—a thing that had never happened before. This last wonder eclipsed, in the opinion of his comrades and of the sergeant of the guard, the wonderful tale by which he accounted for his comatose condition. This is an incredulous and perverse world. It was bad enough to be frightened out of one's senses by the Prince of Darkness, but to have the vision discredited was intolerable to Irish feelings. Michael could not bear to be doubted, consequently the said Muldoony found himself, a few hours afterwards, withdrawn from the tumults and vanities of this outer world into a solitary cell, vulgarly called the *Black Hole*, to expiate the offence of having knocked down and otherwise maltreated one Barnabas Ryan. Now, Barney Ryan's behaviour had been aggravating. He had not scrupled to assert that the vision which Michael supposed himself to have seen was nothing but the last supreme effort of

Domingo in escaping from the bloodhounds. Barney was right though; yet so rudely did he demolish Mike's most effective canteen narrative that they were not drunk under the same table again for upwards of three weeks.

CHAPTER XVII.

To bring up our narrative to this point of the somewhat disorderly entry of Domingo into camp, we must investigate the course of events in Knox's room, to which port we some time ago consigned a very merry party. If you heeded only your ears in that pleasant retirement, you would have thought they were all talking at once: if you gave heed to your eyes and nose in preference to your ears, you must have fancied that each mouth was creating smoke to the exclusion of every other function; so great was the din of tongues, and so palpable was the vapour notwithstanding the open windows. Gonsalvo de Cordova, with an air of extreme despondency, brought in some coffee, and so reduced the general Babel to a more equable conversation.

"Now then, boys," cried Knox, "take some coffee. I'll answer for it, it's good. I've a patent machine for brewing it. Hollo! how's this, Gonsalvo? This isn't the unapproachable quintessence of Mocha—

Edward Knox, sole patentee—to imitate which is felony. How's this, eh?"

"De peccolator break, sar," sighed the great captain, "and me 'bliged to boil him in de pipkin."

"The devil fly away with you, you whining rascal!" shouted Knox. "You've destroyed the best percolator in Jamaica, and degraded me from my supremacy in the preparation of coffee. Henceforth Edward Knox is as other men are. Oh, you long-faced villain!"

"Don't fret yourself, Knox," said Mr Acting Judge. "Ye'll get a better one for a dollar."

"Impossible," sighed Knox.

"Why impossible?" asked some one.

"Perhaps he can't raise the dollar," suggested Melhado.

"He may draw on me at three months for that amount," said Judge Blake, benevolently.

"Fait," said Pat, "he might draw on ye for six months before he'd draw a dollar out of ye."

"I'll drink some of this rather than be ungracious, though it's certainly nearer a solid than a liquid," said the Judge.

"Not quite so delicate as some of your legal arguments, Mr Judge," responded Knox.

"It's as strong as the arm of the law or the hangman's knot, though," observed old Christy.

"Rather," said Judge Blake, "it's like the quality of mercy, in respect of not being strained."

"It's like Gervaise's hat," ventured Melhado, "it's so greasy."

"And like your d—d head, it's so infernally thick," said Tom, judging his distance, and seeing that the stick could not reach.

"Ye're too funny intirely," said Pat Shane; "but be cautious, boys, how y' emit such brilliant flashes. There's fifty barr'ls of powder in the magazine opposite, and ye'll maybe blow us up. I can see the jokes twistin' and twirlin' about the conductor like a nest of snakes that smelled Saint Patrick. What shall it be now—cards or bones?"

The pasteboard had it; and, three or four barrack-tables having been put together for the occasion, the party sat down to a round game, which at that time was much in vogue, and which caused a very brisk circulation of cash. We have no pleasure in giving the details of the gambling scene which ensued; the general features of it are easily communicated. Each player sat with a little heap of notes, doubloons, pistoles, and dollars before him, and each had a glass of brandy-and-water, the frequent use of which during the excitement of the game caused the cloth to be largely printed with damp rings. Smoking, of course, proceeded; and while some, with moderate fortune or strong facial nerves, preserved a look of indifference, most of the countenances alternated from "grave to gay, from lively to severe." Old Christy enjoyed the thing amazingly, played with spirit, and lost his money with a good grace. Melhado was a loser almost from the beginning, and he got very angry at last. Mr Acting Judge lost and won with a joke for both chances. The youngsters soon got excited and intent upon the game. The elders were not so easily interested, and Pat Shane was so inattentive, and he so disturbed the company by talking loud, that he had to be pulled up several times. Tom Gervaise held his cards and played mechanically, but seemed only half-conscious of what he was doing. Knox, without being rash, played very boldly, and by his courage forced the fickle dame to relent. And so for hours they played and played, until some were sleepy, and some were weary, and some were tired of losing, and others wanted to stop and to carry off their gains. There was a pretty plain intimation that nearly all had had enough of it; but Melhado claimed to have his deal, as the only chance of retrieving in some degree the ill-luck of the evening. He dealt, and forced the stakes up to the highest that the game allowed: but the result was only that fortune declared more openly against him. Nothing prospered with him that night, and he had to disburse the value of many

x

a tin kettle, bumboat, mirror, lead coffin, and bale of cotton. Mr Judge, in putting on a somewhat heavy stake, expressed a doubt whether the value of the store would cover what he was about to win, and proposed a dividend if the effects should be insufficient. Melhado lost his deal at last, and dashed down the pack. "Curse the cards!" he exclaimed.

"That's not poloite," said Pat Shane.

"Damn politeness!" answered Melhado, not with the highest courtesy.

"Being a poloite man meself," said Pat, "I consider meself affronted by that remark."

"You do?" said Melhado. "Why, who the devil ever mentioned your name, or passed the slightest reflection on you?"

"By implication ye did," answered Pat, "when ye spoke in that rude way concerning poloiteness."

"Well, I'll be hanged," said Melhado, exasperated beyond control, "if I ever heard of more bullying, ungentlemanly conduct!"

"That's it, is it?" said Pat. "By the powers, then, me boy, I'll try and tache ye the use of more ladylike words, so I will!"

"No doubt you're quite a professor in that line," said Melhado, with a sneer: "I hope your charges are moderate."

"Maybe ye'll not think them so," answered Pat;

"and, now ye mintion accounts, there's a little favour of yours that I haven't jewly acknowledged yet. D'ye mind the sloight obligation ye put me under at Fort Augusta concerning *Irish blackguards,* bad luck to ye? I've the resate ready and convanient in a mahogany case, and shall have the greatest pleasure in remitting it."

"Well, I think you'd better go to bed now," said Melhado; "you'll view this differently in the morning, I fancy. I'm very sleepy myself, and want to be off; so let's have no more nonsense."

Pat Shane placed himself between Manuel and the door, and said very quietly, "Mister Melhado, as ye don't seem to understand a hint, allow me to mintion in plain terms that ye've insulted me by calling my behaviour *bullying* and *ungentlemanly.* I demand satisfaction."

"Yes, very well," said Manuel, pretending to regard this as a tipsy fancy of Pat's; "let me away now, and anything you wish in the morning."

"Moi wish," replied Pat, "is, that we may meet as early as possible, and that ye'd be good enough at once to name——"

"Oh, bother!" interrupted Melhado, "he'll prate here all night," and he pushed Pat aside and was going out. But Pat sprang to the door in an instant, and, slamming it to, turned the lock with a tremendous clang, and put the key in his pocket.

"Now, sir," said Pat, " I give ye one chance more of behaving like a man of honour; if ye miss that, there's other ways of which I say nothing at prisint : but ye must choose, d'ye see ? "

Christy Arabin now came to Melhado's aid, and said—

"Mr Shane, I feel confident that my friend, Mr Melhado, has been hitherto quite mistaken as to your feeling. He did not, I am certain, believe you to be serious. I am ready to act for him in this unlucky affair, and will have the honour of consulting with some friend of yours."

"Thank ye, sir," said Pat ; " I'm daling now with a man of sinse and discretion. Here's Captain M'Corrigan ready to arrange matters with ye ; and I request that ye'll be good enough to make use of my quarters for your confer'nce."

So the two retired.

Mr Arabin now quite admitted to M'Corrigan that Melhado had been to blame, but said that some allowance ought to be made on account of the excitement of the evening: to which M'Corrigan objected that such a representation would have been irresistible if the disagreement had not gone beyond the first offence offered by Melhado; but Mr Arabin must be aware that, Manuel having since treated the affair with unwarrantable levity, having offered personal violence to Shane, and, moreover, having shown a strong desire to get away without bringing the dispute to issue, it was not advisable for either side to talk of compromise. Christy winced a little under this allusion to Melhado's desire to be off, and said that, as that remark had been made, the sooner his principal met Mr Shane the better. Whereupon M'Corrigan drew attention to the brightness of the night, and said there was not the least need of protracting the affair till dawn, and that the earlier they proceeded, the less they were in danger of interruption.

Christy coincided, and the seconds separated to announce this decision to their respective friends. When Arabin reappeared, however, he was informed that, during his absence, gentlemen had remarked on the impropriety of a person of his age and position taking a prominent part in the affair, and it was proposed to him that, having acted for his friend in the most important negotiation, he might trust a younger man to see the quarrel to an end. After a few objections, Christy gave way to the urgent desire of the whole party, and consented to yield the conduct of Melhado's further case to a young officer named Ramsay, who was willing to undertake it.

Christy determined, nevertheless, to witness the duel, as did nearly everybody else, the Acting Judge included. It needs to be distinctly stated that we are not romancing in exhibiting an elderly councillor, and a high legal functionary, as so easily permitting, and even countenancing, this unseemly quarrel. Those who recollect the period in which our story is laid, will bear witness that no wrong is done to the class to which those gentlemen belonged. Both the intending combatants retired with their seconds to prepare for the encounter, which was to take place so soon as preliminaries could possibly be arranged. The others dispersed to get cool, and put off their evening clothes. Tom Gervaise lay down on Knox's sofa to rest himself till he should know where the fight was to be ; he thought it would just fit in delightfully, and fill up the interval till it should be time to set off and meet Arthur Brune and some other people, whom he was to drive from the foot of the mountains to an interesting rendezvous at daybreak. He, however, fell asleep, and to his great regret missed the fight ; he was, moreover, in a fair way to mar a matter of more interest, to which the fight was only an auxiliary. Well aware of Tom's infirmities, Knox contrived not to be Pat Shane's second, expressly that he might see Tom off at the right time, and be free to adjust any screw which might happen to go wrong. He was never in better heart for assisting an adventure. His spirits were at the highest, for he had won enough to dispel his embarrassments, and a great weight (which, by the by, he thought that he had borne very well) was lifted from his heart.

An open space to the eastward of Up Park Camp was fixed upon as the place of meeting, and thither some score of misguided individuals proceeded by moonlight to see two men aim at each other's lives as gaily and unconcernedly as if they had been going to a merry-making. Captain M'Corrigan had provided pistols, and a couple of saddle-horses were taken to the ground to facilitate escapes in case of *accident;* a young surgeon was also among the spectators.

Melhado leant on Christy Arabin's arm. The time which he had had for reflection had by no means caused him to view the affair more pleasantly than he had done at first. Here he was, a man the most envied, perhaps, in the island, on the very eve of attaining a much-improved position, a handsome dower, and a lovely and accomplished wife, about to expose himself in a paltry quarrel to be shot by an Irishman, a term convertible in Melhado's vocabulary with " professed duellist." Besides the unlucky circumstances which made the case so hard just now, he had, as has been hinted, no peculiar liking for hostilities. Even now he insinuated as broadly as he dared to old Christy, that there might be a chance yet of composing the matter without fighting ; but Christy's answer was so short that it put an end to all discussion of compromise. After that, he walked on, alternately shaken by fear and flushed by anger at the unlucky quarrel into which he had been drawn. The more he thought, the more his meaner and worse passions gained possession of him. The chance of quelling his antagonist in fair fight was altogether insufficient for his base revengeful soul: he racked his brain if haply by some subtle but foul device he might make sure of his enemy's blood. The man was a murderer in his heart.

Pat Shane, on the other hand, went to the meeting like a bridegroom. He was aware that he was in some way serving a friend, though he didn't exactly know how; and he was sure that he was doing a most chivalrous and praiseworthy act in endeavouring to rescue an enchanting girl from a spiritless fellow that didn't deserve her, and in devising chastisement for a presumptuous and disagreeable coxcomb. Pat's feelings, therefore, were of the most self-approving and complacent kind.

The skill and experience of Captain M'Corrigan and Mr Ramsay prevented the loss of much time in preliminaries after they reached the ground. They tossed for pistols, measured their distance, and placed their men with great ability; or, as Pat Shane expressed it, "mighty nate." Melhado's face was seen in the moonlight to be of an ashen hue. The spectators withdrew to a short distance, and the seconds placed the pistols in the combatants' hands. "I shall count three, gentlemen," said Mr Ramsay. "You will fire together at the word *three*, and you will not look at each other till you fire. Are you both ready?"

"Ready!"

"*One : two : three ! !*"

The wretch Melhado was seen to make a half face towards Pat, and look fixedly at him for a moment; at the word *two* he raised his pistol and fired. When *three* sounded, Pat Shane fired, and the contents of his weapon struck Melhado's face, who fell. So disfigured were his features by a crimson stream which flowed over them, that it was impossible for the surgeon to ascertain the exact nature of the wound, and as he breathed and had a pulse, it was determined to carry him back to camp on a hospital litter, which M'Corrigan's forethought had provided.

"Be off now, Shane," said M'Corrigan.

"Will I be going before I hear what's happened?" asked Pat.

"Yes, away with you at once. I know where you're to be found; and you shan't be long in hearing from me. Good-luck to you." And Pat, who was by this time in the saddle, received and returned a strong grip from M'Corrigan's fist, and betook himself to the hills. He could have trotted along very pleasantly but for the recollection of the villanous attempt Melhado had made to shoot him by firing prematurely. "The murderin' robber!" thought he; "but maybe I didn't pay him off!" Haunted by this thought, Pat had got some way into the hills, before the day broke, without meeting a soul.

The solitude and the time had a good effect on him. Even wild Pat Shane felt calmed and sobered. He couldn't resist the influence of that dawn among the mountains. Who could? There is life and freshness in that hour. He is not wise who sleeps such gift away. It is short, yet very precious; for all of energy that the clime affords is drawn in from its influence. No rising mist is there, no murky cloud. The arch of heaven, where the hills allow it to be seen, is clear from the zenith to the horizon—clear, and faintly blue. Slowly the moonlight pales before the coming day. There is a cool revealing of dim objects, such as overspread the world's young forms on the first day ere yet the Great Light was—grey hills, grey plains, grey heavens, and grey sea. The dying night-wind with trembling fingers gently moves the leaves. But the many sounds of night are ended, and all is calm repose, for the life of day is hardly roused; no wing disturbs the air, no voice the hush. There is the soothing of a gentle peace upon the heart; and pure, and merciful, and holy thoughts descend with the early dew.

Now came a timid sound. A chirrup quavered for a moment, and, frightened by its own voice, fled back into the mighty stillness. Then whispered a soft cooing from the woods; then rustlings and low murmurs, few and single. These were Nature's preludes ere she brake forth in her song of the morning.

As the light increased, Pat saw before him, coming down the path, two young negroes who were going to their work, and who, as they had not been up gambling and drinking and fighting all night, were in a fresh and sportive mood as they came forth to meet the young day. One of them carried a matchet, or short cutlass used in that country for clearing the bush, and was bounding round his fellow, aiming make-believe cuts and thrusts at him as he did so. This shocked the prudence of Pat Shane, who reined up his horse and said—

"Look here, Julius Sasar, me man: ye shouldn't be cutting them capers: ye might kill or injure a fellow-creature, and then ye'd never forgive yourself!"

"Yes, massa," said the young nigger; and Pat rode forward. He had not got many yards, however, before he turned round and called upon the darkie to stop.

"Except 'twas in fair foight, ye know, Julius," added Pat to his former admonition, "and then it's all honourable and lagal." After which addendum Pat faced about once more, and gat him up into the mountains.

The scene had already changed. As the dull sober chrysalis flutters forth the gayest and the gaudiest of winged things, so had the one-tinted placid daybreak changed to a splendid day. The magic touch of *colour* was on earth and sky and sea—crimson and azure, emerald and gold; and dazzling spots, the earliest kisses of the sun, gleamed on prominent points and ridges. The minstrelsy of birds and insect voices now send up the full chorus of the woods. A burst of beauty and of life which animates and warms, and says, *Lift up your hearts;* for it is a time of radiance, of reviving, and of gladness. Such a change has gladdened greater than mortal hearts. It repeats the original splendour which followed the creation of the sun and all heaven's lights, which purest beings hailed with adoring rapture, when the morning stars sang together, and all the sons of God shouted for joy!

"Bedad it's iligant, so it is," said Pat Shane; "a man that niver seen Killarney 'ud say 'twas sublime.

And to think of that miscr'nt firin' before he got the word! The immorality of this world is past comprehendin': and yet to see it on a mornin' like this, you'd think butther wouldn't milt in its mouth." Whereupon he felt musical, he didn't know why, and began whistling "Savourneen Deelish," making a pause-rest at every double bar to keep his light in.

He lay hidden for some days, after which a mysterious communication from M'Corrigan informed him that he might reappear, but that it would be prudent not to ask questions or to make any observation concerning Mr Melhado, who was supposed to have gone on a long voyage to pull up after a serious illness.

CHAPTER XVIII.

KNOX'S share in aiding and abetting the doings of Arthur Brune had been, however, limited by a cause which he did not expect, and owing to which many hearts beat anxiously before sunrise. It has been said or sung that Knox held himself free from the duel purposely, that he might be Arthur's ready confederate in case of need, and especially that he might stimulate the energies of Tom Gervaise, who had a part to play in the business of the night, and who was very little likely of himself to think of any business whatsoever. Knox, after getting his room clear of the company, was resting for a few minutes in an arm-chair, thinking of the escape he had made from ruin, resolving never to play again, and listening to the snoring of old Tom, who lay on the sofa. He was disturbed by the appearance at his door of a small bandy-legged negro, and the thin weak voice of Sampson besought him to come to the other end of the verandah and speak to Mr Lorton, who was very ill, and wished to see him. As Tom's time was not yet up, and the duel appeared to be working smoothly, Knox thought he could afford ten minutes, and so he walked down the gallery to see what Lorton wanted. On arriving at the room, his spirits, just then so buoyant, encountered a shock. At the very first glance he was smitten by that awe which proceeds from the presence of death, either when he is wrestling for his prey, or when he has set to his seal. There were several persons in the chamber, all but one earnestly employed; and yet there was a hush—and a gloom, and an oppression, and disorder. The air was faint with a smell of vinegar, those who moved went softly, and looks and signs did the work of speech. On the narrow officer's bedstead, from which the mosquito-net had been thrown back, lay poor Lorton, his eyes glassy and staring, his head, which had been shaved and blistered, wrapped in a kerchief: near him sat Malvina, the stout brown nurse, attending to his wants, brushing away the insects, or obeying the signs of the doctors, of whom two were present. Mr Grant also was there observing the sufferer, and Sampson was keeping hot bottles to his feet. A chair near the bed was littered with a mustard plaster recently taken from the sick man's chest, and, besides medicine and ointments, the table held a brandy and a champagne bottle, these stimulants having been used to raise the patient's pulse. Very dim the apartment seemed after the glaring scene which Knox had just quitted; but his eyes soon were tempered to the dull light, and he felt a thrill as he saw Lorton staring at him with a fixed gaze. There was no speculation, though, in that fast look: the soul was yet awake within, but her communication with the outer world by the senses had become a labour. Lorton clearly heeded but little of what was passing ; his spirit was gathering itself together for its supreme flight, and the limbs moved feebly and listlessly without a guide, as they had done in infancy. Doubtless there had once been joy unspeakable communicated by the first languid motion of those limbs, when a fair and well-favoured baby was shown to many longing eyes in a country-house in England not so many years ago. The mercy of Providence allowed no one then to associate the little stranger's appearance with aught but gladness. None could have entertained the idea that after a few, a very few years—alas, how unprofitably spent!—the helplessness of his first hour would return, among strangers and hirelings, in a far-distant island, with no mother's hand to smooth the pillow, and no kindred ear to listen to the parting words. It must be hard to die thus. Many, many things must have risen to the tongue, which, if said to those near and dear, would have been a solace to the ebbing soul; but no fond familiar breast was nigh, and there was no utterance for his thoughts, save probably in those communings which he held so constantly with Heaven. Now and then, however, some local matter would still interest him for a short time. Knox caught the eye of one of the surgeons, with whom he would have retired to be informed of the patient's actual condition, when, making a sudden rally, Lorton inquired if Knox had been sent for. Knox approached the bed and spoke.

"You are Brune's friend," said Lorton; "I have done Brune wrong, for which I trust I shall be forgiven. *He* has already forgiven me, but he could not remain here till I could put him in possession of the source of the injury, and of the means of annulling it. Mr Grant has found every necessary document." (Mr Grant here handed Knox a packet.) "To you I consign these papers in trust for Brune. Brune is named in my will. I wish you to understand that his name stands there by my deliberate and well-considered wish. Let him know this. I trust—I trust"—here the voice became a murmur, and the eyes lost again the intelligence which had temporarily lighted them. Lorton put out his emaciated hand and plucked nervously at the bedclothes. The nails were dark red, and drops of blood were literally oozing from under some of them. The doctor intimated that he was not to be further disturbed, and gave him a little brandy, feeling the pulse at the same time, and observing that the stimulant scarcely affected it. Lorton seemed in a doze, and the voices of the bystanders became a little more free than they had been. Then he was heard to say, " I'm perfectly sensible—perfectly sensible." At this moment there was a loud disturbance in the room below, which greatly discomposed the dying man. Knox stole softly out, and ran down to put a stop to the clamour. On entering the negro room, whence it proceeded, he found Domingo exhausted, torn, and groaning on the ground, while the occupier of the room and another negro were exclaiming after their wont, and pestering him with questions.

"Silence, and be hanged to you!" burst in Knox, in a low whisper; "Mr Lorton is dying over your heads. What's the matter with this fellow? Get up, will you, and behave yourself properly!"

But Domingo could not rise. He tried to gasp forth an apology, and to beg that he might see Massa Arabin. That name reminded Knox of the business he had well-nigh forgotten. He informed Domingo that Mr Arabin had left camp for a time with Mr Melhado (alluding darkly to the duel, of the result of which he was as yet ignorant), and that it was of no use to seek him; and then he went to rouse and hurry off Tom Gervaise: for instead of ten minutes, he had been half an hour in Lorton's rooms. Tom's slumbers had been very little disturbed. Once a cockroach who had come down from a beam, seeing his mouth open, looked in, causing him to splutter and give voice to that kind of prayer which Shakespeare ascribes to military men: after that he slept again, and when Knox came up and roused him, he seemed to be exceedingly comfortable, and resisted with all his might the process of waking. On finding what a laggard he had been, Tom, who had a certain respect for Arthur Brune, exhibited symptoms of compunction, and actually shook himself with some alacrity, postponing even the glass of brandy-and-water, for which he was longing, till he should be about to start. Knox, expecting every minute the return of the shooting-party, kept spurring him, and at last had the satisfaction of seeing him depart. Then Knox returned to see how it fared with Lorton. Only Lorton's mortal remains were there. The spirit had passed but a few minutes before, and Mr Grant was now closing the eyes. Pray, reader, that a stranger, however kind and feeling, may not perform that office for you. Poor Lorton!—there remained the tearless funeral and the muffled drum, and this world would know him no more!

Mr Grant accepted Knox's invitation to rest in his room, and take some coffee. Soon after daybreak they both left for the church at Halfway Tree.

CHAPTER XIX.

BUT where, all this time, was dear Violet Arabin? Escaped, as we left Violet, from one peril, the miseries of that night were not yet over for her. Overwhelmed with terror and fatigue, she had sunk on a bank in the field after being relieved from the pursuit of the dogs. There Leander and Rosabella, believing now that their ill-luck was too strong to contend with, would consult on no basis but that of an immediate return home. Violet herself saw no other course, and wanted only the strength to set forth. While she delayed, mustering her courage, the enclosure was suddenly entered by eight or ten negroes, male and female, headed by old Menelaus, who grinned horribly as he approached the party.

"Beg for you pardon, Miss Wily," said Nick, "I think dere is some mistake here. Tink Missy lose her way."

"You are right, Chitty," said Violet, with firmness, after collecting all her courage. "I have lost my way, and am about to return to it. Do not alarm any one if my weariness makes me long in reaching home, and take away all these people. Leander and Rosabella will protect me. Now go!"

Mr Chitty cast a withering grin at Leander and Rosy as he replied, " Missy not know her faitful sarbint. I afraid dese two is wortless. Massa will expec' Nick Chitty for see young Missy safe home."

"I am much obliged, Chitty," answered Violet, "but I had rather walk alone. You may follow at a distance, if you please; but these people cannot be required, now that you have found me, and I desire that you dismiss them at once."

Seeing that Nick did not obey immediately, Violet said, " Good people, I thank you all for the trouble you have taken in seeking me. I am quite safe, and beg that you will leave me."

" 'Top, 'top," exclaimed Chitty, seeing the negroes about to obey (for so general is the habit of obedience to a command of the kind, that none contemplated an objection)—" 'top, men; big massa desire we is not to leave Missy till she safe home. Hear'ee?"

Then, turning to Leander, he hissed, " Ha, boy, ole Nick too many for you; he 'poil for you 'port yet. My! de whipping you will get!"

Violet could scarcely believe in Chitty's assurance, and commanded him again to take his party off.

"Me is acting in de name of big massa," replied Nick, forging a commission for an object which he considered to justify the fraud. "De nyoung lady berry petickly wanted at home jist now. If him is tired ánd not able for walk, perhapsin we can carry him lilly bit."

"Come near me at your peril, Chitty," said Violet. "Leander, protect me from this fellow, and explain to the other people that he is deceiving them. I will insure you forgiveness and reward for doing so."

"Supposin' I let him go, you will marry me tomorrow, my 'pring-flower?" asked Mr Chitty of Rosabella, who was nearly wild. "Now de time for say *yes*."

"Go to de debil, ole hangman!" screamed Rosy. "I wish you could a dead."

"Hah! berry well," grinned Nick, showing both his gums; "berry well. Now den, my friends, me mus' beg you for gently lift dis nyoung lady, and carry him safe to Crystal Mount. Beg pardon, Miss Wily. You will tank old Nick for dis some day."

Saying which, Mr Chitty stretched forth his arms as offering to lift poor Violet off the ground, who, terrified beyond measure, uttered a scream, and turned to flee with what little strength remained to her. At that instant, however, Mr Chitty, instead of laying hands on her, fell backwards, and rolled fairly heels over head, struck mightily by a new actor who had come unperceived upon the scene.

The attendant negroes exclaimed, "Hei, de buckrah!" while Leander, jumping about like a maniac, shouted, "Massa Brune! Massa Brune!" and Rosy, with a remarkable volubility, commenced a detail of their misadventure and of Nick Chitty's insolent conduct.

Violet was weeping and speechless upon Arthur's shoulder. He saw pretty plainly how matters stood, and knew that this was no time for questions and explanations. The negro gentlemen, after witnessing Mr Chitty's discomfiture, shrank away unperceived with astonishing rapidity, and returned to their incantations. Nick himself, after a minute or two, arose with a frightfully disfigured countenance, and, approaching Arthur softly, asked, "Why you 'trike so hard, massa? Me only wantin' to see de nyoung lady safe home."

"Disappear, you old rascal," said Arthur, "or I'll stop your lying tongue for the next six weeks."

Whereupon Mr Chitty entered into a spirited colloquy with himself touching the whole transaction, and retired while the argument was in its most animated stage. We have had a hint of where Arthur had been delaying. Lorton had summoned him when he should have been hurrying to the hills, and had, with the eloquence of a dying man, entreated him again and again to remain yet another minute, and listen to the confession which contained Brune's own vindication. The situation and the subject had imposed upon his better judgment, and caused him well-nigh to lose all that made life or reputation valuable. Here he was at last, however; and Violet's strength seemed all to return when she leant upon his arm, and heard his voice, and partook of the confidence with which he chose his way, and supported her along. After a long, but not a tedious, walk, they found themselves close to a little negro hut at the mountain's foot, before which should have been standing a carriage ready to convey them to Halfway Tree Church; but, alas! all was still and lonely. Old Tom had failed to keep his appointment, and all that had been achieved with so much toil and danger was like to have been achieved in vain. Once more alarmed and shocked, Violet rested in the hut. She had now the calm decided voice of Brune to reassure her, though; and her fears but half possessed her. Leander was despatched to Kingston to travel at the top of his speed on Arthur's pony, which was tied behind the hut, with orders to bring out a carriage without a moment's delay, and with the promise of a rich reward if he did so in time. Violet's eyes could be seen by the bright moonlight suffused with tears; but she made no lamentation, nor otherwise added to the perplexity of a situation already sufficiently embarrassing. Even then Brune remarked that she would be in her right place as a soldier's wife. Miserable she certainly was, and, after so many misfortunes, unable to believe in a happy result; yet she nerved herself, and did what appeared to be her duty. Far otherwise it was with Miss Rosabella. That young lady, being no longer called upon to use bodily exertion, was not disposed to place any restraint upon the exhibition of sentiment. Her tears, her voice, her gestures, indicated the profoundest despair. She threw herself on the floor of the hut, tore her hair (she really had hair, not wool), and screamed and raved after a fashion indulged in in this country by none but lunatics.

Arthur sat supporting Violet, and whispering hope and the certainty of a good result. He looked often at his watch, and counted the minutes in which Leander could possibly accomplish his ride to Kingston. Long before the least period that he allowed, however, his ears were greeted by the sound of wheels and hoofs. We know that Gervaise, though long behind time, was under way at last; and accordingly Leander had not ridden far before he met Tom tooling along at a great pace; whereupon he returned and essayed to gallop forward and announce Tom's coming beforehand, which he could hardly accomplish, so cleverly did the old fellow put them over the ground. It was not many seconds before the equipage, with all its passengers safely bestowed, was on the road back to Kingston.

CHAPTER XX.

MELHADO—dying or dead, it was uncertain which— was borne gently along towards camp. The doctor of course took the direction, and he declared that, if life remained, the only hope of preserving it lay in preventing a shock of any kind. Thus the return was necessarily very slow, and allowed ample time for the escorting party to collect their thoughts. None of them could have had very pleasant reflections, for they were all now liable to be confronted with the stern face of the law, and it was not impossible that they might stand together in the dock as criminals. To be sure, colonial juries were very lenient in matters of this kind—more especially after a little time had elapsed; but then to gain time it was necessary to flee immediately into hiding, and that was not very convenient. To Judge Blake especially the consequences promised to be ugly; for, supposing him to have come safely through the ordeal of a trial, he yet ran a great risk of losing his appointment after being mixed up in such a transaction. This could not have been an agreeable thought; howbeit, the Judge, like many of his countrymen, had the talent of banishing care, and looking at the bright side of things, so he didn't fret. But the man most to be pitied of the whole group was undoubtedly Christy Arabin. Here, stretched on this wretched canvass, lay all that remained of the young man in whom centred so many of his schemes. He must now face a prospect very different from that which he had imagined a few nights ago as he lay and smoked, and thought that he should never be cast down. Besides, he would have to be the bearer of these sudden tidings home — to announce to his daughter that she was, as it were, a widow ere she was a bride. Then a pang of another complexion shot through him as he thought that his wife would not consider this a very heavy visitation — that the fates were fighting her battle against him, and putting him to shame in his own house in a very unhandsome way! A hundred other vexatious considerations rose up, but in his present agitation he could only glance at them in the gross and see how formidable they were: a dark array indeed!

Altogether there was a terrible revulsion of feeling since they formed a merry party an hour or so ago. And they marched along in moody silence, each absorbed in his own reflections, when on a sudden from the bier came forth a plaintive voice—

"I don't feel in very great pain!"

"Silence, as you value your life," said the doctor; "do nothing but breathe, and do that as softly as you can."

"Melhado's alive; we mayn't have to run for it," thought the bulk of the party.

"Manuel's alive, and his wound may not be mortal," thought old Christy; and he presently began to calculate whether, if he only lost his nose, that must necessarily upset the long-revolved schemes. Mrs Arabin would be strong against a noseless son-in-law, but, d— her, was she *always* to have her way?

With these cogitations they arrived at the barracks, into the first room of which they turned—a servant's room on the ground-floor. The bier was laid upon a table, and the doctor proceeded to clear the room of all but two or three of the curious beholders. Christy Arabin, of course, claimed the right to stay; Judge Blake pleaded that his observation of the case might suggest a legal wrinkle or two in the event of difficulties ensuing; and M'Corrigan and Ramsay could hardly with decency be denied. These, therefore, remained in the room. The rest, after some strong remonstrances, dispersed on a promise that an early bulletin should be promulgated.

"Now, then," said the doctor, as he unlocked his instrument-case, "somebody get a basin of tepid water and a sponge. I should like a saucer too and a table-knife, or something of that kind, to clear the clotted blood away."

"Do you think it's mor—?" groaned Melhado.

"Let me entreat you," interrupted the doctor, "not to attempt to speak. You shall know everything I can tell concerning your case as soon as I understand it. Remarkable, isn't it? though not uncommon," he added, turning to the bystanders, "that a bullet through the brain is sometimes so little felt at first! Here is a case where for a time even the intellect is unimpaired!"

"I beg your pardon, doctor," said Christy Arabin; "might I entreat you to attend to the sufferer now, and we can hear these interesting observations another time?"

"Yes, attend to me, that's a good man. Tell me if I shall die."

The doctor was ruffled—first, at the interruption of his lecture; secondly, at the disobedience of his patient.

"By ——," he said, "if you don't keep still, the undertaker, not I, will have to attend to you!"

His irritation subsided immediately, and he set carefully and tenderly about his work. Melhado's countenance was so discoloured and coated that it was not possible to determine the precise position of the wound. The doctor, therefore, proceeded to work round the outer edge of the stains, removing large coagulated masses, and gradually circumscribing the area. "Strange," said he, "I don't see yet where the bullet entered." He patiently went on again till he had cleared all but a space no bigger than a florin. "In the very centre of the marks," he mused, "the last spot that I expose," and so saying, he removed the remaining particle, and scraped his knife against the saucer's edge. The wound was not manifest though. Then he plunged the sponge in the basin and washed the whole of Melhado's pale countenance. After that he opened the patient's mouth and nostrils, and examined them attentively. "Where the deuce can all the blood have come from?" exclaimed he, completely puzzled. "I can find no wound."

"Are you sure," asked M'Corrigan—"are you quite sure that it is blood?"

"Blood! of course it's blood," the doctor answered; "what the devil else?"

"Don't know," M'Corrigan said. "I've been looking at it, and I have my suspicions."

"Let me see," said the doctor. "I never thought—why, I declare, what's this? Well, it is curious!"

"If I weren't in the presence of a professional man," put in Blake, "I'd say 'twas guava jelly."

"It looks wonderfully like it," said Christy Arabin.

"It *is* guava jelly," said Mr Ramsay.

"Then I'm not shot after all," said Melhado, briskly, as he sat up on end.

The relief of their apprehensions was so sudden that the ridicule of the affair had not yet struck them. M'Corrigan, turning his back upon Melhado, said, "Gentlemen all, be pleased to understand that Mr Shane is entirely ignorant of what his pistol contained. Cartridges—very harmless ones, as you perceive—were manufactured for the occasion, with the view of preventing bloodshed. I need scarcely remind you that, had they not been resorted to, we should have had not only bloodshed, but death. It will be for you to decide whether or not you will enlighten Shane as to the transaction. If you do, I shall of course be ready to answer for the deceit practised upon him. But I imagine that if *we* are content to keep the secret, nobody will wish to divulge it on the part of this—this—person." And M'Corrigan, with a look of supreme contempt, pointed over his shoulder at Melhado, who still sat astonished on the table. "The best advice I can give this person and those who are interested in him," continued he, "is, that he disappear for some time, and pretend to be dead in fact, as he really is in reputation. By the time all of us are off the island, his

z

rascally conduct may be forgotten, and he may show himself to strangers."

"The charge of the pistols shall remain a profound secret with me," said Blake.

"And with me," said the doctor; "but few of those who witnessed the affair will be disposed to ask many questions, or to talk about it, for their own sakes; and a nod or a wink from me will make them fancy they understand the end of it."

Having heard which, and having bowed to Christy Arabin, M'Corrigan went out, followed by Ramsay. Judge Blake, who held that the code of honour and any other code whatever must give way to a joke, went up to Melhado, and, looking him solemnly in the face, said—

"Upon my soul, sir, this is a most unlooked-for resurrection. Receive my congratulations on your having been so wonderfully *preserved*." Then bidding good-night to Arabin and the doctor, the learned gentleman went home to rest, confirmed in his belief that it is better to keep off care and apprehension till they force themselves in.

The doctor was the next to depart, leaving Christy and his high-minded young friend to a *tête-à-tête*. As long as Manuel appeared to be dead Christy felt that he would give anything to have him alive again: now that he was surely alive and unhurt, the old gentleman began to think it had been better if he had died. Always shrewd and practical, though, he immediately decided that reproaches were utterly useless, that he would want a little time to consider what should be done, and that what he had first to effect was the withdrawal of Manuel from Camp, and the concealment of him at Crystal Mount or somewhere in the hills. He therefore said, quietly—

"I think we had better have our carriage out and get away as quickly and quietly as possible. The day is breaking: let us go to the coach-house, where no doubt the servants are asleep, and set off at once."

The tone Christy used brought a great relief to Manuel, who had been feeling like a detected cur. He couldn't understand the old fellow, but began to fancy that there was little harm done after all; and he answered, jauntily—

"Yes, come along. I'm dreadfully sleepy."

So the two stole out.

A little way from Up Park Camp, as you go to Halfway Tree, four roads meet—that is to say, the road from the mountains to Kingston crosses at right angles that which leads from Camp to Halfway Tree. At daybreak, after Clutterbuck's champagne, two carriages were approaching, and near to meeting, at the cross roads; one was travelling from Camp, the other from the hills. They did not exactly meet, however, as the latter, which was perceived to be driven by Tom Gervaise, quickened its speed suddenly, and turned to its right into the Halfway Tree road, before the former reached the cross. The other contained old Christy Arabin and Mr Melhado, and it also turned to its right, but towards the mountains, taking the opposite direction to that which Tom had just left. They were soon far asunder. Neither Christy nor Melhado was in a peculiarly amiable humour, yet the old man had not completely lost interest in passing matters. He nudged the morose Melhado, and, pointing to the carriage that passed them, said—

"Isn't that Gervaise? What can the fellow be about at this time of the morning? He's got women aboard, too, sly dog! Shouldn't wonder if we heard more of this affair, and had some scandal out of it!"

"I hope to heaven that he's run away with somebody's daughter," growled Melhado, "and that the parents 'll go distracted, and that the runaways 'll hate each other and be miserable!"

Christy soon ceased to think of Tom Gervaise; he had to determine what should be done with Melhado. The wise plan obviously was to conceal him for a time. Those who knew of his being unhurt had declared their intention of keeping the matter secret. His rascally behaviour in the duel it was nobody's wish, of course, to conceal. But a man believed to be dangerously wounded might be much more leniently dealt with than one known to have escaped unscathed. Perhaps, when Manuel should appear again as one recovered from an almost mortal wound, his iniquity might be forgotten. Clearly, therefore, the best course, under any circumstances, was, that he should seek retirement, and Christy thought he had better quietly leave the island for a while. This reasoning seemed sound enough when he reviewed it; and yet he saw an objection which one can scarcely comprehend his admitting under such circumstances. Manuel's retirement *must* cause the postponement of the marriage; and the postponement of the marriage was Mrs Arabin's suggestion. He almost determined to face all the opprobrium and ridicule that would greet Melhado's immediate reappearance, and to push the marriage through according to the original programme, trusting to the wealth and influence of the two houses to silence all reproach ere long. Between the whispers of discretion and the wish to thwart his wife, he remained in two minds till he got home, and when he arrived there he had something else to think of; so this momentous question was never decided.

In half an hour from the time when the carriages passed the cross roads Violet Arabin was saluted as Mrs Brune, and she and her husband were off to a house in the recesses of the island, where they lay hidden and very happy for a week or two. Lorton's bequest turned out to be a legacy of £5000, which came most opportunely to the young couple, and set them going, while old Christy was digesting the liberty that had been taken with his domestic arrangements. He did completely get over it at last, and learned to love his son-in-law, and to congratulate himself on the way in which events were ordered.

Mrs Melhado, though dreadfully disappointed and angry, was at the same time moved with admiration at the spirited course taken by the lovers, which, she said, resembled the matches that were made when she was young, and was worth any quantity of your staid formal courtships. To her chopfallen son the old lady afterwards recited the proverb that *there are as good fish in the sea as ever came out of it*, and recommended him to run away with the next promising girl that came in his way, and not to wait till another did it for him. Upon the whole, she admirably maintained her reputation as a strong-minded woman, and, whatever she felt on the subject, let no annoyance appear, and was ready with a grin for everybody, and maybe with a smart retort if any observation appeared pointed at her disaster.

Her son thought proper to make a voyage to the United States of America, which, though it may have dispersed his chagrin, did not improve his manners and sentiments. On his return he never showed again in good society; and when his mother died (which she did soon after his reappearance in Jamaica), and he was left to his own guidance, his feet turned speedily into the broad path that leads to ruin. He still retained his love of finery; he was fond of pleasure and idleness; and he had but little capacity for business. So he became the leader of a low gambling set, called to that bad eminence through his good looks, affectation of fashion, and reputed wealth. Once on a downward path like this, the end is certain. Descending from one depth to another, his father's infirmity got possession of him, as the shrewd old lady had feared it might; and he was known as a drunken, gambling ruffian, about low haunts in Kingston and Port Royal. It ended in his paying a quarter dollar in the pound, and becoming a bookkeeper to an estate of which he had been attorney.

Arthur and his incomparable wife, with Leander and Rosy married and in their service, remained but a short time longer in Jamaica. The whole party left when the regiment was ordered home, and commenced a series of adventures, such as must have been known to many an officer who married about the same period. Scarcely ever parted, Arthur and Violet visited many climes; they knew the vicissitudes of heat and cold, of pestilence and scarcity, and of danger and death, interspersed with bounding life and happy hours. Brune, as soon as he got work to do, made his way in the profession, as people had prophesied that he would. He is at this moment holding a high staff appointment, and known and respected for his achievements and character. There is plenty left in him, too, to do still greater things, and win a still higher name, if the clouds which now darken the horizon should end in war, and oblige Great Britain to draw the sword. His wife (she isn't *Mrs* Brune any longer) is, to our mind, who are not so young as we were, even a more fascinating person than was the Violet Arabin of old days; and the comparison is not made with a vague shadow of the past, for there sits beside her another Violet, whose every look or gesture brings up a crowd of recollections, and transports one back to youth, raising the shades of Crystal Mount and old adventures, and half-forgotten faces, and merry days. The youngsters appear to think Miss Brune a more charming person than her mother: they will get wiser some day. Arthur has a son a captain in his father's regiment, and another is preparing for his competitive examination with a view to entering the service.

Pat Shane was purposely kept out of the way for some time after the duel, by being left in doubt as to

Melhado's fate. As long as any of those connected with the affair remained in the regiment, all who were cognisant of the catastrophe behaved most honourably, and never let Pat know that Melhado was unhurt; though, of course, it was known that he didn't die. After a time, however, some indiscreet comrade let out the story, and Pat's indignation was, we understand, of a very appalling kind. He only wished that M'Corrigan and he might meet before he died, and then—Neptune's *quos ego* was nothing to it. They did meet many years after, when Pat had taken to himself a wife (we believe it was the little divil with the purtiest feet in the world), who, in a dangerous illness that followed the birth of their first child, had bound Pat by a solemn obligation to abstain from private encounters. 'Twas in India that he met his *quondam* second, who was on the march through the station where Pat's regiment lay. As soon as they recognised each other, Major Shane broached the matter, which had lain heavy on his heart for many a day; and the other, who had well-nigh forgotten it, said he believed something of the sort did happen—he had a slight recollection of it.

"If ye'd met me two years ago," said Pat, whose brogue had acquired additional richness by time and matrimony, "ye'd surely have had to confront me in the field; but at present there are raisons, don't ye see, and I'll lave ye to th' upbraiding of your own conscience: we'll not foight, ye know; but as the priests and philosophers tell ye, that when ye're debarred from one amusement, ye shouldn't sigh over it, but take the next best that offers, come and dine wid us at six; we'll talk over ould toimes. Mind six," said Major Shane, at parting; and then he added, in a confidential tone, "I'll show ye the foinest little boy seven months ould ye iver seen, and give ye a glass of clar't that hasn't its aiqual out of the same bin!"

Though Pat had forsworn duels, he was under no restriction as to the enemies of his country, as Siks, Ameers, Affghans, Russians, and Pandies knew to their cost. The 'London Gazette' made frequent mention of the services which Major, and afterwards Colonel, Cornelius Shane (his name wasn't *Pat* at all) had performed. He is at this present writing unemployed, and surrounded by Shanes male and female of all sizes in Ireland, where he likes to talk of the many scenes that he has gone through—Indian and Crimean experiences not a few; but it would seem that the old Jamaica life is, upon the whole, the favourite reminiscence; for when he gets back that far, he generally exclaims, " Ah, them was the days, after all."

Tom Gervaise returned to England, but he never broke himself off the bad habits he had contracted in the West Indies, and they killed him before long.

Though he died at an early age, he survived by many years his cherished hat, which, in the plenitude of its rich absorptions, was removed by cruel and violent hands, while yet warm from the head of its owner. It had been felt in the regiment that neither gods nor men could longer tolerate its appearance; and one day, while Tom was eating or dozing, or otherwise profoundly occupied, the hat was surreptitiously abstracted and arraigned before a kind of Venetian Council or Holy Vehme, summarily assembled in one of Knox's lower rooms. We, the writer, assisted at this solemnity. The court being assembled and sworn, the doors were locked, and the lower sashes of the windows secured to prevent profane intrusion or attempts at rescue. Then the unhappy hat was brought in on the point of a stick (tongs being scarce in that land) and deposited with much ceremony, and in imposing silence, upon the table. Judgment did not pass by acclamation, because such a proceeding would have been incompatible with the gravity of the members and the greatness of the occasion; but a unanimous verdict was recorded, and instant execution prescribed. None of the judges could of course act as finisher of the law, and there were reasons why none of them wished for that office; therefore a young lady of colour, who happened to be about the barracks, was called in and charged with the demolition. It was to be a cutting in pieces as complete as that which overtook King Agag in Gilgal. The first squeeze of the scissors showed why the handling of the victim was not pleasant work—the original material had attracted innumerable foreign impurities not worth mentioning. As Pat Shane remarked, "it may have been *felt*, but cannot be described." Contemplation of the convict was, however, interrupted by a heartrending spectacle, which appeared at the window; the outraged Tom himself, standing on tiptoe to get a full view of the proceedings, his head bare to the sun, his eyes upturned, his hands lifted on high, and an expression of the strongest emotion on his face, while, with imprecations of the foulest character, he demanded the surrender of his tile. Even this harrowing appeal was insufficient to shake the firmness of those righteous judges. Miss Graves, immovable as Atropos, plied her relentless shears, and the disintegration of the hat was accomplished. It is nothing to say that the hatter who made it would not have known it; that recognition was long ago impossible. Its destruction was like that of ancient Babylon—it had become heaps. And the court summoned Gonsalvo de Cordova to gather together the pieces with his besom, and commanded him that they should be burned with fire, and their ashes scattered to the four winds of heaven!

It was many months before Tom became resigned to his loss; and, as long as he refused to kiss the rod, the members of the Vehme kept beyond the reach of his stick. He was comforted at last; and as regarded earthly retribution, the conclave escaped vengeance. But there is one of the judges who is, we know, still expiating, and to expiate, the stern fulfilment of his duty. Oft when we ourself retire to rest, refreshed with oysters and porter, with a Welsh rabbit, or with well-spiced kidneys and brandy-punch, ere we have composed our thoughts, comes the shade of old Tom Gervaise, with his stick in his hand, and in terrible accents, he demands his hat. In conscious impotence and terror, speechless and immovable, we shrink within our narrowest limits, and desire that the earth may open and cover us from the dreadful presence. But there is no escape for us in earth or heaven, or in the waters under the earth. Tom seizes on our quailing body, and, laughing fearfully, springs with us to the realms of space. And we are in a tandem fashioned from a thunder-cloud, whirled along by dark and dreadful steeds. Old Tom is on the box, his stick exchanged for a mighty whip, his hatless head shining like a celestial globe, and studded with pimples of all magnitudes for stars. His weed blazes with the fire of Ætna, and ever on us he turns a look of undying revenge. Lashing his weird coursers with indefatigable wrath, he causes them to hurry us ten thousand and again ten thousand stages through space—onward and onward, reaching nowhere—though the whip, between the lashes, is pointed as towards some awful goal. We are consumed with thirst, and yet, just beyond our fingers' reach, runs a cool and limpid stream which we may not touch. And on we go, and on, through horror and despair, till, struggling, shrieking, we awake, and, behold, it was a dream!

Old Clutterbuck, considering the liberty we have taken with his name and liquor, certainly deserves a word at parting. He left the service without further accession of rank, and took to civil employment. There is, in one of the midland counties, a natty, thin, erect, gentlemanly, bald-headed chief of constabulary, who might be thought to resemble him.

Mr Nicholas Chitty quitted the service of Mr Arabin a year or two after Violet's marriage, that he might fulfil two important designs. One was to "jine relijan," *i.'e.*, to become attached to one of the denominations of Christians; the other was to open a mart for the sale of wine and spirits and malt liquors. This emporium was contained in a wooden hut, upon wheels, about eight feet square, which was usually anchored somewhere near Up Park Camp, in order that the troops, as well as Mr Chitty's religious connection (which was a thirsty one), might reap the benefit of the establishment. One corner of it, about five feet by three, formed his private apartment, where, surrounded by a numerous family, he and his fourteenth wife lived in great comfort and respectability. The last Mrs C., aged eighteen, was an interesting catechumen, who overlooked Nick's age in contemplating the rigid principles which he enounced, and his high estimation in the religious world. He is an elder of his communion, and devotes whatever time he can spare from his secular occupation to denunciations of "de world, de flesh, and de debil." He professes to "lub eberybody, 'pecially de saints," spite of the old-hyænaish grin which still appears frequently upon his venerable countenance. He it was who once announced to his meeting that "on Toosday nex' dere will be a callection for de ministry of dis church—God willing and weather permitting; and on Wednesday whether or no." Nick's crown is silvered now with the rime of age. He must be approaching ninety years, and will probably live to be a hundred, or even more. Like all eminent people, he has more than once been assailed by the venom of detraction. Graceless sinners and envious saints have hinted ungenerously at some thorns in the elder's flesh, and once or twice arose an imputation of serious backsliding. But these Mr Chitty regarded with his wonted superiority, and we have the pleasure of reporting that he has lived them down, and is now in the enjoyment of all that which should accompany old age, including the ability to take a pint of rum at a sitting with perfect steadiness.

Gonsalvo de Cordova, at his particular request, came to England when Knox, his master, returned home. It was the poor fellow's fortune to reach the mother country at the time when the negro question was exciting considerable interest; and as his sad air and whining voice were well calculated to arouse compassion, he became at once an object of great interest in the neighbourhood of Knox's residence. The enthusiasm of one fair creature, a maid-servant, was so intense as to force her pity into love; and she finally, after taking very active measures to that end, bestowed on the great Captain her person and worldly goods, amid the plaudits of a liberal and sympathising community. They retired with great *eclat* to a little shop set up by joining the bride's savings to a donation contributed by Knox—and everything seemed to promise a happy career. Unfortunately, however, other questions began to occupy the public mind; and Mrs De Cordova, finding her spouse no longer an object of great attention, began to flag in her devotion to him. She even got, at last, to open expressions of regret for her folly in marrying him, and to upbraidings on his colour and nation. She would set forth the great matches she might have made, and how she had been fool enough to throw herself away on a stinking blackamoor who didn't know the value of her. This caprice nearly broke the Captain's heart; and, if he was melancholy before, he became now a monument of woe. After he had suffered some time in this way, on a sudden there appeared an American work which raised up for black people a sympathy which they had never excited before. Once more did Gonsalvo become an object of interest to the whole vicinity; whereupon, we are happy to say, his wife's affection returned, and she appeared most devoted. He was repeatedly solicited to recount the wrongs and atrocities of which he had been the victim, and large sums were offered for his simple appearance at indignation meetings, where other people undertook to speak for him, and to recount his unparalleled sufferings, and set forth his divine perfections. Poor Gonsalvo, however, who was both truthful and meek, gave great offence to his intending sympathisers, and omitted the tide in his affairs which promised to lead on to fortune. Had his invention been more acute, or had he possessed a little more impudence, he might have been the centre of attraction to thousands, and received contributions without end. Mrs De C., who perceived the opening, used all her influence to induce him to make use of it; but in vain. Whereupon she attempted to do a little business on her own account as the loving wife of a negro, too heart-broken to speak for himself, or even to meet the public gaze. This vicarial appearance, however, by no means satisfied the prevailing appetite, which was stimulated to a frightful degree. The lady, therefore, could only bewail the loss of this splendid chance, and, in the second place, abuse and torment poor Gonsalvo more than ever she had done. When much irritated, as she not unfrequently was, she would buffet the poor fellow unmercifully. More than once he ran to his neighbours for protection, and thus gave them opportunities of exhibiting their sensibility, which he had denied to the public. All took the husband's part, and so did not soothe the temper of the wife. One day, having read an account of a less scrupulous black man, who at a monster-meeting had realised a heavy sum, she went home perfectly furious, and, commencing with abuse, she lashed herself from injury to injury till she ended in laying her poor spouse senseless with a poker. So great was the general excitement at this outrage that the perpetrator was given into custody by those who now took the matter out of the injured husband's hands. As the officers bore her off, she turned, with all the *naïveté* of a Cincinnatus, to poor Gonsalvo, saying, "I'm afraid your vile throat must remain uncut for a short time!" Somewhat to her astonishment, she was committed to prison for the assault, and never came to trial, for her ungovernable temper brought on a violent fever, which destroyed her. Gonsalvo, when he heard of her illness, obtained permission to see her, in the hope that he might be able in some sort to assuage her sufferings. He was admitted to her cell during a lucid interval, but so great was her rage at the sight of him, that it brought on a paroxysm from which she never rallied. To the last she raved fearfully, and was accustomed to shriek out, "Wherever I go, they can't be blacker than that rascal." After her death Gonsalvo disposed of the little business, and gladly resumed the service of his old "Massa," with whom he still continues, melancholy and pensive, but happier than in his married life.

Knox kept very fairly to this resolution concerning gambling, and now allows himself only an occasional quiet rubber. He, too, is on the shelf; for, imagining that the service promised nothing in the way of promotion, he left it just before things began to mend, and took to lounging about a club and perpetrating small literature. He can rejoice in the fortune and honours of his old comrades, particularly those of his true and tried friend Arthur Brune, of whom and his delightful wife he is frequently a guest. His writing, though of an unpretending character, sometimes enjoys immense honour. He now and then—hem! he now and then gets a paper into 'Blackwood.'

THE END.

www.ingramcontent.com/pod-product-compliance
Lightning Source LLC
Chambersburg PA
CBHW020301240426
43673CB00039B/667